The Career Development Handbook

The Foundations of Professional Career Practice

Tristram Hooley, Rosie Alexander and Gill Frigerio

trotman | **t**

The Career Development Handbook

This first edition published in 2024 by Trotman, an imprint of Trotman Indigo Publishing Ltd, 18e Charles Street, Bath, BA1 1HX

© Trotman Indigo Publishing Ltd 2024

Authors: Rosie Alexander, Gill Frigerio and Tristram Hooley

British Library Cataloguing in Publication Data
A catalogue record for this book is available from the British Library.

Paperback ISBN 978 1 911724 26 1
Hardback ISBN 978 1 911724 34 6

Printed and bound in the UK by Ashford Colour Press, Gosport, PO13 0FW

All details in this book were correct at the time of going to press. To keep up-to-date with all the latest news and updates and to access the online resources that accompany this book, use the QR code or visit **trotman.co.uk/pages/the-career-development-handbook-resources**

Contents

Figures and tables

Figures

Tables

About the authors

Tristram Hooley is a researcher and writer specialising in career and career guidance. He is Professor of Career Education at the University of Derby and the Inland Norway University. He is also the author of the Adventures in Career Development blog (https://adventuresincareerdevelopment.wordpress.com/).

Tristram's work focuses on the intersection of career, education, technology and politics. He believes that career guidance can have a profound and positive influence on the lives of individuals and can help to make the world a better place. But, to make this happen, governments have to put their hands in their pockets and pay! In the light of this, much of Tristram's work is spent helping politicians understand why career and career guidance are so important.

He has published over 100 books, papers and articles on careers and related subjects.

Dr Gill Frigerio is Associate Professor in the Centre for Lifelong Learning at the University of Warwick and leads the Centre's qualifications in Career Studies and Coaching. Gill's teaching and research interests cover theory and practice in career coaching, working with vocation and calling, women's career development and researching career development practice.

She has written on a range of career development practice issues for a variety of audiences. She is particularly committed to increasing the diversity of the career development profession and ensuring it is an inclusive and welcoming space for everyone.

Gill's doctoral research developed a framework for incorporating vocation and calling into career development practice at the interface of faith and work. She enjoys working with new and experienced practitioners to help them develop their insights and critically evaluate their effectiveness, as well as managing their own well-being and career development.

Dr Rosie Alexander is a researcher specialising in career guidance and development. She has published widely, with a focus on best practices in careers provision and on the geographical dimensions of career and career guidance.

She currently holds a postdoctoral fellowship at Aarhus University in Denmark, where she is exploring career guidance innovations in island communities. Previously, she was a lecturer on the Career Guidance and Development programme at the University of the West of Scotland. Prior to her academic career she worked for over 15 years as a career adviser in both England and Scotland with young people in schools, community settings and universities.

Acknowledgements

Thank you to all the students and all of the colleagues who we have worked with on training programmes for career development professionals. We have tried to take all of these discussions and distil them down in this book. We hope that the book can stimulate the next generation of career development professionals, trainers and educators to further debate, discussion and, of course, high-quality professional practice.

Thank you to Claire Johnson from the Career Development Institute for her comments on an earlier draft of this book and to Alexandra Price from Trotman for her endless patience and encouragement.

Foreword

Being a career development professional is a multi-faceted, fascinating and challenging role. Enabling clients of any age to consider their circumstances, values and aspirations; confront any challenges; strengthen motivation; build resilience, confidence and curiosity; develop new perspectives; learn about relevant careers, jobs and the labour market; justify their thinking and be happy with the plan that they make to achieve their career goal requires a wide range of skills and knowledge.

The role also involves working with other professionals; networking; advocacy and working with organisations and systems to support career development. Understanding how government policies affect the economy and society and how career development activities delivered by professionally qualified people can support clients to navigate these is also key.

Reading this book will show everyone how vital this role is and what a rich resource career development professionals are.

This book has achieved the near impossible feat of being accessible to a number of different audiences.

For those people who are considering a career in this sector it explains in a very accessible way what being a career development professional involves and the different ways in which people qualify to work in the sector.

For students of career development qualifications this book will become a well-thumbed resource as it covers the foundations of the knowledge and skills needed for working in the sector as well as inspiring a thirst for further knowledge.

For experienced career development professionals this book will revitalise your skills and knowledge and remind you, if you need reminding, just what an incredible profession this is, enabling you to advocate for the invaluable work that you do.

Drawing on the vast experience of its authors, this book includes a wealth of references. Its engaging style imparts knowledge, encourages reflection and provides useful summaries. Whether you read the book from cover to cover or dip into those chapters reflecting your interests or particular areas of study this will all be time well spent.

As someone who has worked in this profession for forty years, thirty of which involving designing, delivering and developing many of the initial qualifications and supporting the continuous professional development needs of the sector, I have no hesitation in recommending this inspirational book to everyone.

Claire Johnson, RCDP and CDI, ICCI and NICEC Fellow.
CDI Head of Professional Development and Standards.
October 2024.

Glossary

Adaptability. An ability and willingness to change to suit different conditions. Career adaptability is the quality of changing yourself to thrive in different work environments and career contexts.

AGCAS. The Association of Graduate Careers Advisory Services. The organisation that represents career services and professionals in higher education in the UK.

Apprenticeship. An apprenticeship is a form of work-based training which combines paid work, on-the-job training and classroom instruction. It is often, but not always, associated with the training of younger people.

Boundaries. Professional boundaries are the legal, ethical and competency limits beyond which a professional should not venture. Boundaries exist to protect both the professional and their students or clients.

Career development. The term 'career development' is variously used to describe the process of personal and professional development that an individual goes through, the interventions that can be made by professionals to help people develop their careers, and the professional field which encompasses career counselling, career education and other career interventions.

Career Development Institute. The professional body representing people working in the career development sector in the UK.

Career education. Pedagogic activities that help people to learn about and develop their careers. This can include classroom-based learning and a wide range of other forms of learning, for example, online learning and experiential learning.

Career guidance. Can be used as an overarching term to describe all kinds of interventions designed to help people to choose, manage and develop their careers. It is also sometimes used to refer specifically to one-to-one interventions, instead of the terms 'career counselling' or 'career coaching'.

Career management skills. Are the skills, competences and personal qualities that you need to choose, manage and develop your career. They are sometimes organised into career management skills frameworks, which provide a list of the key skills and competencies that an individual might need.

Client. The individual who receives career development services (usually used in relation to career counselling and coaching).

Cognition. The process of thinking about information and experiences.

Competence/competency. A skill or ability that has been developed by an individual.

Continuing professional development (CPD). Activities that a professional engages in after initial qualification to develop their competence and keep up to date.

Contracting. The process of agreeing on aims, objectives and ways of working that takes place at the start of a career counselling or coaching session. Contracting can also be undertaken prior to any other career development intervention.

Critical thinking. The act or practice of applying reason and questioning assumptions to solve problems, evaluate information, discern biases and make decisions.

Curriculum. A collection of courses and other educational activities that are structured to lead to particular learning outcomes. This can be applied to a career curriculum which defines the organisation of a programme of career education, but is more usually used to describe the wider programme(s) of learning that students follow and which provide the context for much career learning.

Data. Information, evidence and observations that can be used to inform career decision-making, the assessment of the impact of career interventions or any other kind of decision. It is important to be clear that data does not just describe quantitative information (statistics) but also encompasses a wide range of other forms of information.

Economically inactive. A policy term used to mean those who are neither working, studying nor looking for work. This can include a wide range of people who may have very different reasons for being economically inactive.

Employability. Individuals' capacity to find and keep work. It can be used to describe some forms of career provision (e.g. employability programmes or employability adviser) particularly in the context of higher education and public employment services.

Employer. The individual or organisation that employs workers/employees.

Employer engagement. The range of ways in which educational institutions and careers providers can engage with employers and working people to support career development and achieve a range of other purposes.

Entrepreneurship. The ability to develop new businesses or enterprises through the investment of skills, money and contacts. It can also be used to describe a competency (entrepreneurialism) which comprises a mix of creativity, risk taking and problem solving and which can be used in any context.

Epistemology. The theory of how we know what we know about the world.

Ethics. A code of morality and behaviour that govern an individual's behaviour. Mainly used in this book in relation to the professional ethics which discuss how a career development professional should act within their professional role.

Evaluation. Using data and observations to identify the impacts of your services and think about what can be changed and improved.

Experiential learning. The process of learning by doing.

Holland codes. A taxonomy of interests which suggests that people's vocational interests can be broken down into six main categories: Realistic (Doers), Investigative (Thinkers), Artistic (Creators), Social (Helpers), Enterprising (Persuaders), and Conventional (Organisers). It is often known as the RIASEC model based on the first letter of these types.

Industry. The type of employer that someone works for. In the UK it can be defined by the Standard Industrial Classification.

Internship. An opportunity to undertake career learning and personal and competence development within a workplace. Internships are usually offered for a time-limited period and may be paid or unpaid.

Job shadowing. Following an employed person for a day or two to observe how they work for career learning purposes.

Labour market information (LMI). A range of sources of information about what is happening in the world of work. This may encompass both quantitative and qualitative information, as well as government data, research and various forms of naturally occurring and informal information.

Learning outcomes. A description of what a particular educational activity, course or programme is designed to achieve.

Managing up. The process of influencing your leaders and managers and taking a leadership role even from lower down in the organisation.

Memorandum of Understanding (MOU). A formalised agreement setting out mutual responsibilities and expectations between two parties.

Metacognition. The process of thinking about how we think, learn and act.

Monitoring. Using data and observations to check that your services are being delivered as you planned.

Normative. Relating to social norms, standards and assumptions. It can also be used to describe the setting of standards or targets, e.g. defining that all young people should be in education or employment.

NEET (Not in Education, Employment or Training). Policy term used to describe young people who are neither learning nor earning. It often describes a group who are not eligible to receive the full range of benefits and support available to unemployed people.

Occupation. A kind of job. Typically used to organise a variety of different forms of work into standardised categories; in the UK this is through the SOC (Standard Occupational Classification).

Ontology. The theory of the nature of reality.

Opportunity structure. The systems and structures within which people develop their careers.

Paraprofessional. A person trained to assist a professional or to undertake more basic tasks associated with a profession, but who is not trained or recognised as a full professional.

Person-environment fit. The idea that there is an optimum alignment between an individual and their (work) environment which can be both measured and improved.

Placement. A short-term opportunity to learn in a workplace, typically provided as part of a wider programme or course of study. This can be for the purpose of career exploration or for the purpose of vocational skills development.

Policy. A set of decisions and actions about what a government or an organisation will do (or not do). Often set out in policy documents.

Professional. A person recognised by wider society as trained and qualified to undertake a particular occupational role.

Psychometric. Relating to the measurement of human psychological concepts and capabilities.

Public employment services. The government agency tasked with supporting individuals to secure and remain in employment, and supporting employer engagement with the labour market. This is typically strongly focused on supporting unemployed people to find work.

Qualitative data. Non-numerical information that might include pictures, narratives and case studies.

Quantitative data. Information that can be counted and represented in statistical form.

Regulatory bargain. The agreement that a profession has the right to regulate itself and does not need intervention from government or wider civil society.

Reflective practice. The ability to reflect on one's actions so as to engage in a process of continuous learning.

Resilience. The capacity to withstand or to recover quickly from difficulties.

RIASEC model. See Holland codes.

RQF (Regulated Qualifications Framework). The framework for the accreditation of qualifications in England, Wales and Northern Ireland.

Sector. One of the main areas into which the economic activity of a country is divided. This usually comprises multiple industries and can be described in the UK by the highest level of categorisation offered by the Standard Industrial Classification (SIC).

Self-efficacy. An individual's belief in his or her capacity to execute behaviours necessary to undertake different tasks and achieve different outcomes.

SIC (Standard Industrial Classification). A standardised description of the range of different industries in the UK.

Skill. The ability to perform a specific task, job or activity.

SOC (Standard Occupational Classification). A standardised description of the different types of jobs that exist in the UK.

Social justice. The view that everyone deserves equal economic, political and social rights and opportunities.

Social mobility. The ability to move up or down in the social hierarchy. This is usually understood in terms of the likelihood of individuals moving into higher (or lower) status and earning occupations than their parents.

Social reproduction. The reproduction of social structures, systems and hierarchies. In this sense it can be understood as the opposite of social mobility.

SQCF (Scottish Credit and Qualifications Framework). The framework for the accreditation of qualifications in Scotland.

Traits. A distinguishing quality or characteristic, typically one belonging to a person.

Triage. A preliminary assessment of clients' needs to determine the nature of the services from which they might benefit.

Work-based learning. Structured opportunities for learning in and about the workplace.

Unemployed. Someone who is not working in a paid role, but who wishes to find such a role (be employed).

Vocational education (and training). A form of education which is focused on a particular occupation or group of occupations. Sometimes shortened to VET.

Chapter 1
Exploring careers and the career development profession

Introduction

If you are reading this book, you are likely either already a career development professional or are studying to become one. This means that when you've introduced yourself at a party or to a family member, you will probably have received one of the following responses.

> Well, you won't want to talk to me, because I've never had a career, more just a collection of random jobs.

> OK, so what should I do with my life then?

> When I was at school my careers adviser told me that I should be a quantity surveyor/landscape gardener/ undertaker, but thankfully I never listened to them.

> My son dropped out of school last year and has just been sitting on his Xbox ever since then. Can you make him go to university/get a job?

Sadly, these kinds of responses betray quite a bit of misunderstanding on the part of the general public about what career development professionals do and even about what the term 'career' actually means. This book is going to explain what careers are, how they work and what the role of 'career development professionals' is in helping people to develop their careers.

Given this, it is worth starting by teasing out some of the enduring myths that inform the kind of popular understanding of careers that is found in the responses above.

This book is a handbook for career development professionals. In it, you will learn a lot about careers, how people develop their careers, what we, as career

Table 1.1. Deconstructing career myths

Myth	Reality
A career is an orderly progression through ever more senior jobs in the same industry or sector.	Most people pursue their careers across many different jobs and sectors. It is very common to move sideways, and sometimes downwards in terms of money and status. It is also common to take career breaks (e.g. to have a family) and to change direct on more than once in your life.
Careers are only for high-status occupations, not for 'ordinary' jobs.	Careers are not just the preserve of the professional classes. While you can have a legal career or a medical career, you can also have a career as a footballer, a pop star, an administrator or a cleaner. Your career belongs to you, not to your employer or your profession. So, if you quit your job as a stockbroker and become a teacher, you have developed your career in a different direction, rather than ended one career and started another.
There is a right job for everyone, and you will only thrive if you can find it.	While individuals undoubtedly have aptitudes and interests that suit them for some jobs more than others, human beings are incredibly flexible. There are lots of different jobs and lots of different ways to do those jobs. It is probably best to give up looking for the perfect job and focus much more on how you can develop yourself and your current situation to make the most of your interests and talents.
Careers are all about paid work.	Your career starts when you are born and continues until you die. It is about how you spend your time along the way. During that time, most people will spend a lot of their time in paid work, but they will also spend time in studying, looking after family, taking holidays, following their interests, considering whether to set up their own businesses and undertaking a host of other activities. Making choices about how to allocate time between these activities (sometimes described as *work-life balance*) is one of the most important decisions of your career. So, even if you never work in paid employment, you still have a career.
Career development professionals tell you what to do with your life.	Career development professionals support people to think through their careers, to educate them about what is possible and to motivate them to make good decisions. They are not there to tell people what they *should do* nor to *predict the future*. However, it is important to recognise that when people talk to career development professionals, they might have assumptions about what this encounter is for that are unrealistic or just wrong. This is why it is important, as a career development professional, to explain what you can and can't do for people.

development professionals, can do to help people in their career development and how the careers profession works and what some of its main challenges are. By the end of it, you will be able to easily dispel all the abovementioned myths and deal with any other misunderstandings or difficult questions that people throw at you. However, first, it is important to dig a bit deeper into the central idea that we are working with, that of *career*.

CASE STUDY

In this book we are going to provide a series of fictionalised case studies to bring some of the concepts to life. Let's start by meeting a man in the middle of a career crisis called Petr.

Petr came to the UK to live about 15 years ago as a young man. Since then, he has mainly worked in the kitchens of a succession of small restaurants. During that time, he's become pretty experienced and acquired the title of 'chef' in his current workplace (but none of the formal qualifications that often go with that title). Despite the progression that he has achieved, he still isn't very happy with what he earns and is starting to get tired of the long, unsociable hours. He has a young family and is keen to make a change in his life so that he can spend more time with them.

He goes to see Shona, who is a career development professional based in the community centre near his house. He's not sure that she is going to be the right person, as he doesn't really want a career, just a new job with better pay and more sociable hours. He's hoping that she can help him write a CV (which he has never done before).

Shona talks to him about what he likes and doesn't like about his current work, why he dropped out of his apprenticeship, went travelling and ended up in the UK, and what he is looking for in a new job and in his life. The conversation is much wider-ranging than he's expecting. She says that before they start working on a CV, it might be a good idea to do some research into what jobs he's interested in and to think about whether he is interested in doing some retraining.

She keeps using the C word to describe his life, the decisions that he's made in the past and what he's looking for in the future. Petr feels that he got a bit more than he bargained for, but it is all worth thinking about. Maybe just jumping into a new job isn't the right thing. It might be worth considering what kind of career he does want.

So, what is a *career*?

The word 'career' has its origins in the Latin terms *carraria* (a road or track) and *carrus* (chariot). But from the 16th century, the term entered the English language denoting both a course and the idea of travelling along this course at speed. Career is both the road *and* the vehicle travelling along it, but it is often a vehicle that is only just under control.

By the early 19th century, the term had started to be applied to the lives of individuals and particularly to their professional lives. At this point, career still had the sense of an out-of-control carriage; it was an adventure, beset with challenges. It wasn't an orderly, pre-organised and pre-ordained experience. But by the middle of the 20th century, there was an attempt to tame careers and turn them into something predictable. The metaphor was no longer the high-speed carriage hurtling down a track; it was now the career ladder. The career ladder suggested that careers were predictable, that your journey only went in one direction (up), that the steps were logical and that once you got onto a ladder, you couldn't get off. Most importantly, the career ladder put paid work in an organisation at the centre of the picture.

Increasingly, this kind of thinking has become discredited, with careers now recognised as complex and multi-faceted. It is questionable whether the career ladder or career path ever really described the experience of the majority, but it certainly doesn't now. The business coach Robin Linnecar famously described modern careers by saying *'there is no such thing as a career path – it's crazy paving and you lay it yourself'* which we think captures some of the reality of contemporary careers. However, other commentators use different metaphors and emphasise different things, with an important strand of thinking highlighting the way that social structures shape and limit the choices that you have available. In other words, you can't just lay any path that you want; your career is always a question of balancing aspiration with possibility.

💡 Resources

If you are interested in the debates that exist around the definition of a career, some of the following articles and books might offer you a good starting point.

Kerr Inkson writes interestingly about how we define careers. See his article 'Images of Career: Nine Key Metaphors' in his and his colleagues' book *Understanding Careers*.

It is also worth looking at Tony Watts' paper 'Reshaping Career Development for the 21st Century' where he discusses the origins and future development of the term 'career'.

Note: In these resources boxes we will just provide the name of the author and the title of the book or article. You should be able to find the full reference in the reference list at the back of the book.

Given all of these myths and debates about terminology and meaning, it is important to find a clear definition that we can use as a starting point. Thankfully, the recent *Oxford Handbook of Career Development* summarises a lot of this discussion and provides us with a good definition of what a career is (and what it isn't).

> Career is not a single moment of decision when we choose one job over another. It is deeply woven into the ongoing fabric of our lives. Our careers are conducted continuously and they develop in social and political contexts that provide contrasting opportunities and limitations. Career is all around us and there is no escape from it, because it describes the coming together of our life, our learning and our work. Career is important to the lives of individuals across the world and to the societies in which they live.[1]

This kind of definition of career is democratic (everyone has a career), lifelong (it is an ongoing process across our lives) and lifewide (it is not just about paid work, but about all aspects of our lives).

Reflection

Think about what the term 'career' means to you. Do you tend to use it just to mean paid work, or do you think about it more broadly? Do you associate it primarily with certain *types* of work?

Why do you think that helping people to develop their careers is important work? How do you see your role in doing this?

How does being, or becoming, a career development professional fit into your own career, both in terms of the other work that you have done and in relation to the other aspects of your life (family, interests, learning and so on)?

Career development work

Lots of texts about 'career' will present career development work in its current form as relatively new while also reminding us that consideration of how to make sense of choices in life has ancient roots. We can go back to Greek philosophers and Zen Buddhism for evidence that people have long been concerned with what to do with their lives. That said, historical accounts tend to locate the emergence of formalised career support, at least in its recognisable form, in the early 20th century.

At the start of the last century, social and economic changes created challenges for people in choosing and securing work, and social reformers responded with new forms of help. During this period Boston was undergoing significant industrial and political changes as the United States emerged as one of the economic powerhouses of the world. Part of this was dealing with mass migration, mechanisation and urbanisation all at the same time. Into this tumult stepped the social reformer and failed politician Frank Parsons. He established vocational bureaus to help Boston's new and existing citizens find work suitable for their talents. In his book *Choosing a Vocation*, which was originally published in 1909, Parsons outlined a three-stage process: understand yourself, understand work requirements and use 'true reasoning' to create a match between the two. This matching process and some of the techniques set out in his book remain influential more than a hundred years later. Parsons' starting points of activism and social justice are worth remembering, as the thought that career development work can help to make the world a better place also endures today.

At the same time as Parsons was setting up his vocational bureaus in Boston, other social reformers around the world were engaging in similar activities. For example, Maria Ogilvie Gordon was at work in the UK creating a network of labour exchanges, facilitating dialogue between education systems and employment, Etta St John Wilemon was innovating in Canada, and both Edith Onians and Carolyn Chisholm were busy with voluntary activism in Australia. Onians' story is particularly inspiring as she worked with 'newsboys', who were precarious child workers who sold newspapers in the street. Onians developed programmes that improved these boys' literacy, skills and employability and helped them to move on to new and better employment. Ultimately, her work developed into the *Victorian Vocational Guidance Centre* (Victoria being the Australian state, not the monarch).

In many other places, from Germany and Norway to Japan and India, it was this kind of philanthropic work that laid the foundations for the emergence of public career services. The economic and social crises at the start of the 20th century meant that people had more choice about what to do with their lives than ever before, but that they also needed help in exercising this choice. Career development work emerged as a way of helping people and ensuring that societies could function even when the world of work was changing and becoming more complex and difficult to navigate.

Reflection

What are the challenges faced by our current society? How many of them interact with questions about how people manage their careers?

Where can people turn for help with their careers? Are contemporary career development services fit for purpose?

In the 21st century most developed countries around the world have established professional, publicly funded career development services. In some countries, these are embedded into the education system or into public employment services (like Jobcentre Plus in the UK), and in each country, you will find variation in how the system works and who is able to access it. In many countries there are also career development services which are not provided by the government but instead by employers, trade unions and professional associations or which can be purchased on the private market. Understanding the diversity of provision out there, in your country and overseas, is very important as a career development professional. The careers profession is bigger than many people realise, and career development work is even bigger as it also involves many people who aren't professionals.

In this book we use the terminology of the *career development professional*, but in the real world, you will find a bewildering array of terms and terminology. Some people will talk about this work as *career guidance* others about *career counselling* or *careers education*, still more will use alternative terminologies like *employability*, *progression* or *transition* support or *life coaching*. Some of these differences reflect national traditions; *careers advisers* and *guidance counsellors* are used in the UK and in the United States, respectively. Other differences reflect the sector that you work in, with, for example, *career consultant* a much more popular terminology in higher education and the private sector than it is in schools. Still more differences are related to differences in approach, with some *career counsellors* and *career coaches* arguing that they are using radically different methods to work with clients. We will discuss all of these issues further as we go through the book, but as a point of principle, we believe that the profession is stronger if it includes people working in a range of sectors and roles and using diverse approaches, but also if we recognise and emphasise the commonalities between our work, rather than focusing on the differences and dividing into tiny tribes organised around different terminology and philosophies.

So as a career development professional you stand on the shoulders of generations of others who worked to improve the lives of individuals, to reform the education and employment system and to make the world a better place. You are also part of a massive international family of professionals working to support others in the development of their careers. This work matters for individuals, for organisations and for societies.

> ### 💡 Resources
>
> If you want to find out more about the origins and history of career development work, you could read Frank Parsons' *Choosing a Vocation* or Mark Pope's 'A Brief History of Career Counseling in the United States'. In the UK, David Peck's *Careers Services: History, Policy and Practice* and Michelle Stewart's edited volume *A History of the Careers Services in the UK from 1999* are both well worth a look.
>
> If you are interested in the contemporary organisation of career development work in different countries, then the websites of the OECD (https://www.oecd.org/education/career-readiness/), Cedefop (https://www.cedefop.europa.eu/en/projects/lifelong-guidance) and the International Centre for Career Development and Public Policy (https://www.iccdpp.org/) provide some very good starting points.

About the book

This book is a handbook for career development professionals and others interested in career development work. It is ideal as a textbook if you are taking a course to become a career development professional, but it will also be useful if you are already engaged in career development work (either as a qualified professional or learning on the job). The book is organised in 12 chapters. In this section, we are going to briefly talk you through the twelve chapters, as it will help you understand how the book is organised and what it is trying to achieve.

You've already made it through most of Chapter 1. In this chapter we've tried to introduce you to the two big concepts that are at the heart of the book: first, 'career' and secondly, 'career development work'. We hope that this has excited you about the career development field and encouraged you to start thinking deeply about the work that you do.

Chapter 2 focuses on how you can study to become a career development professional. Career development is a very practical field, but it is underpinned by a lot of theory. If you are training to become a career development professional, you will probably have to demonstrate that you can work with clients one-to-one or in groups and show that you have read some of the main theories and can write about them as well as integrate them with your practice. If you have been out of education for a while, or if you never got on very well with education the first time around, then this might sound scary, which is why we've included a chapter focused on the skills you need for this kind of professional learning.

In Chapter 3 we talk about the role of the career development professional. This includes discussion about how the profession is structured, what the main tasks of a career development professional are, ethical issues and continuing professional development. We then move on to Chapter 4 to talk about the wider context for career development work, for example, how the education and employment system works, and then in Chapter 5 to talk about career development systems and policies and think about why that matters.

Chapter 6 moves on to look at career theory. This looks at how we understand ourselves and our clients, how we understand the wider context and its implications for career, and importantly how people learn about their careers and manage and develop them. Many people are anxious about studying theories, but the aim of all of these theories is to simplify the world in ways that will help you to practice more effectively, so try and enjoy it.

The next few chapters get increasingly practical, with Chapter 7 focusing on career development work with individuals such as guidance, counselling and coaching, Chapter 8 on working with groups and developing and delivering career education and Chapter 9 on using career and labour market information and other resources. In Chapter 10 we look at working with organisations and systems, including thinking about the building of internal and external partnerships and how you can influence and shape the organisations and systems that you are working with.

Chapter 11 asks you to think about how you can be involved in the development, management and leadership of career services. At the start of your career, this is about understanding the organisation that you are part of and thinking about how to make a positive contribution to it, but as your career develops you are likely to take on more leadership and management positions. So, it is important that you think about how you are going to fulfil these roles as part of your practice as a career development professional.

Finally, in Chapter 12 we conclude the book by summarising key learning and contemplating on how you can continue to develop as a career development professional and support the continued development of the profession.

The book is also supported by a glossary and a full bibliography.

How to read the book

Some people may want to sit down and read this book from cover to cover, but we imagine that most people will dip into the sections that interest them or relate to topics that are being covered in their course or issues that they are facing in practice. This is fine; you are welcome to use it in any way that you find helpful.

As you read, you will notice four recurring features that appear in all the chapters.

- *Resources* which provide you with further reading and links to websites and other resources. This is backed up with a reference list at the back of the book, which draws together all the texts that this book is based on and which you might find useful in your work.

- *Reflections* which encourage you to think about the issues raised in the main text. Most of these reflections take the form of a question that asks you to relate the content of the book to your life and your practice.

- *Case studies* which present fictionalised examples of issues raised in the text. The aim of these case studies is to bring some of the more abstract issues to life. While they are fictional, they are based on the real experiences of the authors and their research with career development professionals.

- *In a nutshell* is a feature which closes out each chapter by providing a summary of the key learning in that chapter. It will provide you with a tool for reviewing your learning once you have finished the chapter.

In a nutshell

This chapter has introduced you to two of the main concepts that will be critical to this book and then set out how the book itself will be organised. It has covered:

- what the concept of *career* means, and argued that we should adopt a broad and democratic definition of the term as the individual's pathway through life, learning and work;

- the origins of the *career development profession* and encouraged you to think about why this work came about and why it is still important more than a hundred years later. As a career development professional, you are part of a global family of people who help, educate and support others to develop their careers;

- how *The Career Development Handbook* will be organised so that you can read it strategically to support you in your study and learning.

Chapter 2
Studying to become a career development professional

Introduction

This chapter explores the process of engaging with an educational programme to become a career development professional. We recognise that many people decide to train as a career development professional after spending a long time outside of the education system, so we are going to try and break down some of the basic study skills here. But even if you have only just finished a degree, there are likely to be ways that studying for a professional course like career development is going to be different from other kinds of study that you might have done in the past. That is not to say that studying career development doesn't require some deep thinking, but just to notice that a lot of the time you will be thinking as much about how to apply some of this deep thinking in practice.

So, in this chapter we are going to talk about academic study skills, reflective practice and the challenges of moving from theory to practice and back again.

How you can train to be career development professional

If you have picked up this book to help you consider whether and how to become a career development professional, it is important to understand that there are a range of different pathways that you can take to achieve this aim. Even if you are already on a training programme, or already working in career development, it is useful to understand the different ways that people can train to be career development professionals. These people will be your colleagues, and it pays to appreciate how a diversity of prior experiences can be useful. It will also help you to consider how further training and development might be available to support your own career and professional development.

As we discuss in more detail in Chapter 3, career development work is 'weakly professionalised' in most countries, which means that there are not normally formal requirements to demonstrate the required skills and capabilities to do the work (whether that is demonstrated by qualification or by some other means). Employers can ask for whatever level of qualification or prior experience they want and in theory anyone could set themselves up as a career counsellor or career development professional. We will talk more about the pros and cons of this system in the next chapter.

In practice, there are a range of reasons why getting a formal qualification is a good idea. First and foremost, it should give you confidence that you are doing the right thing, offer you theories and strategies to lean on and help you to convince employers and other regulatory organisations that you know what you are doing. In England, the Department for Education and the Quality Assurance Agency for UK higher education both recommend that careers staff should be appropriately trained and qualified. In the UK people who hold a graduate level or above, 60 credit or more, qualification in career development, can also join the Register of Career Development Professionals (RCDP), a voluntary listing held by the Career Development Institute. The upshot is that there are advantages to being qualified, both in terms of your own employability and the quality of your practice. The pathways to qualification will vary depending on the sector you are working in and the country where you work, but broadly they can be divided into the following categories.

- **Apprenticeships** in which employees are supported by their employers to engage in both on-the-job and off-the-job learning. In England, apprentices are expected to meet the Higher Apprenticeship Standard, which specifies nine 'core duties' of career development professionals and then lists the knowledge, skills and behaviours apprentices need to demonstrate that they are able to fulfil these duties.

- **Work-based qualifications.** Many career development professionals are trained on the job by undertaking a work-based qualification at degree level. These qualifications can be at a range of levels from the level of a high school education to graduate and, less commonly, postgraduate level.

- **Academic programmes** which are typically delivered by universities. These programmes may be linked to formal professional accreditation (such as the Qualification in Career Development in the UK) or have particular specialist foci such as work in higher education or one-to-one counselling and coaching.

- **Professional accreditation as a career development professional.** In some countries it is possible for people with a lot of experience as a career development professional to seek professional accreditation by providing robust assessed evidence against a competence framework.

Depending on the training route, some evidence of prior study may be necessary. To study at postgraduate level, for example, typically requires individuals hold a degree or demonstrate equivalent levels of qualification. Having some relevant work experience or evidence of prior learning in an associated role can also be helpful, depending on course providers. Some individuals, particularly those in paraprofessional roles, may undertake additional training or qualifications at a lower level before progressing into full professional training.

The best route for you will depend on your combination of prior experience, goals and available options. And, of course, there are combined routes, usually as an employee and a part-time student, where you can get a relevant qualification as well as draw on your working context. There are pros and cons to whichever route into career development work you take. Studying for a postgraduate qualification will put an academic award as well as a professional qualification on your CV. This will be reflected in the way the course is delivered and assessed: you will be a registered student and have access to all the services the university has to offer, and will likely have to write long-form assessments at a postgraduate level. A work-based route enables you to earn and study and connects your learning with your current work context as you gather evidence in a portfolio. This may bring the course content to life in particular ways, but you may miss out on opportunities to learn about other contexts that may interest you in the future.

Even after initial qualification, it is possible to progress through qualifications up to the doctoral level. Master's degrees will usually involve conducting research and writing a dissertation, which serves in turn to strengthen the evidence base for your work. While doctoral work usually involves undertaking an extended research or development project over a number of years.

CASE STUDIES

Shona, whom we met as she worked with Petr in Chapter 1, works in a community centre. Shona graduated in sociology and social policy and found work in her university town in a job centre, helping unemployed people find out about local vacancies. Through this she realised how complicated careers could be, and so decided to pursue a master's degree which included the Qualification in Career Development offered by a nearby university. She funded this through a government-based postgraduate master's loan.

Graham worked in graduate recruitment for a FTSE100 employer, which involved liaising with university career services, attending careers fairs and supporting schemes designed to boost the diversity of their graduate intake. Through this, he got interested in the way university career services support their students. He saw a career consultant role advertised at a university 20 miles from his home. He was able to demonstrate the skills and qualities to secure the post and was offered the chance to undertake a graduate-level work-based training route alongside his work.

Aleesha had held a variety of business admin roles and was working in a recruitment agency when she saw an advert for a trainee career development professional with a group of local schools, using the apprenticeship route. She took 18 months training 'on the job', with time off work to attend courses and for private study, and gathered evidence from her work against the specified knowledge, skills and behaviours in the apprenticeship standard. She had regular meetings with her line manager and apprenticeship tutor to monitor her progress. After 18 months she was awarded a qualification and was able to take her apprenticeship 'end point assessment', which she passed. As a result, her contract was made permanent, and she got a small pay rise.

💡 Resources

If you are in the UK you can find out more about the training routes to become a professional on the CDI website: https://www.thecdi.net/professional-qualified/qualifying-to-work-in-the-career-development-sector

---

Challenges of returning to study

If you have been out of the education system for a while, you are likely to experience some of the following challenges when you return.

- **Feeling nervous.** It is normal to feel a bit nervous when you go back into any kind of study programme. Take your time and try and build your confidence slowly. You won't be the first student to experience any of the problems that you are facing. Talk to your tutors and ask for help where you need it.

- **Not knowing the rules or expectations.** When you enter any new environment it can be challenging to know exactly what is expected of you. Most programme providers will hold inductions and produce things like course handbooks or guides. Try and make the most of these things to help you to decode the rules.

- **Connecting with other students.** It can feel difficult to make connections with other students, particularly if you are older or studying remotely. It is really worth trying to connect with others, as building a community of learners will give you another resource to aid in your learning. Make sure you attend any additional social activities if you can, reach out to other students and take time to help others where you can.

- **IT and systems.** Studying in a professional programme is probably going to ask you to expand your IT skills and introduce you to some new systems. This can be frustrating, but rather than avoiding the systems, take a deep breath, try to adopt a positive approach and ask for help when you need it.

- **Finding the time.** When you study as an older student, you will probably find that your life is considerably more complex than when you were last at school or university. You will need to be an excellent time manager to juggle work, family and study. One of the most important tips is to talk to all the people in your life (work, family and friends) about what you are doing and why you might be a bit more time-pressured for a while. Remember it won't last forever!

- **Meeting the standard.** It is very easy to get anxious about the requirements of your programme. The fear is always that you won't be good enough and that you will crash and burn. Remember that no one (not you, your employer nor your lecturers or trainers) wants you to fail. Everyone is rooting for you to succeed, so use the study advice offered in this chapter and by your programme staff to learn new skills and develop your capacity to succeed.

Reflection

How have any previous experiences of study shaped your preparedness for the programme that you are studying?

How will you manage your time and energy for study alongside your other life roles? Who are the significant people in your life whose support you will need and how will you make sure this is available?

Can you speak to anyone who has been through the programme that you are studying? What advice do they have to give you?

Study skills

Undertaking any kind of study programme requires you to develop more than just subject-specific knowledge and skills. So, as well as learning a lot about career development, while you do your programme you are also going to learn a lot about reading, writing, note-taking, research and a host of other study skills. In this section we are going to look at some of the most important study skills that you are likely to need as you engage with your programme. One of the most important things to remember is that no one is born knowing about essay writing or any other aspect of academic study. You need to learn how to do it and, like anything else, the more you do it the better you will get. So, don't be discouraged if you don't get an A+ on your first assignment.

Resources

There are lots of books and resources which can support you in developing your study skills. We recommend Stella Cottrell's books, e.g., *The Study Skills Handbook*. For a broader look at transitioning into higher education, in particular, Lucy Tobin's *A Guide to Uni Life* is well worth looking at.

Getting motivated

Unless you are a robot, you will notice that how you feel about tasks has a direct impact on your ability to find time to do them. You might be an enthusiast who says an excited 'yes' to every project you are invited to get involved with, only to then find you are mentally overloaded and practically overcommitted, and struggle to find time to complete last month's ideas. Or you might be a slow starter who struggles to get going, particularly if, in the early stages of a project, it seems overwhelming.

However motivated you are feeling, identifying a few small tasks and then ticking them off can get you on a roll, giving you the satisfaction of accomplishments and a sense of achievement. With tasks that you don't like, this is sometimes referred to as 'eating the frog', the idea being that the thought of it is off-putting, but once it is done, we can move on with our day.

Getting organised

Adding study into your life is going to require some thought on how you will organise your time, your space and your commitments. Some top tips to help you get organised include

- **Break tasks down into small goals.** It is easy to get overwhelmed with the amount that there is to do. However, every big task is really just a series of small tasks, so start by figuring out what you have to do and work through the tasks one at a time.

- **Focus on what is in your control.** None of us can deliver our absolute best all the time. Life has a way of messing up our plans. So you would like to produce the perfect assignment, but the kids are ill, and you have to pick up your mum and you just don't get as much time as you hoped. Be kind to yourself and recognise that this might mean that you don't get top marks for every piece of work because that's not a realistic goal for you in the time that you have available.

- **Developing good habits.** A lot of effective time management is mainly about using time efficiently. This means things like developing good note-taking approaches, managing your file store carefully and noting down the references of everything you read. If you get into these good habits, you won't waste lots of time looking for things that you read but can only half remember.

- **Learn to prioritise.** You might have come across the matrix of urgency and importance, sometimes known as the Eisenhower matrix. There will always be some things that are urgent and important and need to come first. But always addressing the urgent without considering importance can create a way of working where you respond to demands but never get time to think and learn better ways to work in the long term. Maybe it's urgent to someone else, but not to you? The idea is that the more time we can spend in the plan phase, the more we will be able to identify what needs doing and when, and fewer things will emerge in the DO NOW box (see Figure 2.1).

Building networks

Networking is not always listed as a study skill, but learning is a social process, and students who are connected to others have many more resources to draw

Figure 2.1. The prioritisation matrix. See Stephen Covey's *The 7 Habits of Highly Effective People* for more information.

on. The networks that you build while you are studying can also pay off after you graduate. Key relationships to develop include

- **Your tutors.** Getting to know your tutor and feeling comfortable asking them questions will be invaluable as you make your way through your programme. They can also become invaluable members of your professional community long after your course has finished.

- **Student support professionals.** The institution where you are studying is likely to have a range of student support professionals whose main role is to help you with your studies. These will include people who focus on study skills as well as people who can support students with disabilities, learning difficulties, welfare issues and a host of other problems. It is worth gaining an overview of what is available to you early on in your studies.

- **Fellow students.** Finding a study buddy or two can help you create accountability and provide the support you need to keep making progress. Other students on the course will have different experiences from you and serve as a source of insights and fresh perspectives. You may also need to work together with other students for group assignments.

- **Career development professionals.** While you are studying, you should also be trying to build professional contacts who are currently working in the field. You are likely to have to interview people and maybe undertake a placement as part of your course if you are not currently in practice. View this as a starting place for building a powerful professional network.

- **Colleagues.** If you are already in practice and training through a work-based route, you are likely to be surrounded by other colleagues who are career development professionals or members of allied professions. Use these contacts as another starting point for building a professional network in your workplace and beyond.

Reading

Whatever programme you are following it is likely you will be given reading lists and material by your training provider, which is your starting point for background reading. There is also a wide range of background material and wider reading that you will become aware of once you start (including the material that we suggest in this book). How widely you need to read will vary depending on your qualification and your own personal goals. Generally, academics and course tutors will provide you with more material than you *need* to read and trust you to make sensible decisions about what are the best texts to focus on.

It is worth making sure that you are reading smartly, which means keeping a record of what you read with some brief notes. This serves two key functions, firstly helping you to think while you are reading and secondly, providing you with a record of what you have read for later. If you are at a university you will probably be able to access reference management software, like Endnote or Zotero. These enable you to record what you read, import citations and then generate reference lists automatically. But even if you decide not to invest the time in learning to use such a tool, a simple Excel spreadsheet of what you read can be enough to keep track, noting your reactions and connections to other literature in a searchable format.

Resources

There are lots of reference managers for you to choose from. This article from the Bodleian Libraries (https://libguides.bodleian.ox.ac.uk/reference-management/comparison-tables) summarises the strengths and weaknesses of the main options out there.

Researching

Most programmes will ask you to do some kind of research. Research skills refer to the ability to search for, locate, extract, organise, evaluate and use or present information that is relevant to a particular topic. These are probably things that you do every day for a host of different reasons, from finding a restaurant to go to, to choosing the course that you are now studying.

So, when it comes to research, you are already building on strong foundations. Undertaking research for a professional programme probably asks you to do to two new things that you may not be used to. First, your tutors will be concerned with the quality of the information that you refer to, and they are likely to want you to go beyond Google and dive into academic sources of information, including journal articles and books. Second, they are likely to want you to engage with *original* resources (which means not just second-hand opinions but original texts) and to engage with a range of resources to make sure you get a balanced perspective. You may also be engaged in applying your research and potentially starting to generate new knowledge by going out and talking to career development professionals and their clients.

Resources

It is beyond the scope of this book to introduce you to research methods and research management processes, but there are lots of books out there that might be useful for this. Something like Catherine Dawson's *Introduction to Research Methods* might be a good place to start.

Succeeding in assignments

When you are studying to become a career development professional, you are likely to encounter a wide range of different assessment approaches. These may include traditional forms like essays and exams, but you are also likely to be expected to produce group assessments, presentations, and to be assessed on your practice, for example, having an interview observed or a lesson plan that you have written graded.

Your course provider will be able to provide more detailed guidance on the types, level and style of writing that they expect, but you should expect that many of the ways in which you are being assessed will differ from any previous academic study you have done. Ultimately, in a professional course, it is your fitness to practice that is being assessed, and this can't normally be done by just producing a series of theoretical essays. Your tutors are likely to be most interested in how you integrate theory with your daily work. In such cases, it is often hard to talk about what you do without using the first person, so the use of 'I' in your assignments is usually stylistically acceptable (although it is worth checking with your tutor).

Moving from one assessment approach to another is likely to be challenging, but if you remember the following tips, you will have a very good chance to succeed.

- **Read the assignment carefully.** The biggest reason why students fail assignments is that they have done the wrong one. They have either not answered the question that they were asked, or done it in too many or too few words. So, spend some time analysing the question that you've been given and make sure that you have identified all the different elements of it. If you have access to the learning outcomes for the assignment or the module, look at them as well as they will give you a good idea of what the assessor is looking for. And if it isn't completely clear, ask your tutor.

- **Think critically.** Students are often told that they need to 'think critically' or 'be more critical'. This doesn't mean that you have to be negative about everything. What tutors mean when they say 'critical' is that your writing should firstly link to the existing literature which has discussed the subject, and secondly that you should try to evaluate the various different perspectives that exist on any particular issue and explain which position (or combination of positions) are most convincing.

- **Learn to reference.** Referencing is about being clear where you got your information and ideas from. If you read something and used it in your assignment it should be referenced. Referencing is a difficult technical process and requires you to follow rules and include particular types of information. You should check whether your training provider has referencing guidelines and then follow these strictly. If no guidelines are available find a good advice page (e.g. the Purdue OWL https://owl.purdue.edu/).

- **Read everything you write four times.** No one can produce a good piece of writing first time. Plan to read everything you write four times. The *first* time is when you are writing it, the *second* time is the next day after you have written it and you should be looking for whether the whole piece says what you want it to say and thinking about whether you need to restructure it. The *third* time you are looking at whether it is well written, so try reading it out loud and amending it so it is easy to say. Finally, the *fourth* time you are proofing it, checking for spelling, grammar and mistakes. Use the tools in a word processing programme like Word to help you with this.

- **Hand the right thing in on time.** Most learning providers have pretty strict deadlines these days. If you miss the deadline you run the risk of failing the assignment or losing marks. So get it in on time! What is more, it is important to stick to the word limit and any other key requirements. If you want to hand it in late or vary something like the word limit you will have to ask for permission and will need a very good reason.

- **Treat feedback as feedforward.** When you get feedback on an assignment, don't think of it as explaining why you got the mark that you got, try and focus on what it tells you to do differently (or the same) next time. The purpose of feedback is to fuel your learning so see it is a resource for you to improve.

Moving from theory to practice (and back again)

One of the important things about undertaking a professional programme is that you will usually need to develop some experience of practice alongside your engagement with theoretical content. There are a range of ways that programmes typically help you to do this.

- **Reflecting on existing or current experience.** If you are on a work-based programme or are currently working in a relevant role, the provider may encourage you to try out many of the things that you explore in theory in your current work context. Assessment tasks might be crafted to require this integration.

- **Engagement with career development professionals.** Ideally, your programme will give you a number of opportunities to speak and talk with career development professionals working in different kinds of settings. It is important that you make the most of these encounters and think about what you want to ask people who are actually working in the field.

- **Visits and job shadowing.** You may get the opportunity to visit workplaces where career development work takes place or to follow an experienced practitioner. This can be a great opportunity to learn how things work in practice.
- **Placements.** Many programmes will arrange for you to undertake placements which will give you one or more short opportunities to work as a career development professional. Typically, you will be provided with a workplace mentor who will guide you and provide you with feedback on this placement.

All of these different kinds of engagement with practice are valuable aspects of your course. Professional education is about the coming together of theory and practice, and these moments provide you with an excellent opportunity to draw together some of this learning. To make the most of these opportunities, consider the following tips:

- **Remember you are in a workplace.** While this is a great learning opportunity for you, you need to remember that you are in a real workplace with real clients. So dress and act professionally, be respectful of professionals and clients and be careful not to step into office politics.
- **Listen to your mentor.** Your mentor is your key learning resource. They are probably giving up their time to help you for free, so listen to them and the feedback they give you carefully. You don't have to agree with everything, but it is all useful input.
- **Focus on what you can learn from the practice context.** You've got lots of interesting new theoretical knowledge that people might be interested in, but the main point of being there is to learn from those in practice.
- **Make notes or keep a journal.** It is important to take some notes about what you notice in a practice context. One of the most important things is to reflect on what you do, see and are told and think about how it relates to what you have learnt so far.
- **Build your network.** Any interaction with the field of practice gives you an opportunity to meet people and build your network. Make the most of this: talk to people, connect with them on LinkedIn and remember that these people might be interviewing you for a job in a few months' time.

Reflective practice

As you follow your programme you will be asked to reflect on your practice and to consider how you reflect in practice. When we are learning a professional skill, you can think of it as moving through a series of stages of competence (Figure 2.2).

Unconscious competence | You can just do it right 'automatically' because you have become so comfortable and competent in your skills and knowledge

Conscious competence | You know what you know, but it takes effort to do it right

Conscious incompetence | You know what you don't know, but you don't have the knowledge and skill to do anything about it

Unconscious incompetence | You don't know what you don't know.

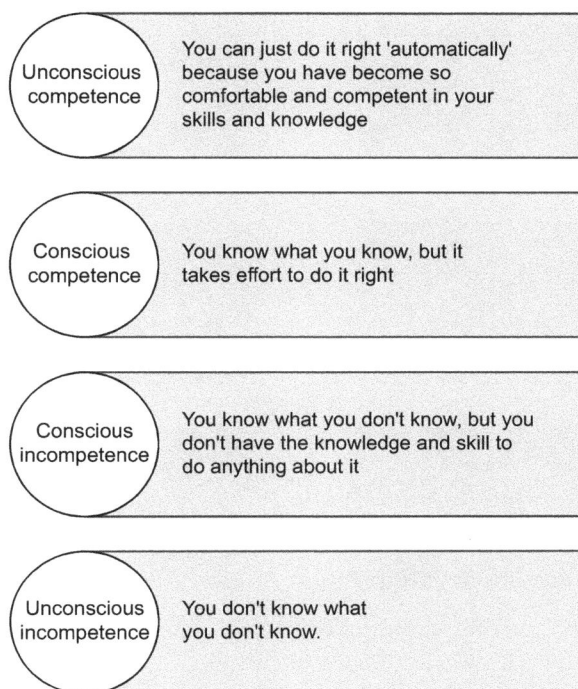

Figure 2.2. The four stages of competence. First proposed by De Phillips et al. in *Management of Training Programmes*.

Moving up this ladder of competence is not just about the accumulation of new knowledge and skills but also about rethinking your ideas and assumptions in light of this new information. This is where reflection comes in. One way of thinking about the purpose of reflection is to view it as the place where you put all the elements that you have learnt together. You can think about these elements as follows:

- **Head.** There is a lot of material to wrap your brain around, much of which is covered in this book. From theories of career development to policies and systems that drive how career guidance is delivered, there are things you will need to know and to think about critically.
- **Hand.** There are also things you need to be able to do: ask clients questions, design a learning activity, manage a relationship with a stakeholder in your organisation and advocate to an employer. These are the practices of career guidance.
- **Heart.** There are also values which underpin career development work and which are reflected in our ethical codes. Our own values that bring us to this work will chime with this, as we will explore in Chapter 3.

But how do all these come together and allow us to move forwards? Well, to underline the point about reflection, a mirror allows for each to see the other and for perspectives of hand, head and heart to be integrated in learning.

23

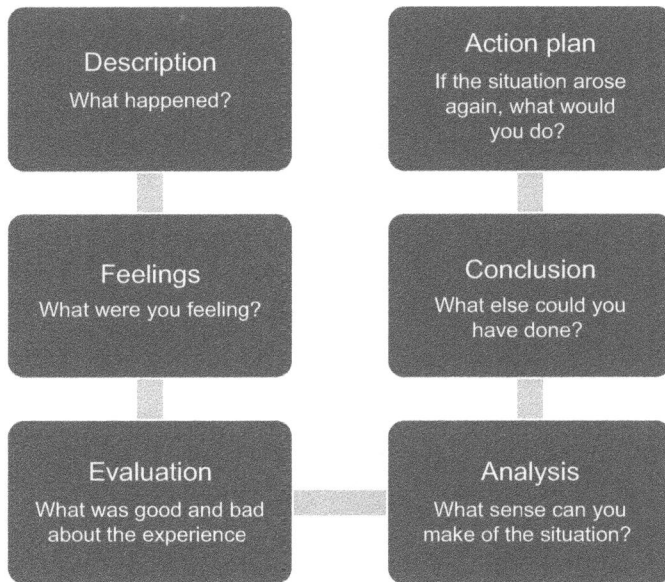

Figure 2.3. Gibbs's structured debriefing model.

Reflection is one of the main phases of learning. In Chapter 8 we will be looking in more detail at the experience-based learning cycle developed by David Kolb, in which reflection plays a key role. For now it is just important to note that there is a lot of evidence that tells us that reflection is a critical part of turning knowledge and experience into behaviour change and professional practice. It is also worth noting the connection between our own learning and the way we as career development professionals design learning materials and experiences for our clients.

There is no one best way to reflect, so here we invite you to consider the ways that will work for you. You might find that discussing particular work-related incidents with a fellow student or colleague can help, or prefer to give time to reflective writing or journaling. This can be done by writing out your thoughts in long form or on an app, or by voice note. Either way, a process can help. Here we offer one which is widely used in professional learning and we all have experience with using on the programmes we are involved with (Figure 2.3).

One criticism of this model is that it can leave you a little isolated. In later chapters, we will be putting a great emphasis on how context and interactions with other people shape our learning and careers, and so it's also worth sharing a model of critical reflection that makes use of the social resources available to you. Stephen Brookfield, in a model for teachers, suggests reviewing a learning experience or critical incident through four critical lenses[1]:

- **Self.** Here we bring our own autobiography into the mix and think about how our lives interact with what we have learnt.

- **Colleagues.** The perspectives of others can give us insights and feedback that can support our reflection and also provide solidarity and support for our learning journey.
- **Learners.** Here we bring in evaluations and feedback from the clients we work with and consider what that tells us about what we have learnt.
- **Theories.** We can also use scholarly literature and theories to underpin our critical reflection.

Hearing your course mates, colleagues or even your tutors' reflections can help with your own sensemaking and help you to identify your assumptions and develop self-awareness.

CASE STUDY

Graham had just been running a session with second-year economics students about looking for summer placements. As he walked back to the Careers Centre he reflected on how it had gone. He had enjoyed it and received a good response from about half the students in the room, who had taken away lots of ideas about their job seeking. But a small group of students seemed bored and like they weren't listening. He realised he had found that a bit irritating; why attend a session if you aren't interested?! It struck him that it reminded him of the feeling he used to get as a recruiter when students made what seemed like half-hearted applications.

Later, he got the chance to talk this session over with an experienced colleague, who asked a few questions about what the students had been expecting. He realised that he didn't know. His session plan had gone straight into the detail of finding vacancies for placements without taking some time to find out more about what the students attending were interested in. He decided to revise the session so that there was a technology-enabled means for students to anonymously comment on what they needed at the start of the session. This felt risky – what if they asked for more than he had planned? Or something different? But then he reflected that he had delivered a session that was positive for the majority of attendees, and this built his confidence for handling this situation, and he realised that even if he had to refer some students to other resources or services, that would be better for everyone.

Alongside reflection, giving and receiving feedback on your work is an important part of the learning process that is worth exploring. Whether it is a fellow student commenting on an observed practice interview, a learner responding to an evaluation form or a tutor formally assessing your assignment, learning involves being open to comments from others. Getting beyond defensiveness or feelings of inadequacy when discussing our developing abilities is a big part of studying any professional practice. This emphasises that learning is an emotional as well as a cognitive process, and taking care of ourselves and our well-being is paramount if we are to manage this aspect of studying.

When giving feedback to fellow students, it's helpful to think about how you can point to a person's specific actions (which can be changed) rather than general behaviours or personality (which are harder to change). '*You asked two questions at once which could have confused the client*' is better than '*you were confusing*'. Providing feedback tentatively can also be helpful. Similarly, when receiving feedback, taking time to consider it and how you can learn from it rather than justifying, defending or taking it personally will help you process it well.

Reflection

What forms of reflection do you think might work well for you? For example, do you think that you benefit most from discussion with a peer (including the giving and receiving of feedback) or from a process like journaling? What do you think is the best mix of reflection strategies for you?

Resources

There is a lot of useful material written on reflection and reflective practice. Helena Košťálová and her colleagues' free book *A Practitioner's Guide to Uncharted Waters of Career Counselling: A Critical Reflection Perspective* is a helpful resource. Barbara Bassot has also done some important work and offers both *The Reflective Practice Guide* and *The Reflective Journal,* which is an interactive guided journal.

If you want something specifically on reflective writing, then Kate Williams and her colleagues' book *Reflective Writing* is very useful.

In a nutshell

This chapter has looked at how to thrive in the variety of study programmes designed to train and develop career development professionals. It has shown that

- undertaking a course in a professional practice like career development work may be different in many ways from any previous experience of studies you may have had. Because of this, you should expect it to be challenging;

- it is critical to develop your study skills and to recognise that this is something that is going to take time and effort;

- assignments are there to support your learning. Try to view them positively, follow the guidance that you are given and learn from the feedback that you get;

- one of the key challenges of this kind of learning is the need to move backwards and forwards between theory and practice. Try and make the most of the opportunities that you have to engage with practice; and

- reflective practice is at the centre of learning to be a career development professional and also to continuously improve throughout your working life.

Chapter 3
The role of the career development professional

Introduction

There are different ways that people learn about career development, such as talking to friends, family, colleagues and managers, as well as from observing other people's career trajectories. However, career development professionals fulfil a particular role in supporting people with their career development. As this chapter explores, professionals are trained individuals with a range of specialist skills and expertise who work in line with agreed standards of practice. This means that the advice they provide can be trusted to be of a certain quality. In the light of this, we are going to use this chapter to explore more about what being a professional means and how you can ensure that you are working professionally.

What is a profession?

There is a lot of debate about what a 'profession' is. On one hand, someone who is a professional is simply someone who completes a task for money. So, you might like to play a game of football on a Sunday, but you would never describe yourself as a 'professional footballer' because no one would pay you to do this.

Other definitions of 'professions' emphasise that it is not just getting paid that makes you a professional, but rather the fact that you have a set of skills and knowledge (usually acquired through specialised training) and that you are recognised by others in society as a professional. So, under this kind of definition, a doctor is a professional, while an unskilled labourer is not, even if they are paid for their work.

One element that is often included in definitions of professionalism is the idea that professionals have the right to regulate their own profession. So professional bodies have a key role, often in negotiation with government, in setting standards, defining training and then policing incompetence and malpractice. This idea of professions as self-governing bodies is described as the 'regulatory bargain' which professions strike with society. Essentially, it is a recognition that professions have the right to manage themselves because they have the expertise to do it well. Such a 'regulatory bargain' requires societies to place a lot of trust in professions and professionals.

Understanding professions in this way highlights some of the potential positives and negatives. Being a professional accords status, privilege and opportunities for greater autonomy and control over your work. But who decides what occupations become professions? How can we be sure that we can trust them? How can people become professionals and what are their rights and responsibilities once they have done so?

Career guidance is often described as being 'weakly professionalised'. What this means is that career guidance is in the process of organising itself as a profession, but not everyone agrees that this is important or necessary. This is why, in most countries, there is nothing to stop you from renting an office, buying a sign and announcing that you are a 'career counsellor' even if you have no qualifications or knowledge in the area.

💡 Resources

John Gough and Siobhan Neary discuss these issues of professionalism more deeply in their chapter 'The Career Development Profession: Professionalisation, Professionalism and Professional Identity'.

Understanding the profession

As discussed in the introduction, the origins of career guidance are typically traced back to the early 20th century. In the early days, there was no profession; instead, people with a variety of backgrounds began to provide career guidance. This included those trained as teachers, social workers, psychologists and other professionals, as well as those with no qualifications at all. But over the years, the range of practices and approaches used in careers work began to become more standardised, and universities and other training providers began to offer training.

The development of the profession has taken different forms in different countries. In some countries, training to be a career development professional happens after training as a teacher or a psychologist, and in others such as the UK, training is open to individuals from a wide variety of backgrounds. The kinds of training professionals undertake and the kinds of jobs they do also vary according to the kinds of contexts professionals work in. So, career development professionals work in the education systems (schools, vocational education and higher education), in public employment services (such as the UK's Jobcentre Plus), in community settings, in organisations and in private practice.

In some countries and contexts, a qualification is required to work as a career development professional, in others a qualification may not be required. As we think about what qualifications are required to be a professional, it is also useful to think about para-professionals and congruent professionals. These are practitioners who are neither complete amateurs nor fully qualified career development professionals.[1]

Para-professionals. Most professions recognise that there are a range of activities within their area of interest which do not require full professional status. In the context of careers work, this might include managing information resources, checking CVs, triaging clients (i.e. identifying who needs professional help and who can be dealt with in other ways), organising speakers and events and so on. These kinds of roles are sometimes described as 'first contact' or 'support' roles, and people doing them may have some qualifications in careers, usually at a lower level than full career development professionals. Such para-professionals would be expected to be working closely with full professionals in most circumstances. Many people who are working at this level may ultimately progress to become full career development professionals by engaging in work-based qualifications.

Congruent professionals. Another area where the professionalism of careers work can be confusing is with respect to the role of congruent professionals such as teachers, social workers, youth workers and human resource management professionals. Many of these roles inevitably undertake some careers work as part of their broader professionalism. It is important that such professionals' initial and continuing professional training should include an insight into careers work. However, such training will usually stop well short of the level of training given to career development professionals. We will explore this further in Chapter 5 where we look at systems and contexts for careers work.

Reflection

Think about some of the different contexts in which career development professionals work in your country.

Schools

Vocational education

Higher education

Work with young people who are NEET (not in education or training)

Public employment services anc work with unemployed adults

Publicly funded adult guidance services

Privately funded career counselling and coaching

Talent management and career development services within employing organisations

Outplacement services for those who have been made redundant

Career guidance in prisons and probations services

Services aimed at special groups such as migrants or people with special educational needs or disabilities

Services that support people with long-term health conditions in the workplace

Other services

What career development services exist in your country across these different contexts? Who is responsible for delivering them? How are these people usually trained?

All of these different contexts for career development work, as well as differences of opinion about what the role is, how it is best done and what it is most helpfully called mean that there are a huge range of different versions of career development professionals performing various different tasks with different emphasis and with different kinds of training. In an analysis of job adverts for career development professionals in the UK, researchers found that there were 103 different titles for career development professionals.[2] If you look internationally, it is likely that you would find even more.

Some of these job titles are associated with particular functions (e.g. Higher Education Adviser or Job Search Specialist) or with particular traditions of practice (e.g. Career Counsellor or Careers Coach) but it is just as often a question of branding. So, one service might describe its practitioners as 'Careers Consultants' while a few miles down the road people are doing the same job and described as 'Employability Specialists', 'Careers Advisers' or 'Future Engineers' all while doing essentially the same job. All of this speaks to a need to be careful about assumptions about people's roles based on the terminology that is used and to take the time to dig down a bit beyond what a person's job title is.

Professional skills and knowledge

Despite the diversity of working contexts, titles and training routes to becoming a career development professional, there have been concerted efforts internationally to define the roles of career development professionals, including the tasks that they undertake and the skills and knowledge needed to work effectively. More than a decade ago, people who were involved in the training of career development professionals from across Europe decided to get together in what was called the Network for Innovation in Career Guidance and Counselling in Europe (NICE). One of the main tasks of NICE was to develop an overarching framework that could guide the training of all European career development professionals. By reviewing existing practices across different countries they concluded that there were five main roles that made up career development professionals' practice. These were then developed into the NICE framework (Figure 3.1).

The NICE framework has been influential because it creates a broad and inclusive framework for the training of career development professionals. It allows for the training of different professionals in different countries and contexts to be organised differently, but it sets some minimum standards. Of course, not every career development professional is going to be equally involved in all the five NICE roles. Many career development professionals will be focused on the giving of one-to-one guidance, and using career information and assessment, while others might be primarily involved in leadership and management. However, everyone should have an understanding of all of these roles and have a level of competence in them.

Figure 3.1 The NICE framework

All career development professionals should understand how to

- use career information;
- support people through one-to-one counselling or coaching approaches;
- contribute to career education;
- engage with organisations and intervene in social systems (such as the education system or the benefits system); and
- help to manage career development programmes.

The NICE framework also helps to clarify what skills and competencies are needed for different kinds of career development work. This is defined in detail in the second volume of the NICE handbook by Schiersmann et al., *European Competence Standards for the Academic Training of Career Development Professionals*.

Drawing from the work of NICE, we have constructed an overview of the key roles and skills and competencies of the career development professional, and we have mapped these to different chapters in this book (see Table 3.1).

The NICE framework has been very influential in shaping the qualifications available in different national contexts.

⌁ Resources

For more information on the NICE framework, see Schiersmann et al.'s *Handbook for the Academic Training of Career Guidance and Counselling Professionals* and Schiersmann et al.'s *European Competence Standards for the Academic Training of Career Development Professionals*.

Both of these documents, and many other useful papers, are available for free at NICE website: https://www.nice-network.eu/pub/.

Becoming a professional

There are lots of ways to become a career development professional, and the exact route that you follow will depend on your background, and your intended professional context (including your country context). Broadly there are three main pathways to becoming a professional.

1. **Pre-service professional education.** This is where an individual trains to become a career development professional prior to starting work in the profession.

Table 3.1. Skills and competencies required by career development professionals

Role	Key skills and competencies	Relevant chapters
General professional tasks	Advocacy for career development services Reflective practice Prioritisation and self-management Ethical practice	4, 5, 10, 11
Career counselling	Contracting and building rapport Building a working alliance Empathy Active listening Supporting career exploration Goal setting and motivation Understanding transitions and personal change and development Supporting clients in the interpretation of complex situations	7
Career education	Designing career learning programmes Presenting Teaching and learning Assessing career management competencies	8
Social systems interventions	Brokering relationships Referring to other professionals and services Networking Advocating Mediating career-related conflicts	10
Career service management	Service development Marketing Coordinating your own work and the work of others Building partnerships Quality assurance	11
Career assessment and interventions	Investigating clients' interests and resources Identifying clients' information needs Assessing clients' needs and capabilities Developing clients' awareness of information sources Developing clients' information literacy Recommending appropriate tools and resources Providing clients with relevant and useful information and sources of information	7, 8, 9

2. **In-service training or work-based training.** This is where someone who is already working in a relevant role undertakes further training to become a professional. This route is often taken by those in paraprofessional roles.

3. **Grandparenting or accreditation of prior learning and experience.** This is where someone has been working in the profession for a long time without formal training and is asked to provide evidence that they have sufficient knowledge, skill and experience to become a full professional without needing to go through a formal training pathway.

In many countries, training to be a career development professional involves studying at a university. In the UK the QCD (Qualification in Career Development) is a key professional qualification and is structured in order to meet the NICE framework we described in the previous section. The QCD is awarded by the professional body (the Career Development Institute) and is delivered as part of recognised postgraduate qualifications delivered at UK universities. This means you complete your QCD alongside university studies. There are also some postgraduate, university-based qualifications which do not lead to the QCD. University studies are typically offered both as part-time or full-time courses and may be taken either face-to-face or at distance (online). These courses can be taken both by those currently working in a relevant role and those who are seeking to enter the profession. The CDI also recognises other routes into the profession in the UK which we have discussed in Chapter 2.

CASE STUDY

In Chapter 2 we heard that Shona had signed up to undertake a master's degree to help her formalise the skills that she had begun to develop while working in the community centre connecting unemployed adults with work and work-related opportunities.

When she signs up as a student she gets sent information about the professional body (the Career Development Institute). She realises that becoming a career development professional is not just a question of acquiring new knowledge and skills but also about connecting to a huge new professional community (with associated groups on Facebook and LinkedIn).

Even before the course begins, she is starting to feel part of a big professional community, which offers both lots of practical help and a bigger sense of purpose.

Professional organisations

Alongside professional training, a key part of being a professional for many people is an ongoing relationship with a professional organisation. In some regulated professions, membership of a professional body is required to practice; this includes doctors and nurses for example. In the UK career guidance is not a regulated profession, and this means it is possible to practice without a professional membership. However, for many practitioners, membership of a professional body provides a number of advantages. Membership can offer:

- **Professional status.** Being a member of a professional body indicates to potential service users, customers or clients that the services you provide are of a certain standard. You will see practitioners indicating their professional memberships on their CVs, business cards and elsewhere, through the inclusion of a logo or letters after their name.

- **Ongoing training and development.** Professional bodies allow members to become part of a community of practice and to develop networks with other practitioners. They might offer training sessions or information resources (such as newsletters) to help members keep up to date with changes in the sector, and to improve their skills.

- **Support for career development.** Professional bodies often provide access to support or advice for practitioners. This includes things like support with setting up self-employment. In the UK, the CDI, for example, keeps a 'professional register' where registered members can advertise their services, and which can be searched by members of the public.

- **Professional protection.** Professional bodies set standards for the provision of services, and through membership of the body practitioners agree on the standards against which they provide services. This can help practitioners to be clear with clients, customers or service users about what they can expect. Where things go wrong, professional bodies may also handle complaints from clients and provide support to practitioners.

- **Collective action and networks.** Being part of a professional body allows access to networks of other professionals, and membership can help to promote and support the profession.

There are different professional bodies and associations available to career development professionals. In the UK, the Career Development Institute is the main body within career development, however, depending on professional role and identity professionals may choose to be a member of a different organisation. Career coaches, for example, may be members of the International Coaching Federation or the Association for Coaching.

There is also the Association of Graduate Careers Advisory Services (AGCAS) which is a membership organisation for career development and graduate employment professionals working in higher education. Congruent professionals (e.g. teachers) also have their own professional bodies, and for human resource management professionals, there is the Chartered Instituted of Professional Development (CIPD). Other countries will have their own professional associations, and the International Association for Educational and Vocational Guidance (IAEVG) is an international professional association in the field.

💡 Resources

As part of your professional development you should familiarise yourself with the relevant professional bodies and consider which ones to join.

Career Development Institute https://www.thecdi.net/

AGCAS https://www.agcas.org.uk/

CIPD https://www.cipd.org/uk/

International Coaching Federation: https://coachingfederation.org/

Association for Coaching: https://www.acconnect.org/

International Association for Educational and Vocational Guidance (IAEVG): https://iaevg.com

---

In addition to being a member of a professional body you may also be interested in joining a trade union. Professional bodies are involved in developing the profession that they are associated with, including developing the skills of professionals and the public image of the profession. Trade unions represent their members in relation to their employment situation and negotiate with employers about pay and conditions, including things like access to training. Internationally trade unions are also an important provider of career guidance to their members.

💡 Resources

A range of different trade unions represent career development professionals depending on the situation in which they work. In England the most common union for career development professionals to belong to is Unison (https://www.unison.org.uk/), although in higher education it is also common to be a member of UCU (https://www.ucu.org.uk/).

Professional ethics

One of the key roles of professional bodies in career development is to outline the standards that professionals are expected to adhere to. One of the ways that these organisations do this is by setting out ethical guidelines, principles, standards or codes of practice. The CDI, for example, explains its code of ethics as covering '*the professional behaviour and practice required of all CDI members*'.

Ethics can be thought of as moral principles that guide the work of practitioners. Whether or not a practitioner is a member of a professional organisation it is reasonable to expect that they would seek to provide their services in an ethical manner. However, professional associations typically lay out the specific ethical principles practitioners are expected to follow. Most codes highlight things like working in the best interests of the client, being open and honest, and doing no harm.

The CDI code of ethics covers ten principles, which we have summarised below:

- **Equity, Diversity and Inclusion.** Providing services that are accessible to all, actively promoting equity and diversity in their work and seeking to address barriers that individuals might face.
- **Accountability.** Practitioners should be accountable for their services, behave with integrity, honesty and diligence, and not bring the profession into disrepute.
- **Autonomy.** Encouraging individuals to be autonomous in their decision-making and enabling clients to make decisions in their own best interests.
- **Confidentiality.** Respecting the privacy of individuals, being clear about confidentiality (and its limits) at the outset of service provision and only disclosing confidential information with informed consent or when required by the law.
- **Competence and continuous professional development.** Maintaining professional competence through ongoing continuous professional development and being clear about the boundaries of their training and expertise. Maintaining professional competence through participation in ongoing training.
- **Duty of care to clients.** Always acting in the best interests of clients.
- **Impartiality.** Providing unbiased advice based solely on the best interests of the client and independent of any external pressure. Being aware of limits to impartiality and acknowledging these.
- **Transparency.** Being open about the services provided as well as about any assumption, limits or requirements (e.g. associated with funding) that shape these services.

- **Trustworthiness.** Ensuring clients have appropriate expectations of the service and honouring agreements and promises.
- **Fitness to practise.** Ensuring ongoing fitness to practice in terms, including being aware of personal integrity and physical and mental well-being.

Most ethical frameworks are similar to this, although each one is likely to emphasise different things. If your work is governed by a different ethical framework, compare this to the framework above and consider the similarities and differences.

Resources

There are a wide range of different ethical frameworks. It is worth looking at a few different ones to see how they vary. Some suggestions are provided below.

The CDI code of ethics: https://www.thecdi.net/Code-of-Ethics

The AGCAS code of ethics (https://www.agcas.org.uk/AGCAS-Member-Code-of-Ethics) covers higher education in the UK.

The IAEVG international ethica guidelines (https://iaevg.com/Ethical-guidelines).

You might want to search for other ethical frameworks or codes from different international contexts.

As will already be clear, ethical principles extend beyond the legal requirements of practitioners to consideration of what is right or appropriate. A good example is confidentiality, which is a common principle in codes of practice. In the UK practitioners' record-keeping is governed by the legal requirements of the Data Protection Act, which says that records should be accurate, stored securely and so on, but the ethical principle of confidentiality extends beyond this and requires, for example, that services are provided in suitably private spaces.

Because ethical principles extend beyond legal requirements and are focused on the moral or right way to deliver services, they act more as a guide to practice than as a checklist. Sometimes practitioners will face 'ethical dilemmas' which arise when working to one principle might contradict another principle.

CASE STUDY

Shona has been working with a client who is looking to get a job and move to another town. Her colleague who works with the same client on her housing situation asks Shona for some information about the client's plans. Should she try and place her in a new flat or not? As a supportive colleague, Shona might be concerned that her colleague risks wasting time and resources rehousing someone who is going to move anyway. But the principle of confidentiality says that she shouldn't pass this information on without the client's agreement.

The next day Shona sees a young person who has been referred to her by one of the community centre's youth workers. This girl informs Shona that she doesn't want a 'career' and plans to drop out of school and hang around with her friends. She intends to become a famous TikToker and isn't going to need any qualifications for that. Shona wants to respect her autonomy to live the life that she wants but feels concerned about whether this decision is really in her best interests (duty of care to clients).

Shona uses the ethical principles outlined by her professional body to reflect on these situations and work out on how best to proceed.

Despite the existence of ethical frameworks, it is not always clear what the 'right' thing to do is. Ethical frameworks provide a tool to help you think through your practice, consider the nature of the dilemma and work out the best way forwards. They also provide you with a language to help you describe and talk through a situation with colleagues, a supervisor or a manager, and to justify the decision that you have taken. Taking a thoughtful approach to practice is key to working ethically and the principles outlined by a professional body can help practitioners to do this.

Reflection

In the case study above we have given two examples of an ethical dilemma that a practitioner might face in their work. How would you resolve those dilemmas?

Can you think of other kinds of ethical dilemmas that practitioners might face?

> 💡 **Resources**
>
> If you are interested in reflecting more on the complexities of ethical practice then Helen Colley's 'Ethics Work in Career Guidance: Navigating Ethical Principles and Ethical Pressures in an Under-Resourced Service' and Tristram Hooley's 'Impartiality: A Critical Review' both provide a good starting place.

Professional boundaries

In the discussion on ethics above we mentioned the idea of 'boundaries', and it is important to say a bit more about this. Boundaries involve understanding what your role is and how it is appropriate to act within this role. How you speak to a client, for example, will differ from how you speak to a friend or family member, because you are a professional. If and when you see a client outside of a session, your interactions will also be guided by your professional role, so you would not discuss in a public space what you have discussed in the confidential space of a career guidance appointment. Nor would you seek to transgress professional boundaries by meeting up with a client outside of a session for a social activity, or acting as a friend. Because of the lines between being a professional and other relationships, it is also normally advisable not to enter a professional relationship with someone who you know well outside of this role (as a family member or friend for example).

A further professional boundary aligns to the important ethical value of 'competence'. In other words you shouldn't do anything that you don't know how to do or give advice to people about subjects which you know nothing about. Your competence provides you with a boundary for your practice. Thinking about the boundaries of your role is also important (and what you therefore should and shouldn't be talking about) and what other professionals' roles are (and therefore what subjects someone else might be better to deal with).

In many cases these boundaries are quite clear and well understood by both you and your students and clients. So, people don't generally come to see a career development professional when they have broken their arm or if they are having trouble in their marriage. So if someone comes through the door and asks about these things you should suggest that they go and see a doctor or a relationship counsellor. But not all areas are as clearly demarcated as this. For example, many people who are having difficulties in making career choices may also be suffering from poor mental health. You can help them to deal with their career issues, and also allow them to talk about their wider problems, but you are not qualified to start doing therapeutic counselling. So, in this case you should highlight the limits of your practice, and explore with the client what other sources of support they have access to or could access. Where they would benefit from additional support and are not already accessing this you could refer them to mental health services. In some cases, clients may like to self-refer, and in other cases you may make a referral for them with their consent. Where clients are struggling to access appropriate services you may also have a role in advocating for them, and liaising with other services to try and improve access. But you would not step across your boundaries and try and provide these services yourself.

We can summarise the key principles of effective referral as follows.

- Understand the limits of your knowledge and your role, and think carefully as you approach those limits. Be clear with a client about the limits of your knowledge and of your role.
- Build your awareness of other professionals and sources of support and encourage your students and clients to use them as appropriate.
- Where it is helpful to pass on information that you have to another professional, gain the consent of the client to do this.
- Consider whether it would be useful for you to have regular contact with other professionals either to discuss particular cases (with client's consent) or to talk in general about areas of overlap, mutual interest and inter-professional working.
- Make sure that you have accessed appropriate training about referral, data protection and safeguarding, and follow any organisational procedures closely. Where in doubt speak to your manager about the best way to proceed.

The importance of continuing professional development

Being a professional involves not only professional training and membership of a professional body but also ongoing training and continuous professional development (CPD). CPD is part of the regulatory bargain we mentioned earlier, in other words you only get to be a profession and a professional if you keep up to date and continue to develop your skills. Reflective practice, as we discussed in Chapter 2, is key to ongoing professional development. However, CPD may also take other forms, such as attending training courses. Many professional bodies have requirements for CPD. These might be specified as 'inputs', a certain number of days or hours spent in learning, or focus on 'outputs' by asking professionals to record what they have learned. Having a robust mechanism to ensure their members stay well informed is part of convincing society that they can be trusted to regulate the quality of their work. If you are a member of a professional body you should check their requirements for CPD, including how it should be recorded.

The starting point in planning any CPD is to identify your own professional development needs. There are several ways of doing this. One would be simply to note things that you want to know or understand more about or learn how to do. Another would be to review your current knowledge, understanding and skills against a suitable template (such as the list of skills given in Table 3.1). Once you have identified your CPD needs you need to think about how you can find development opportunities that will help you to meet those needs. In some cases, it might be obvious, but at other times it might take some research. Google will sometimes answer your questions and find you a good opportunity, but in other cases there might be a need to ask around and see how other people have addressed this issue.

Reflection

Make a note of some of your CPD needs. Look over your list and consider the following questions.

- Is this a need that you could work on by yourself using self-study resources?
- Is there anyone in your workplace who could help you to meet this need?
- Is there anyone else in your immediate network who could help you to meet this need?
- Is there an obvious course or development opportunity that addresses this need?
- Are there any opportunities that are free?
- How much of a priority is meeting this need?
- How have other career development professionals developed in this area?

As the reflective questions above suggest, engaging in CPD is about a lot more than just attending a training course. That is just one of many forms that it can take. Neary and Johnson list an A–Z of over 60 different forms of CPD in their handbook. It is worth getting hold of that book once you are qualified, but for now we will offer *a top 10* of the main types of CPD activity.

1. **Reading.** Sometimes just reading a book, article, blog or website will provide you with the information and ideas that you need.

2. **Shadowing and visits.** You can learn a lot by watching others in your organisation or by visiting other organisations to see how they do things.

3. **Mentoring and supervision.** It is enormously useful to have a mentor who can help you to structure your learning and allow you to draw on their skills and knowledge. Supervision is a formal relationship with an experienced professional who can guide you through a process of reflection on your practice to identify key learning needs. It is common in a range of helping professions and a requirement for therapeutic counsellors. It is not yet very well established in career development work, but the CDI have produced a helpful resource (by Mallows and Walker) on it, if you want to know more.

4. **Observation.** While it can be worrying to have someone more experienced watch you delivering a career counselling or coaching session or teaching a careers education lesson, it is a powerful learning opportunity. Ideally observations include the opportunity to talk about what is being observed before and after the observation.

5. **Conferences.** The careers world is full of conferences and events. Some of these are free while others are expensive. These are valuable opportunities to access up-to-date knowledge and build a network of contacts.

6. **Short courses.** There is a wide range of courses on different aspects of career practice that variously last between an hour and a day. These kinds of courses are usually relatively cheap to access and can support you to improve your skills and knowledge.

7. **Longer training programmes.** More in-depth training can sometimes be accessed through participating in a course which takes place over a number of days or weeks.

8. **Accredited qualifications.** In some cases longer training programmes might lead you to an accredited qualification. This might be about studying for a master's or PhD in career development or taking a much more specific qualification, for example, becoming a mental health first aider.

9. **Online learning resources.** There is a range of online learning resources available which include blogs and information sources that you subscribe to, self-study courses and online tutored programmes.

10. **Communities of practice.** A huge amount of professional learning comes from having the right network or community of practice around you. Building a network of friends, colleagues and informants is critical to your CPD.

> ### 💡 Resources
>
> A good starting point is Neary and Johnson's book, *CPD for the Career Development Professional: A Handbook for Enhancing Practice*. This is a practical handbook which provides information on ways in which CPD can be undertaken and which helps career development professionals to direct their own CPD.
>
> Professional bodies typically provide access to information, expertise and training courses. In the UK, the Career Development Institute (CDI) provides a monthly CPD bulletin, an extensive programme of training courses (see https://www.thecdi.net/training-and-events) and several online communities of interest (see https://www.thecdi.net/communities-and-networks).

Professionalisation and professional advocacy

Finally, it is worth noting that becoming a professional comes with responsibilities to your profession. As well as developing the skills and knowledge you need, ensuring that you are up to date and working ethically, you should also be an advocate for the careers profession every day of your life.

Career development professionals should work to exemplify the values of the profession and speak out about the value of the profession. This could include everything from challenging your employer if they are asking you to behave unethically, to arguing against cuts to your budget, to writing a letter to the newspaper if it has published an article attacking careers advisers, to suggesting to friends and family when they may benefit from seeking career advice.

Being a professional is about something more than just doing a job. It also speaks to our identity and our values. In a world where the concept of career is often poorly understood and career development services are often underfunded, we all must become advocates for our profession.

In a nutshell

This chapter has discussed the idea of career development as a professional activity. It has argued that

- being a professional is about more than just doing a job;

- that while everyone can help people to develop their career, there is a special role for a trained and qualified career development professional;

- career development professionals work in a range of contexts but should all be able to give one-to-one career support, provide careers education, intervene into social systems, manage and develop services and make use of information, assessment and resources;

- there are a range of routes to becoming a career development professional, but once you are qualified you need to continue to engage in CPD; and

- ethical practice is at the heart of professionalism, and a key part of this is knowing where your boundaries are and referring as appropriate.

Chapter 4
The context for careers work

Introduction

Career pathways are always developed in relation to the world around us. They are shaped by the kinds of schools we go to and the educational systems that we go through. They are also shaped by the kinds of employment opportunities that are available to us, the economy and the structures of different professions.

In this chapter we introduce and explore the nature of the contexts for our career development, focusing particularly on the role of education systems and the labour market. Understanding these systems is important because as a career development professional you are involved in helping to support individuals as they navigate their educational and working worlds.

Understanding the world within which careers take place

The contexts we live and work in shape the ways our careers develop. This influence is direct, as educational and employment opportunities shape what is possible for us; but it is also indirect because the kinds of opportunities we engage in will influence the ways we think about ourselves, the skills we develop and how we understand our position in the working world. Understanding how our contexts shape our career ideas is something that many theorists of career development have considered and is a topic we return to in Chapter 6.

As a career development professional, it is important to build awareness of the systems that our clients engage in and the nature of the opportunities that they provide. This helps us to understand what kinds of pathways are possible and how people can move through education and employment. Understanding where to get accurate and up-to-date information about education and labour markets, and how and when to provide this to clients, is also an essential skill for career development professionals (see Chapter 9) and a core part of career development services.

In this chapter we explore the nature of labour markets and educational systems. Here, we recognise that these systems can be quite different in different countries (and sometimes vary regionally as well), and that they change over time. So, the kinds of experiences that you personally had in engaging with these systems as you have developed over your career will not necessarily be the same as the kinds of experiences or opportunities your clients can access. This is why it is important for us as practitioners to stay up to date with the world of work. This chapter aims to introduce different concepts and ways of thinking that will help you make sense of the workplace and educational systems in your context, and that of your clients.

Reflection

Think about your experiences of career development. What kind of opportunities were available to you at school and when you first entered the workplace?

- What qualifications did you obtain?
- What educational or work opportunities were available to you after school?
- What kinds of training or career pathways were available?

How might these be different from clients you might work with as a career development professional?

The labour market

The terminology of the 'labour market' is something that you will come across a great deal in career development work. But what do we mean by this term? At first glance we might think of the terminology of the 'labour market' as referring to the kinds of jobs that are available in a specific place or a specific industry. But this is not quite the whole picture. The term 'labour market' focuses on the world of work as a marketplace. There are 'buyers' of labour (employers) and there are 'sellers' of labour (individual workers), and the 'labour market' is the marketplace where buyers and sellers interact.

Thinking about work in terms of a labour 'market' highlights how work is a negotiation between what someone is willing to sell their labour for, and what an employer, or a purchaser of goods or services (in the case of self-employed people), is willing to pay. It is also the case that the wider systems and structures around employment impact these negotiations. This includes ways of regulating or organising the labour market, such as when a government 'regulates' a profession, setting a standard or qualification that someone needs in order to be employed in a particular role or when it regulates the whole labour market, for example, by setting a minimum wage or deciding what age people are allowed to leave education.

The education system has a key role in the labour market as it is how individuals gain the skills that employers look for and which are required in some professions. The education system also has an important role in accrediting these skills through qualifications. In addition, as we will see later in this chapter, the welfare system has a key role in supporting, and at times compelling, those who are out of work to access the labour market; and employment legislation regulates the behaviours of employers and employees in the labour market.

It is worth stating that selling labour through employment is only one way in which people spend their time and resource their lives, albeit the most common. Others might sell goods and services to a range of buyers (i.e. be self-employed), be financially supported by others or live by income from capital and investments, such as pensions.

Understanding the labour market

If a key role of a career development professional is helping people to understand and navigate the labour market, then it is important to develop a strong understanding of labour market structures and systems. One particularly important point to note is that although we often talk about the 'labour market', the labour market is not really a single market. Instead, it is composed of different labour markets which overlap to a certain extent.

The idea of *labour market segmentation* is important here, as it helps us think about how there are different labour markets for different industries or occupations and in different geographical areas. So, for example, people do not move freely between different regions and occupations, and if a job for a nurse arises in London, this is of little consequence or interest to a teacher in Edinburgh. Recognising that different parts of the labour market function somewhat separately, we might think about the importance not just of understanding national labour markets but the labour market in particular industries or professions, and in particular areas or regions.

An associated idea is that of the *dual labour market* which thinks about how labour markets are divided into two key parts – the primary part which is characterised by professional jobs that require a level of training and the secondary labour market which is characterised by short-term contracts, low-paid and low-skilled work. Again, these labour markets can be thought of as relatively distinct from each other. The idea of a secondary labour market is particularly important when it comes to considering equality and diversity, as minority and disadvantaged groups tend to be disproportionately represented in the secondary labour market.

The ideas of labour market segmentation and the dual labour market highlight how different people have quite different relationships to the labour market depending on their social, occupational and geographical position.

Occupations and industries

The complexity of the labour market has resulted in different kinds of concepts or tools we can use to help us understand it. Recognising geographical variation in labour markets, when we talk about 'regional' labour markets, it is typical to use commonly agreed geographical boundaries. So, we might talk about the 'South West labour market' or the 'Welsh labour market' or the 'Manchester labour market'. When it comes to thinking about the segmentation of the labour market in terms of types of work, it is common to speak in terms of 'occupation' and 'industry'. In the UK these terms, for example, are used by the Office for National Statistics (ONS) to categorise jobs. But what do we mean by these terms?

Occupation. An occupation is a broad grouping of jobs according to the kinds of tasks they involve. Sometimes an occupation can seem to be very clearly defined, especially when an occupation is aligned to a profession which requires specific professional training. However, in other occupations, there can be a lot of variety in terms of job titles and specific duties (as we have already seen is the case in career development). In the UK, Standard Occupational Codes (SOCs) are used to classify occupations into different groups, by both skill level and skill content. The idea of 'skill level' is important here, as it recognises different levels of employment, and SOCs are currently used (in combination with salary levels) to determine eligibility for skilled work visas for those people coming to the UK.

Industry. When we think of 'industry' we often think of manufacturing companies. However, thinking about labour markets, the term has a much wider meaning. All jobs in a labour market can be classified by industry; by the setting in which they take place. In the UK, just as we have SOCs for occupations, we have SICs (Standard Industrial Classifications) for industries. Some occupations are closely linked to certain industries; for example nursing is associated with healthcare, and teachers with education. However, other occupations are found across different industries; for example human resource professionals will be found in companies working in all different industries.

Occupations and industries are, effectively, the *what* and the *where* of jobs – what is being done and where it is being done. Although these terms are important ways of understanding the labour market, there are other terms too which are equally important to understand. One of these terms is 'sector'. A sector, simply speaking, is a group of similar industries, for example it is common to group industries that are funded by the government, such as teaching, social work, and the civil service, into the *public sector*. Sometimes you might come across analysis of the labour market by 'sector'.

Skills

One of the challenges with ideas of 'occupations' and 'industries' is that these can seem like fixed and distinct categories. For example, using SOCs and SICs, each job can be given a particular code. However, in practice, for workers, jobs are not always quite as distinct from each other as these categorisations might suggest. During the course of their life, an individual might work in a number of different occupations and industries.

An alternative way of thinking about the labour market is to focus on the kinds of skills, qualifications and knowledge that different jobs require and recognise that these might, to some extent, cross over. As a career development professional, if you work with adults, you will almost certainly be asked at some point in your professional career '*what other jobs can I do with my skills and qualifications*'? Here the idea of '*skills*' is particularly important. Skills are often understood as coming in two different varieties:

- **Transferrable skills.** Those that 'transfer' between different occupations and industries. For example, language skills, critical thinking, business awareness, literacy and numeracy are often understood to be 'transferrable'.
- **Occupationally specific skills.** Those that are specific to a particular occupation and do not easily transfer between occupations.

In recent years, there has been some discussion about whether labour market analysis needs to move away from thinking just about set industries and occupations and develop ways of defining and mapping skills across the labour market.[1] Thinking about 'skills' in this way highlights how individuals might move between different sectors and industries depending on their capacities and interests. However, it is also important to remember that movements between some sectors or occupations might be more possible in some cases than in others, depending on the level of occupationally specific skills that are necessary, and whether or not different professions are regulated.

Resources

There are some useful papers that explore the labour market from the perspective of career development professionals, such as Marcus Offer's 'The Discourse of the Labour Market' and John Killeen's 'The Social Context of Guidance' although both of these are now getting somewhat old.

There is an extensive academic literature that discusses the labour market, but this is probably beyond what you are likely to need. A basic text like

Peter Cramp's *Labour Markets* might be a good starting point if you want to dig into this more deeply. Alternatvely, there are basic introductions on the *CIPD* website at https://www.cipd.org/uk/knowledge/factsheets/economy-labour-market-factsheet/ and the Investopedia website at https://www.investopedia.com/terms/l/labor-market.asp

If you are based in the UK, it will be useful to familiarise yourself with some of the labour market statistics produced by the Office for National Statistics (ONS) (https://www.ons.gov.uk/). Other countries will have equivalent national statistics agencies which should have major sections on education and employment.

The education and training system

A key part of understanding the labour market is understanding the education system and how it relates to the world of work. Increasingly, as countries pursue 'high skill' economies or 'knowledge economies', governments are investing more and more in educational provision, and individuals are spending longer in the education system before they enter the workplace. There is also increasing diversity in the kinds of educational pathways that are available in modern education systems. A good understanding of the education system and the routes through it is therefore central to working as a career development professional.

Educational structures

As children we often take for granted schooling and the structures of the education system. We don't think about when we start school, the age at which we move into secondary schooling, the age at which we take exams and what these exams are. However, there is considerable variation internationally in education systems, including variation between the home nations of the UK (Scotland, Wales, Northern Ireland and England). Young people in Scotland, for example, start school and transfer to secondary school at a different age to those young people in England and take different qualifications.

In understanding education systems, it is useful to recognise that despite their differences, national education systems typically comprise three different levels of education:

- **Basic education** is often split into 'primary' and 'lower secondary' education and is compulsory for young people. In some countries, there is no break between primary and secondary schooling, and so basic education is completed in the same school. In the UK basic education includes school provision up to GCSE level in England, Wales and Northern Ireland and National Certificate level in Scotland.

- **Upper secondary education** is education delivered after compulsory schooling, typically between the ages of 16 and 19. It is often divided between (academic) pathways that prepare young people to enter higher education and those that are focused on vocational and technical education. In England this includes provision that leads to A levels, T levels and other qualifications, and in Scotland to Highers and Advanced Highers. Wales and Northern Ireland's systems offer A level and other vocational qualifications like BTECs, with Wales also offering the Welsh Baccalaureate. Upper secondary education may take place in a school or in another kind of institution, such as a vocational or further education college.

- **Tertiary education** is education delivered after the upper secondary phase and includes higher education as well as a variety of forms of vocational education. 'Tertiary education providers' in the UK are colleges of Further Education, Independent Training Providers (ITPs) and universities.

There are different kinds of pathways through these levels of education, and it is common to think in terms of 'vocational track' education and 'academic track'. Vocational track education, sometimes called vocational education and training (VET), is training related to a specific trade, occupation or profession. It can be undertaken in a school, further or adult education setting, or in a workplace.

In the UK and many other countries, *apprenticeships* are a key form of VET. Apprenticeships are delivered by employers and training providers in partnership, as a combination of on-the-job training and study towards specific qualifications. Although apprenticeships are often associated with initial training and induction into a new occupation, they can actually be taken at any age and lead people to a high level of skill and qualifications; for example in the UK apprenticeships go up to master's level. The key differentiator between apprenticeships and other forms of education is that they are, first and foremost, a *job*, so that means that people wishing to pursue them need to be employed and stay employed throughout the apprenticeship.

Academic track education is less vocationally oriented and is often aimed at progressing into university. Although vocational and academic tracks are often seen as distinct, in practice there is not always a firm dividing line between these kinds of education. It is the case, for example, that degree courses at university can also have different levels of vocational focus – a degree in nursing or veterinary medicine, for example, is vocationally very specific. Furthermore, vocational qualifications undertaken at school or college can be used as entry qualifications to get into a university degree course. The increasing number of routes from vocational courses into higher education provision is just one way that education systems have been adapting to the needs of a high-skill labour market.

In practice, then, education systems have become more and more complex, with different routes available through them. As systems have grown in complexity, countries have developed qualifications frameworks which act as maps of the education landscape. These frameworks are helpful for demonstrating to all stakeholders (individuals, employers, career development professionals and others) how different qualifications relate to each other. They can also help individuals plan their routes through education and can support career development professionals in explaining how the education system works to their clients.

💡 Resources

You should make sure that you are familiar with the qualifications framework in your country, as this is important for understanding the way that qualifications are structured.

- To find out more about the RQF in England, Wales and Northern Ireland, you can look at https://www.gov.uk/what-different-qualification-levels-mean/list-of-qualification-levels.
- You can find information about the Scottish Credit and Qualification Framework (SCQF) at https://scqf.org.uk/.
- And the European Qualifications Framework (EQF) at https://europa.eu/europass/en/europass-tools/european-qualifications-framework.

To get a better understanding of the apprenticeship system in the UK, Ben Rowland's *Understanding Apprenticeships* is invaluable.

Understanding client contexts

As a career development professional, you will be working with clients who are seeking support in navigating through education systems and labour markets. In supporting individuals to navigate their pathways, it is also important to recognise the importance of wider contextual factors. In this part of the chapter, we explore the importance of the welfare system, educational funding and employment legislation in influencing someone's position in relation to the labour market. As a career development professional, it is very important to have some understanding of these areas as they can be significant in an individual's pathways. However, do remember that you should be careful about straying beyond your knowledge base and your professional boundaries (see Chapter 3); advice about entitlement to benefits and rights in the workplace are specialist areas of knowledge that should be referred to professionals working in these areas.

It is important to note that welfare systems, funding arrangements and employment law are all highly contested political issues. They differ not only from country to country but also from year to year as new governments come and go. Because of this, it is important for career development professionals to pay close attention to policy debates and changes in laws and funding regimes. Relatively small changes can often have big (and sometimes unintended) consequences for your students and clients.

Welfare systems

Welfare systems exist in countries across the world to support people in meeting basic human needs, such as food and housing. These systems are particularly important sources of support for people who do not have the ability to earn enough money to live on, either because they cannot work, cannot find work, or cannot access work which is sufficiently well paid. The approach to welfare provision varies globally with some countries providing a great deal of support and others providing less. Support includes things like unemployment benefits, as well as housing benefits, child benefits, and disability benefits. In the UK some of these benefits are currently combined into 'universal credit'.

Although career development professionals do not give advice on welfare systems, it is important to have a basic understanding of the availability of welfare support and benefits as this can impact the position of a client in relation to the labour market, and the kinds of employment or education choices that are possible for them. Typically, people fall into the following three main categories.

- **Employed or self-employed.** Someone who is employed is working under contract for an employer; someone who is self-employed works for themselves. It is useful to remember that issues of low pay or low hours in some jobs mean that even when someone is employed or self-employed, they may still access support from welfare systems.
- **Unemployed.** These are individuals who do not have a job *and* who are available to work, and are actively looking for a job.
- **Economically inactive.** These are individuals who are not employed but who are also not seeking work. This includes, for example, people who are unwell, people who do not need an income (such as the independently wealthy and those who have retired early) and people who are taking time out of work to raise children or provide care.

How a person engages with the labour market will depend on their situation and the benefits they are claiming. For example, in the UK, people who are unemployed or on a low income can claim universal credit, but as part of this, they complete an agreement which commits them to specific activities to help them find work or increase their earnings. This is known as *benefit conditionality*, as access to the benefit is made conditional on certain activities. As people increase their earnings, their entitlements to benefits will also change, and this can also impact the kinds of work that people might seek and the implications of engaging in work.

As well as unemployment benefits, individuals may also access other support from the welfare system. This includes support to access housing and healthcare. For example, social housing may be provided to some individuals in some countries, and healthcare may be provided either free of charge (as it is in the UK) or subsidised for some people.

Educational support

With education options expanding and people spending longer in the educational system before entering the workplace, most countries make significant provisions for financing education. However, the way that education is financed varies. In some cases, people are expected to pay for their education directly; sometimes it is subsidised, and sometimes individuals can access grants or loans. It is essential for career development professionals to have a good understanding of how different forms of education are financed.

Basic education, which is mandatory in most countries, is typically provided free of charge. However, the funding landscape for post-compulsory education is much more mixed. Upper secondary or college education is often provided free of charge to young people, with some additional funding available to support living costs. In England this is currently through the 16–19 bursary fund, and in Scotland, Wales and Northern Ireland through educational maintenance allowance (EMA).

Adult learners often have less entitlement to free education, although this varies by country and qualification. In England a new funding regime for post-18 student finance has recently been launched called the Lifelong Learning Entitlement (LLE), which provides loans for a wide range of different vocational and academic further and higher education programmes. Sometimes training grants might be available, either through national programmes or sometimes through charities or trusts. Courses in basic skills such as literacy and numeracy are also often funded. For adults in employment, some forms of training may be paid for or run by their employer, especially where there is a clear benefit to the business. However, in practice, adults often pay for their own training.

Support for accessing higher education varies considerably by country. In the UK, for example, higher education is more heavily subsidised in Scotland

and Wales than in England. In England in the past higher education was largely funded through grants made to universities and individuals. However, now individuals have to borrow money from the state to pay for their tuition and their living costs. Funding can also vary by subject of study; for example bursaries or grants may be available for people entering higher education to train to be teachers, medical professionals or social workers.

Employment rights

As career development professionals are involved in supporting people's journeys through work, a final area of knowledge that is important is that of employment rights. This includes rights to work and rights at work.

Rights to work. The first area to be aware of is that not all individuals in a country have the right to work. This particularly applies to international migrants and young people who fall below a minimum age. In the UK, for example, asylum seekers do not have the right to work, but if they are granted refugee status, then they can work. Visa regulations in some countries determine who can and cannot work in a country, with those in highly skilled jobs, shortage areas or highly paid work more likely to be granted access. With regards to young people, legislation often sets minimum ages at which people can work, as well as limits on the amount and kinds of work people can do.

Rights at work. The second area to be aware of is that individuals who are employed have certain rights. In the UK, for example, this includes the right to a minimum wage, the right not to be discriminated against, the right to a safe working environment, the right to time off and so on. These rights are enforced by various acts of parliament including health and safety legislation and equalities legislation.

Under the Employment Rights Act 1996, everyone in the UK also has a right to a written contract. This contract sets out expectations of employers and employees and often, but not always, provides additional rights, including rights to more than the statutory minimum expectations around holidays; salaries; maternity, paternity and adoption leave and so on. These are known as '*contractual rights*'. Contracts can be negotiated, and employees have the right to request flexible working or other adjustments. However, a contract cannot be changed without the agreement of both the employer and the employee. Sometimes a union might also be involved in negotiating contract changes, especially on behalf of a number of employees, sometimes called 'collective bargaining'.

As a career development professional, it may be important for you to be able to explain to clients their rights at work, as well as help people to think about how to ask for contractual changes and ways to approach contract negotiations.

CASE STUDY

Tina is currently unemployed and claiming benefits (universal credit). She has an agreement as part of her benefits claim to engage in a certain number of job search activities every week and has regular meetings with her job centre adviser to support and monitor her activities. As Tina has expressed uncertainty about what kind of job would suit her, her job centre adviser refers her to speak to James, a careers adviser with a local service.

James speaks to Tina about her background and her interests and helps her clarify the specific kinds of work that might suit her. This conversation helps Tina to focus her job search in a specific area – administrative work. Together, James and Tina explore various local options, and Tina identifies a specific job at a specific local company she is interested in. She expresses concern, however, over whether the job would allow her the flexibility to pick up and drop off her children at school and about whether she could access time off to support one of her children who has ongoing health issues. James discusses her options with her. He explains that as a parent, she has some rights at work to have time off to care for children. He also explores her preference around working hours and identifies that she would ideally like part-time work. He explains that in this case, she has a number of options:

She could call the employer directly to ask if they were willing to consider part-time hours before she makes an application. Alternatively, she could make an application, and then if she is offered the job, she could talk to the employer about whether they would be willing to employ her on a part-time basis. While Tina is nervous about this, James explains that this is all part of the normal contractual discussions that follow a job offer.

Finally, if full-time work might be an option, she could consider what after-school childcare is available in her area and used by other carers and parents, such as childminders. Tina rules this out for now on the basis that she and her family need time to get used to her working outside the home but acknowledges that full-time work is an option for the future.

Tina thinks that negotiating part-time hours seems like a good idea but expresses a concern about whether working part-time would allow her to earn enough money to live on and whether she could continue to claim benefits. James explains that even if she is working, she may be entitled to some benefits if her earnings are low; however, he suggests that she speak to her Jobcentre adviser about this and also gives her the number for the local Citizens Advice service for additional support.

Two weeks later, Tina phones James to thank him for his support. She tells him that she was offered the job and has agreed with the employer that she would work part-time. She also checked her benefits entitlement and can continue to claim some benefits to help her cover some of her living costs.

Resources

Information about eligibility for welfare and employment rights is available in the UK from Citizens Advice (https://www.citizensadvice.org.uk/)

You can find the location of your local Job Centre Plus at https://www.gov.uk/contact-jobcentre-plus

To find out more about applying to higher education in the UK, use the UCAS website https://www.ucas.com/

In a nutshell

This chapter has discussed the contexts within which people develop their careers. It has argued that

- career development professionals help individuals to navigate the world of work and, therefore, an understanding of the labour market is essential;

- labour markets can be understood and analysed in different ways, but common conceptual tools include the ideas of occupations, industries and skills;

- the education system has a key role to play in the labour market as it generates knowledge and skills that are important for employers and employees. Structures of education vary internationally, but there are broad commonalities;

- as well as an understanding of the labour market and the education system, career development professionals also need a good understanding of the wider contexts in which individuals make decisions. This includes an understanding of the welfare system, educational funding and employment rights; and

- as careers provision is often supporting people to address not just their current circumstances but to think about their futures, understanding how the labour market is changing is also essential.

Chapter 5
Understanding
guidance systems

Introduction

Working as a career development professional means working within a community of practitioners and services. Exactly who you work for will shape the work that you do, and your work will also intersect with the activities of many other providers. Understanding the national context for careers provision, including what kinds of services are delivered, where and by whom, and the ways that services are organised together into a system, is an important part of your professional role.

Many career development professionals will work for the government in one way or another, for example, through a national career service or via the publicly funded education system. But even if you are working outside of these public systems, they still set the context for your work. So, if you are in private practice, you are likely to be more successful if you provide services that the government does not provide or if you provide them to people who cannot access any public services.

In this chapter, we explore how career services are organised in different national contexts. We highlight some similarities and some differences. A central point in this chapter is that, in most countries, career education and guidance services are largely publicly funded. This means that, one way or another, the money that pays for these services is government money. It might come directly from the government in the form of a government-funded national career service, or it might come indirectly from the government with services offered as part of the work of schools, colleges or other institutions which are recipients of public money. Because governments are largely responsible for funding career provision, their reasons for supporting career provision are important in shaping the kinds of services that are provided and the work that practitioners do on the ground.

To understand how government priorities shape the career systems we work in, in this chapter we argue that it is important for practitioners to understand public policy, particularly career-related policy. We define policy broadly here as anything that a government chooses to do or not to do, and note that it can take the form of legislation, guidance, strategy documents, funding or regulation. These policies typically shape the way in which services are organised and delivered. Although policy contexts differ, we identify how in most countries career development work is funded to support the functioning of the labour market and the education system, but exactly what is delivered, how and by whom varies a great deal between nations.

Why do governments fund career development services?

Career development services are often understood to be both a public good and a private good. Helping an individual to think about their future and identify their best options will benefit the individual, but helping lots of individuals to think about their best 'fit' in the labour market will also help the overall functioning of the labour market itself, bringing wider benefits to the economy and society. The benefits of career development work might also extend to intermediary organisations such as schools or employers in the impacts it has on their learners or their workforce. When career development professionals are working with individual clients, they will be primarily focused on the person in front of them. However, for career service funders, the wider economic and social impacts of careers provision are a key reason for funding provision.

In most countries career services are almost entirely publicly funded. This means that what services are provided and how they are provided are heavily shaped by government priorities. Because governments have a limited amount of funding, decisions about how much money should be spent, what it should be spent on and how are often challenging. Although in an ideal world we might think everyone should have access to limitless career development support, governments might argue that this funding could also be spent elsewhere, such as on healthcare, education, roads and infrastructure. Because governments are accountable to their taxpayers for the decisions they make about funding, they need to justify that the funding they allocate is appropriate and helpful in meeting national objectives, not just something that is nice to do.

In deciding what career services to fund and how, governments are concerned with meeting public policy goals. Career development provision is typically understood to address three main policy goals relating to education, the economy and social equity.

- **Education.** Providing career services within the education system is often understood as valuable for increasing the engagement and progression of learners. The thinking is that if young people understand where they want to go in the future, they will be motivated to learn and more likely to progress. They are also more likely to progress into courses which are aligned with their skills and interests, further increasing their achievement and motivation.

- **The economy.** Providing career services for people at the points where they are making transitions into the labour market or within the labour market is often understood to help ensure the success and sustainability of these transitions. Key transition points might be from school to the workplace, from university to the workplace or from unemployment to employment. Often the focus is on keeping people 'economically active' and contributing to the labour market, and reducing the cost to the state of financial support for those who are unemployed and unable to find work. However, career services may also be understood as important for supporting individuals not just to find any work but to find work where their skills match the needs of an employer, ensuring that their skills are of most use within the economy. Services may also have a role in supporting workers to progress and develop in their roles, again maximising their ability to contribute economically.

- **Social equity.** Providing career services is often also considered valuable in addressing issues of inequality in the labour market. Recognising that some individuals face more barriers to accessing work than others, career guidance can help address and reduce those barriers. Practically speaking, this can result in the development of career services for particular target groups, perhaps individuals facing health challenges or with disabilities, in deprived communities, with family and caring responsibilities and so on.

Reflection

Consider your experiences of your own career development. What kinds of choices have you made? What evidence can you see for how your career choices might fulfil your own needs, but also fulfil wider policy goals of education, the economy and social equity? Can you see any potential or actual conflict between these goals?

Sustainable development goals

Although economic and educational priorities are perhaps the most prominent rationales for funding career guidance provision, career guidance can also potentially address several other policy priorities. One recent development that has been influential in how countries think about their policy priorities has been the development of the United Nations' Sustainable Development Goals (SDGs). There are 17 sustainable development goals which are intended to be relevant across different international contexts and support global development. These goals were adopted by all UN member states in 2015:

1. No poverty

2. Zero hunger

3. Good health and well-being

4. Quality education

5. Gender equality

6. Clean water and sanitation

7. Affordable and clean energy

8. Decent work and economic growth

9. Industry, innovation and infrastructure

10. Reduced inequalities

11. Sustainable cities and communities

12. Responsible consumption and production

13. Climate action

14. Life below water

15. Life on land

16. Peace, justice and strong institutions

17. Partnership for the goals

Looking at this list, we can see that some goals have a clear and direct relevance to the economic, educational and social equity goals we have discussed so far in this section. This includes the goals around decent work and economic growth, quality education, reduction of inequalities and gender equality. However, we could also argue that career guidance has a role to play in other goals. This includes, perhaps, the contribution career guidance can make to good health and well-being, because being out of work or being in a job that is unsuitable for us can have health implications. We might also argue that career guidance can impact climate goals, particularly through proactive encouragement for people to consider the skills they need and the role they can play at work in addressing the climate emergency, and to peace and justice goals, for example, by helping to align skills in periods of post-war reconstruction or in helping those who have been in the criminal justice system to integrate into society.

Drawing on the Sustainable Development Goals, Pete Robertson has suggested that career guidance can be thought of in relation to six primary goals: (i) labour market goals, (ii) educational goals, (iii) social equity goals, (iv) health and well-being goals, (v) environmental goals and (vi) peace and justice goals.

💡 Resources

There is extensive discussion of the rationales for funding career development services. A good place to start is Pete Robertson's chapter, 'The Aims of Career Development Policy'.

There has also been a lot of work on the economic case for career guidance, such as Chris Percy and Vanessa Dodd's 'The Economic Outcomes of Career Development Programmes' or Chris Percy's article with Tristram Hooley, 'Lessons for Career Guidance from Return-on-Investment Analyses in Complex Education-Related Fields'.

You can also find out more about the UN's Sustainable Development Goals from their website: https://sdgs.un.org/goals

---

Evolving policy contexts

Internationally there are some patterns in the ways in which career provision is understood, but the policy goals which are prioritised vary between countries. This can depend on the nature of the political administration and which political party is in power, the economic context and the cultural context. So, for example, where a government is focused primarily on economic growth, the economic rationales for career development might dominate, whereas governments with a stronger focus on equality and social welfare might be more concerned with those rationales. This means that the ways that career guidance is understood and provided are subject to wider political, economic, social and cultural movements.

A particularly important development in the international context for career development services in recent years has come through wider global changes in the organisation of work, influenced by the forces of globalisation and technological innovation. These forces are understood to be radically reshaping the nature of the workplace, as companies move their operations across the globe and technology makes some jobs redundant while creating new skills or job openings. Experiences of economic instability (including global economic slowdown or recessions), the growing threat of climate change and experiences such as the Covid-19 pandemic are all commonly referenced as reasons the world of careers is less stable than it once was. Our economies, the argument goes, need to become more flexible, and individuals also need to become more flexible and adaptable, potentially making many career changes over the course of their lives. Rather than a 'job for life' conducted within a single sector or a single organisation people are understood as operating within 'boundaryless careers', taking place across multiple organisations and changing over time or 'protean careers' where frequent job changes are undertaken. Many of these arguments are contestable, and it is important to look for evidence of anything that people tell you is an unstoppable trend, but they have certainly been persuasive and so have influenced the policy context within which career development services operate.

The argument that education and work have become increasingly complex and that there is a growing need for flexible and adaptable workers has led to many governments to focus on how to equip people for these changes. The concept of 'lifelong learning' stresses the ways that people need to continually improve their skills and learn new skills. In parallel, the concept of 'lifelong guidance' emphasises that adults need access to career services throughout life to manage these changes.

The idea of lifelong guidance clearly raises a range of cost implications for governments. In response to this, some career services have experimented with triage systems, online service provision and other initiatives. For example, a recent trend has seen some services recruit and train para-professionals to perform discrete aspects of a career development role, such as supporting people with CVs, applications or interviews. Many countries have also developed online web resources that people can access freely and without the help of a professional. At the moment the jury is still out on what the relative effectiveness of these different kinds of approaches is and even on whether they really save governments any money.

The concept of lifelong guidance does not necessarily mean that everyone in the population should sit down for a career guidance interview every year. Such a model would be very costly and may not best meet people's needs. Some of the most interesting thinking about career development services has focused on career development as a process of learning and has tried to define what people need to know to be successful in their careers (typically described as 'career management skills').

Career management skills are the skills that people need to proactively manage their careers over their lifetime. They include things like being able to find and evaluate career information, decision-making skills, personal awareness and awareness of the economic environment. Thinking about career management skills also opens up the possibility of funding different kinds of services that develop individuals' capacity to self-manage their careers rather than simply providing support at transition points. So, for example, if schools teach young people the skills to manage their own careers, then some of the pressure on adult career services might be reduced. Rather than needing to go to a career development professional to access information to make a career transition, if someone has career information literacy skills then they may be able to access, evaluate and understand career information available on the internet themselves and not need access to one-to-one support at all.

A number of countries have developed national blueprints or career management skills frameworks. These include frameworks in Australia, Canada, England, Norway, Scotland and the United States. Although all the frameworks have similarities in the kinds of skills they identify, they are distinctive for their national contexts. A framework typically outlines a number of learning areas (or skills), as well as sometimes offering levels for these skills to articulate what an individual should be able to do at different stages in their career journey. They can then be used in schools, further and higher education settings and adult settings in order to structure careers delivery. These kinds of frameworks aim to provide a nationally agreed standard for the delivery of career services that can be shared between providers. Articulating the impact of career services in relation to career management skills also offers a framework that can incorporate different forms of service such as guidance, education and information provision.

The growth of concepts like career management skills, an understanding that careers provision extends beyond one-to-one interviews, and the possibilities offered by new technologies have created more complexity in the career service landscape. Careers provision is understood as important for everyone but may be delivered in different ways, by different people or organisations.

💡 Resources

For a discussion of career management skills, try Tristram Hooley and colleagues' article 'The "Blueprint" Framework for Career Management Skills' or Ronald Sultana's 'Learning Career Management Skills in Europe'.

For an exploration of the relationship between public policy and career guidance, see John McCarthy and Tibor Borbély-Pecze's chapter 'Career Guidance: Living on the Edge of Public Policy'.

Career guidance systems across the world

With career provision meeting a range of policy goals, being delivered by a wide range of organisations and individuals, and being delivered in a variety of forms, careers systems are highly complex. For governments, this raises key questions about how to organise career services so that they are relatively coherent and consistent, and to reduce the potential for duplication or conflict. In the sections that follow, some ways in which services are organised in different national contexts are considered.

All-age guidance systems

One way to organise career services in a country is by developing a single service with responsibility for careers provision across all ages. This kind of service is apparent in Scotland and Wales as well as other nations. In large international reviews of career guidance provision conducted in the late 1990s and early 2000s, this kind of all-age service was identified as a very strong basis for the development of a coherent careers guidance system.[1] With adult services and young people's services delivered by the same organisation, we might assume that services will necessarily be reasonably consistent and delivered to high national standards.

However, it is important to recognise that even in nations with an all-age service, some careers provision will necessarily be provided by other organisations and individuals. For example, even if there is a national career service, teachers remain a very important source of career information and education for many young people. Employers are also key sources of work placements and career education. Therefore, where there is a large national careers organisation, it needs to focus not just on the delivery of career services but also on supporting wider career-related provision delivered by other organisations, including schools.

In countries with an all-age guidance service, sometimes careers provision in schools might be largely left up to the career service. However, the evidence suggests more effective provision is through a *partnership* model, whereby schools develop a partnership with the service. This partnership involves identifying and dividing the responsibilities of each partner, sharing information and working together to ensure that the needs of pupils are met. For example, in Scotland, schools have a duty to provide career education in line with the Career Education Standard, but Skills Development Scotland provides one-to-one career guidance to young people and supports with resources and input to help schools meet their duties. Proponents of partnership models of school delivery argue that the use of an external agency to deliver career guidance ensures a professional and impartial service which has a stronger connection to the labour market than is possible for schools. However, critics note that partnership models are only as good as the partnerships they are based on. If there is not a 'true' partnership between a school and an external organisation then the system risks becoming disjointed.

Age and stage-related models

Despite suggestions that all-age services are a good way to organise career development systems, most countries do not pursue this model. In schools, for example, an alternative to the 'partnership model' is an in-school model. In this model, schools have responsibility for arranging all elements of their career provision, including guidance, education and other activities. A good example of this is in the Republic of Ireland, where guidance counsellors in schools are responsible for leading all careers provision alongside teachers and other school staff. England has a bit of a mixed system, with most provision delivered by the school, but some support provided by The Careers & Enterprise Company and a range of other partners. There are risks associated with in-school models, which include inconsistency in delivery between schools, low investment in career services, disconnection from the labour market and a lack of impartiality. However, proponents of in-school models argue that they can, potentially, be more effective than partnership models because they bring together all aspects of careers delivery in a school into the responsibility of a single organisation and ensure that all delivery is done by professionals who know the students and have an ongoing relationship with them.

Recognising the risks of in-school models, countries that pursue these models might choose to introduce additional advice or regulation to address these issues. In England, for example, the development of the Gatsby Benchmarks has attempted to provide a clear framework for schools about what they should be delivering and how. The eight benchmarks are

1. A stable careers programme

2. Learning from career and labour market information

3. Addressing the needs of each pupil

4. Linking curriculum learning to careers

5. Encounters with employers and employees

6. Experiences of workplaces

7. Encounters with further and higher education

8. Personal guidance

In these benchmarks it is possible to see how different elements of career delivery, including career education, information, guidance and employer activities, are drawn together into one coherent framework. The additional guidance for each benchmark also includes some references to what good quality provision in each area looks like. In relation to personal (or one-to-one) guidance, for example, there are references to professional qualifications and standards for provision. Although the development of standards and guidelines is very useful in addressing issues of consistency, it has been pointed out that unless the activities of schools are monitored, it is difficult to guarantee that such standards are being met.

If schools have responsibility for school provision, then alternative services need to be offered to adults. In many countries, adult guidance services are provided primarily through public employment services (PES). In the UK, the public employment service is known as Jobcentre Plus and mainly exists to support unemployed workers while career guidance is provided by other national organisations.

Resources

For more information on the Gatsby Benchmarks, see Gatsby Charitable Foundation, *Good Career Guidance* or visit the organisation's website on the Benchmarks at https://www.goodcareerguidance.org.uk/. The organisation also provides bespoke resources for vocational/further education colleges and for special schools.

Coordination structures

From the previous sections we can see that whether or not a country has an all-age service, a diversity of organisations and individuals are involved in career-related provision. Trying to bring these organisations and individuals together and address issues of potential inconsistency, countries often develop different kinds of national structures to support collaboration. In Europe, for example, the European Commission has encouraged the establishment of national lifelong guidance forums to enable careers providers to come together in one place and work together. Cross-national initiatives such as the European Lifelong Guidance Policy Network (ELGPN) have also been developed to allow for collaboration between national contexts and to support the sharing of best practices. The idea of these forums is to develop joint initiatives and build understanding between different organisations. At a regional or local level, different kinds of forums might also be supported to facilitate joint activities. In Scotland, for example, local employability partnerships are developed at the local authority level, bringing together different organisations involved in the career, employability and skills sectors.

Other kinds of frameworks that can support consistency in delivery include the development of different kinds of national standards, quality standards or competence frameworks. This can include nationally agreed qualification frameworks for career development professionals. The development of national quality marks for career services, or information resources is also sometimes available. These frameworks aim to support consistency in service delivery. However, it is worth remembering that if such standards are optional, they may not *guarantee* consistency in service. National Career Management Skills frameworks, as previously discussed, may also offer a way of trying to build consistency between different providers.

💡 Resources

There is a lot of work that looks at the way different kinds of career development systems are organised. Useful summaries of this work can be found in Tony Watts and Ronald Sultana's article 'Career Guidance Policies in 37 Countries' and Watts' 'Cross-National Reviews of Career Guidance Systems'.

If you are interested in taking your reading further, you might like to refer to the publications from a number of supra-national organisations that have produced guidance for countries in designing their career provision. This includes the 2004 publication from the Organisation for Economic Co-operation and Development (OECD) *Career Guidance and Public Policy*. The International Labour Organisation's (ILO) work includes Ellen Hansen's handbook *Career Guidance: A Resource Handbook for Low and Middle Income Countries*. And various publications from the European Lifelong Guidance Policy Network (ELGPN), including various toolkits for policymakers on how to implement lifelong guidance policies: https://www.elgpn.eu/.

Deirdre Hughes has written a paper comparing the organisation of career services in the UK home nations, which provides some insights into the different strengths and weaknesses of different careers systems, *Careers Work in England's Schools: Politics, Practices and Prospects*.

How career development professionals can work with, respond to and influence policy

So far in this chapter we have explored how the public policy context shapes the delivery of career services within a national context. We have also seen how a country's cultural, social, political and economic context can shape the evolution of career-related policies. In this last section of the chapter, we turn to thinking about what this means for you as a career development professional.

The first thing to be clear about is that as a career development professional, your work will be heavily shaped by the public policy context in your country.

The kinds of activities you are asked to undertake by your employer, what you are asked to report on, and the tools and resources you use to deliver your service will all be shaped by your policy context.

It is also important to remember that policy often begins with high aspirations, but in practice is not always implemented. A particular issue here relates to under-resourcing. For example, governments may introduce a policy that says all schools should provide career guidance for pupils, but unless there are resources available to a school, this may be difficult to achieve. Whether or not services are delivered in line with policy expectations relies on factors such as available resources or funding and also on other policy levers like whether or not there are regulations or legislation that make activities or outcomes mandatory.

As a career development professional, you are at the interface between policy and practice, and understanding the policy landscape is important for you to be able to respond effectively.

Understanding policy in your context

To understand your career policy context, it is important to start off by thinking about how you can find out about relevant policy. As we have seen, career services meet a wide range of public policy goals, but in itself, it is not often a primary focus of public policy. Instead, it tends to sit between the larger policy agendas of education and economic policy. So, understanding the career context in your country is likely to involve understanding at least something about the wider public policy landscape.

A good place to start is to look for national strategies or policies that are specifically related to career guidance. Within these national documents, you will often find references to wider educational and economic policies that are relevant. Another approach is to start by identifying how career services are delivered in your country, because how they are delivered is likely to be shaped by the public policy context, and then look for appropriate policies. You might also find country reviews in the wider literature, including those gathered by intermediary organisations like the OECD, which may include your country and others that you are interested in. Other organisations like national career development organisations or professional bodies often have an interest in interpreting policy changes for practitioners as well as seeking to respond to or influence policy. Reading articles in the professional press, and joining an association or membership body, can help to ensure that your knowledge remains up to date about changes in the policy context.

Recognising that policies are not always implemented, it is valuable to think critically about the policy landscape in your country. This might involve asking yourself questions about how far the aspirations in a policy are likely to be achievable, whether the evidence always backs up the claims that policy documents make, and how policies seek to define the problem that they claim they are trying to solve.

Influencing policy

Policy does not have a direct impact on individuals. Instead, the implementation of policy relies on organisations, and ultimately individuals, to enact it. As such your work as a career development professional is inherently political. You will make decisions about how to respond to the requests your service makes of you, and ultimately the directives of the government. Like other professionals whose work is shaped heavily by public policy, a career development professional has sometimes been described as a *'street level policy maker'*. This is not to say that in your work you have complete freedom about what you do; indeed, you need to work within the law, and if you want to retain your job, you have to work within the terms of your contract and your employer. However, typically workers retain a level of autonomy. For example, you might be required to meet a target of a certain number of appointments with a specific target client group, but you may have scope to offer other clients some support at your discretion. You may have access to tools and information resources, but how and when you use these, and how you explain these to clients may be up to you. In practice, although services will often be designed to target national needs such as increasing levels of employment, you will have some latitude in your work about how you deliver services to your clients and what you discuss with them.

As well as policy framing your work, your role as a career development professional can also involve feeding back into the policy context and advocating on the basis of your practice experience. Policies, as we have already seen, are developed by governments to address national priorities. But how and when policies are developed and what they contain depend on the identification of a 'problem' that needs to be fixed. So, for example, if a country had 100% employment, there might be no 'problem' of unemployment, and therefore no need for a policy intervention. However, if unemployment rises, then it may start to be seen as a problem that needs intervention. How a government identifies a problem that needs intervention depends on a range of factors. Governments will receive expert input from economists or researchers that might help to demonstrate a problem that requires intervention. Or, because in a democracy governments are reliant on voters to keep them in power, if there is evidence in media discourses or elsewhere that the public perceives that there is a problem, a government may respond to this, even if this perception is not completely accurate. Another really important influence on the policy context is the role of professional and sector organisations who might lobby governments for policy changes. This is one place where the professional bodies and trade unions that represent career development professionals can have an important role in influencing political change.

As an individual citizen, you have certain capacities to shape the policy landscape, including the decisions you make about whom to vote for; and through lobbying your MP. But as a professional, you can also seek to influence the policy landscape by joining a professional body and responding to calls for information or ideas. Your professional body has a greater ability to impact the policy landscape than you could ever manage as an individual. Alongside a professional association, through your day-to-day contacts with your employer, you also have the ability to provide feedback about service delivery. This may be through your manager, or through special interest groups or other activities. Joining a union can also be beneficial, as unions have a role in representing their members' interests to their employers, lobbying for improved working conditions, and will often have a political fund which enables them to engage in political work.

CASE STUDY

Samira works as a careers adviser in a career service working in multiple schools in England. The schools commission her company to deliver career services to make sure they meet the Gatsby Benchmarks, especially Benchmark 8, which states that '*every pupil should have opportunities for guidance interviews with a careers adviser*', the benchmark also states that '*every pupil should have at least one such interview by the age of 16*'. Samira mainly works at Grantchester Academy and knows that she has to make sure that all young people are seen by the age of 16. But she is also aware that some young people might need more support than others, and that she does not have enough time to offer as many interviews as she would like. She plans her workload so that she interviews every pupil at the age of 15 for 45 minutes. She also keeps one afternoon a week free as a drop-in and another a dedicated time for those who need a follow-up interview.

Samira has access to a database of the pupils in the school, and she notes every time she sees a pupil. This helps her keep track of who has been seen and to make sure the benchmark is met. After Samira has been doing her job for six months, she realises that it will be very difficult to ensure that every pupil *has* an interview because some young people do not wish to attend an appointment or are not very often in school. She discusses this with her boss and she starts to also record when she contacts a pupil or offers an appointment. This helps her to track all her activities and to demonstrate that she has offered appointments to all pupils, even if they haven't always been taken up.

She attends training courses and professional events where she discusses her work with other advisers, and they identify similar challenges in their own schools. When the professional body surveys practitioners about the use of the Gatsby Benchmarks in schools, Samira provides feedback and suggests that the professional body argue that more resources are needed so that careers advisers in schools have time to follow up with students who don't engage.

Resources

If you are unsure about how to find out about your country's policy context, this chapter has given you a few ideas of where to start. You might also like to look up the ICCDPP (International Centre for Career Development and Public Policy). On their site you can find details of their symposia, and the resources include a series of country papers giving an overview of public policy in each country: https://www.iccdpp.org/

In the UK, a number of professional, membership and learned organisations come together as the Career Development Policy Group and are advocating for a Career Guidance Guarantee. You can find out more here: https://careerdpg.co.uk/

Thinking about how career guidance policy is developed and implemented, including exploration of the role of career development professionals, a useful introduction is Tristram Hooley and Lorraine Godden's paper *Theorising Career Guidance Policy Making*.

In a nutshell

This chapter has explored how public policy interests shape the ways that career services are delivered in different national contexts. It has argued that

- career provision meets diverse public policy goals. Although these goals are often economic or educational, the exact nature of these goals is different across national contexts, and these are shaped and reshaped over time;

- because careers systems meet diverse public goals, relevant policy is developed from different policy portfolios, often focused on education and economic policy but potentially from many different sources;

- the complexity of the policy landscape creates a complexity in the delivery landscape, with a diversity of organisations and individuals involved in delivering career services in every country;

- finding ways to create alignment and consistency in the diverse delivery landscape is often a key concern of governments. Different ways of organising systems to try and achieve consistency are apparent, with some countries pursuing all-age guidance services, while others seek to create alignment through other means. Coordination structures, including forums, frameworks and guidelines are common across contexts to support effective systems; and

- working as a career development professional is an inherently political role, as you are situated at the practice interface of the policy context. It is therefore important for professionals to maintain up-to-date knowledge of their policy contexts, to be able to critically analyse the claims of policy interests, and to engage with actions that seek to offer feedback or input to policymakers, and ultimately to inform the development of better policy measures.

Chapter 6
Making use of career theory

Introduction

Career theory is often seen as one of the more challenging elements of becoming a career development professional. Many people feel that they are OK with the more practical elements of the job, but that the theory '*blows their mind*'. In this chapter, we are going to try and introduce you to theory in a way that relates to practice and makes it make sense.

We are also going to make a more fundamental argument that theory is inescapable. Career development professionals always use theory; it's just that sometimes we don't call it '*theory*' and view it as just '*common sense*'. For example, if you say '*you'll find the right job someday*' you are theorising that there is a 'right' job out there and that through a process of exploration, you can increase your chance of finding this job. If you say '*shit happens*' you are drawing on a theory that says random and unexpected events are important to our lives and careers, and that we need to figure out the best way to deal with them.

This kind of intuitive or common-sense theory is sometimes called a 'folk theory', and it is a good place to start, but it is also valuable to look for theories that are based on scientific evidence and established ideas about things like learning, motivation and identity. *Theory* is the process of making observations about life and career, naming them and then discussing what they mean. Where theory is at its most helpful, it can support you to understand careers better, increase your sensitivity to clients' issues and support the development of better solutions and interventions.

While this chapter is designed to introduce career theory, it isn't the only place in the book where you will encounter theories. Most of the theories in this chapter discuss how individuals choose, develop and pursue their careers, rather than addressing what career development professionals do (although of course this distinction is often difficult to make). Later in the book, we will be thinking more about what theories and models we can use in our practice. For example, we will be thinking about counselling, guidance and coaching models, and the underpinning ideas and theories that inform them in Chapter 7, careers education and learning theories in Chapter 8 and theories about the way information is created and used in Chapter 9. Everything that you do requires theory, so what we are going to do in this chapter is mainly to start to name these theories and encourage you to become more reflective about them.

> ### Reflection
>
> What are the basic folk theories and beliefs that you hold about how careers work? Ask yourself some questions such as:
>
> - How important is an individual's personality to their career?
> - How important is the world within which they live, work and build their career?
> - How do the psychological and social aspects of career come together?
> - How far is it possible to plan a career, and how far does it just happen?
>
> You will probably find that you have some strong opinions on some of these questions and less clarity on others. Where you have a notion of how this works already, we bet that you will find a theory that puts that into words. Where you aren't so clear, hopefully, engaging with theory will introduce you to new ways of thinking and expand your ideas about what is possible. The important thing is to reflect on the relationship between your current thinking and the new ideas that you are encountering.

What is theory?

As we've already argued, theory isn't something complex and obscure; it is embedded in our thinking and serves as a way of making sense of the world. Albert Einstein (who was a man who knew a bit about theory and theorising) described the purpose of theory as follows.

> It can scarcely be denied that the supreme goal of all theory is to make the irreducible basic elements as simple and as few as possible without having to surrender the adequate representation of a single datum of experience.[1]

In other words, theory is trying to explain complicated things like physics, the world and careers, in as simple terms as possible. BUT, as theories try to simplify things, they need to be careful not to oversimplify them; otherwise, they end up misrepresenting what they are trying to describe.

In fact, all career theories *must oversimplify* things because our lives and careers are so complex. If you think about what makes a difference to your career, you could start with basic things like the country you are born in, your confidence or intelligence and keep going through things like your qualifications, your wealth, your knowledge about different occupations or your resilience in the face of knock backs. So, where do you stop? Does the football team you support, the way you like your eggs cooked or whether you are a cat or a dog person, also make a difference to your career? *Well . . . probably not . . . but maybe sometimes . . . but how important is it . . . Oh, I don't know!*

What career theories do is look at all this complexity and try and make sense of it. What are the most important factors, issues and processes that we should attend to when we are helping people to develop their careers? Inevitably, you get different answers to this question. For example, Bandura argues that the most important thing to focus on is '*self-efficacy*' which is the individual's self-belief in their ability to do something (like build a career), while Roberts argues that it is the '*opportunity structure*' which is the way that society organises who gets to move into different educational pathways, jobs and life trajectories. Both are right; self-efficacy and opportunity structures are both important, but where you place the emphasis matters.

It is also important to understand that theories are not just practical tools that can be used to solve problems (although they can be this as well). Theories are built on the way the theorist sees the world and how they believe that reality is organised (this is sometimes called *ontology*) and the tradition of evidence and scientific investigation that they believe is useful for finding out about reality (this is sometimes called *epistemology*). This means that the answers to questions like '*what is the most important influence on someone's career*' can sometimes get into much bigger questions about what we know, how we know it and what we believe the nature of reality to be. How different theorists answer these kinds of questions is likely to be strongly influenced by the discipline they are working in, as psychology, education, sociology and economics all make different assumptions, as well as the particular philosophical school that they associate with, for example are they a feminist, Marxist, existentialist or a pragmatist. It is also likely to matter when and where they were writing, who paid for what they wrote and why they ever put pen to paper.

Let's slow down before we blow your mind too much! The important point here is that different theorists disagree on both the questions that they are asking and the answers that they are giving in response to them. They can also disagree at more fundamental levels about what counts as evidence and even how they see reality. This can make it difficult to directly compare one theorist with another as they are doing different things, for different reasons. Of course, it is possible to combine insights from different theories together (and we would encourage you to do this), but at times you may find that you are trying to do a jigsaw where the pieces don't all fit together (and some don't even agree that this is a jigsaw at all).

It is also worth noting that while some career theories claim that they have found the absolute answer to the *problem of career*, a lot of criticisms point out that many theories only work for certain groups and that the assumptions they make can't easily be universalised So, a lot of theory developed in the United States in the 1950s and 1960s is great for understanding and explaining the careers of white men in the United States, who work in corporations and who have relatively stable careers. The more you don't conform to that demographic, the less useful some of these theories tend to be. And, if you are a woman living in Senegal in the 2020s, engaged in precarious work and caring for your family, you might reasonably say that many of these theories are of no use at all to you. Some critics talk about the dominance of Western, educated, industrialised, rich and democratic (sometimes shortened to WEIRD) assumptions in the development of much theory. As a result, there is a growing movement that emphasises the importance of non-Western traditions in theory, as well as feminist and socialist critiques that challenge established theory from different points of view.

Finally, it is also worth noting that there are lots of different ways to organise career theory. In this chapter, we are mainly working with three concepts: *the self, the world* or wider context, and the *relationship* between the two. We are going to place all of the theories somewhere in relation to these concepts. However, you may find that other analyses organise the theories differently. It is important to remember that the relationships between different theories are a matter of opinion; there are no absolute rules here, and it is possible to think about theory in many different ways. You may find other people grouping the theorists in different ways from this book. The important thing is to think about why they have done this and which groupings seem more useful and clear to you.

💡 Resources

This section has introduced a lot of big ideas. If you want to think more about the philosophical issues raised, then you might want to get hold of an introductory text like Simon Blackwell's *Think: A Compelling Introduction to Philosophy*. If you are interested in the idea of WEIRD theory, then have a look at Joseph Henrich's *The WEIRDest People in the World: How the West Became Psychologically Peculiar and Particularly Prosperous*.

If, however, you are just interested in career theory, then both Nancy Arthur and colleagues' *Career Theories and Models at Work: Ideas for Practice* and Steve Brown and Robert Lent's *Career Development and Counseling* provide a good introduction. Additionally, you can find out more about self-efficacy in Bandura's article 'Self-Efficacy: Towards a Unifying Theory of Behavioral Change' and more about opportunity structures in Roberts' article, 'Opportunity Structures Then and Now'.

Matching: A square peg in a square hole

The earliest and, many would argue, still the most important career theories are concerned with identifying a match between the individual and the labour market. We've already met Frank Parsons and the other early 20th-century social reformers who created the career development field. They understood career development processes as essentially about understanding yourself, understanding work requirements and using 'true reasoning' to create a match between the two.

This 'matching approach' to career development has proven to be an enduring theoretical contribution, but it presents some difficulties. How should we define what the relevant aspects of someone's personality are, or decide what skills and other attributes employers might want, and how can we match the two? By the 1950s John Holland was searching for a more scientific approach that could categorise both individuals and jobs and offer a method for putting the two together.

The answer that emerged was the development of six types that could be used to evaluate both individuals and the environments where they might work. These types can be summarised as follows (see Figure 6.1).

Figure 6.1. Holland's theory of vocational personalities and work environments

Because it contains six elements, Holland's model is sometimes described as the 'hexagon' model but is more usually known by the first letters of the categories RIASEC. Holland's approach is supported by a wide range of evidence, deep thinking and research which has both demonstrated the validity of this model of personality and categorised a huge number of jobs into the model. As a result, RIASEC is detectable as the theory which underpins a wide range of computer-based matching tools. There is lots of research that draws directly on Holland or alternative matching theories which has found positive results in terms of things like job satisfaction and motivation when people are able to find work that fits with their interests, abilities and other traits.

However, Holland's work has also received considerable challenge. There are concerns that Holland's theory oversimplifies the world. It is clearly the case that there are more than six types of people and more than six types of jobs. Holland's defenders would argue that he acknowledges this and that by ordering the types by relative dominance, you actually end up with 720 different vocational personality profiles. But this is still creating some massive categories in a world of almost eight billion people. Clearly, the fit between someone's personality and job type is not everything, as it doesn't take into account of education, interests or aspirations. Someone may be both more likely to get a job and better at doing it than someone else who seems to be a better psychological fit for it. There is also relatively little evidence that suggests that fit is what makes you happy and quite a lot that suggests that both individuals and jobs change and develop, meaning that initial fit might not matter for all that long.

Indeed, an important development of, and response to, the kind of person-environment fit proposed by Holland is *work adjustment theory,* which retains a focus on achieving a good match between the individual and their work but views both the individual and the workplace as dynamic. The aim, therefore, is not to find the perfect match between a person and a job on day one of employment but instead to recognise that it is both possible to adjust the work environment and for the individual to change and develop. Ideally, this dynamism brings the person and the work environment into correspondence, and this balance needs to be actively maintained over time.

Resources

John Holland wrote a huge number of papers exploring, developing and evidencing his theories. A good place to start is his book *Making Vocational Choices.*

A comprehensive overview of recent research on person-environment fit can be found in Van Vianen's (2018) article, 'Person–Environment Fit: A Review of Its Basic Tenets'.

Finally, if you are interested in work adjustment theory, then Swanson and Schneider's chapter on 'The Theory of Work Adjustment' is an excellent starting point.

The self

Matching theory is a good place to start because it draws out three very important concepts for thinking about careers. First, the individual; second, the environment and third, the relationship between them. All career theories have to account for these three things in some way, but each theory gives a different account and typically focuses on one or more of these concepts. In this section, we are going to focus on theories which are interested in the individual. What is the nature of a person, and what elements of their personality or other attributes are important as they develop their career?

It is useful to consider how far an individual has free will in their choice of life and career and how far their personal attributes can be changed and developed. Conversely, how far should we view people's personalities as largely fixed at birth, as the philosopher Plato believed, meaning that their careers are pre-ordained? Much career theory has emerged from the discipline of psychology, which is strongly focused on understanding the individual.

Measuring and describing personality

A lot of psychological work is interested in measuring and describing personalities or other attributes in a similar way to how Holland did. For example, the Myers-Briggs Type Indicator (MBTI) drew on the work of Carl Jung to propose that there are 16 personality types, which are based on 4 dichotomies.

- **Extraversion (E) – Introversion (I).** Where do people get their energy from? Is it from the external world (extraverts) or the internal world (introverts)?
- **Sensing (S) – Intuition (N).** How do people absorb information? Is it through an orderly, step-by-step approach which focusses on details (sensing) or more holistically with attention paid to the big picture (intuition)?
- **Thinking (T) – Feeling (F).** How do people make decisions? Is it through an attempt to be objective and rational (thinking) or through the use of empathy (feeling)?
- **Judging (J) – Perceiving (P).** How do people deal with the world? Do they decide on a course of action, develop a plan and carry it out

(judging) or spend more time collecting information and then use this more flexibly to guide their actions (perceiving)?

Based on these preference patterns, MBTI assigns you a four-letter code and organises you into 1 of 16 personality types, for example, ENTP. MBTI isn't a career theory as such, but it is enormously influential in the careers field and often used in workplaces as a development tool. Inevitably, there is a lot of debate about the scientific basis of MBTI. Many psychologists use alternative measurements like the *'big 5* or *OCEAN'* which measures people on their *openness, conscientiousness, extraversion, agreeableness* and *neuroticism* but which does not then focus on preferences for one or the other, preferring to view all of these traits as a continuum.

It is worth thinking why these kinds of descriptions of personality are important and attractive for many people thinking about their careers. Your personality is an impossibly complex thing, so much so that even you often don't really understand it. Assessments like the Holland types, MBTI and the big five give you a language to understand yourself and a framework for thinking about how you are different from other people. They then go a step further and provide you with a supposedly objective judgement on what you are *actually* like. This can make them attractive tools for individuals when they are making decisions and for employers during recruitment processes. However, this does not mean that they are always appropriate or valuable. For example, the providers of MBTI state that it should not be used in selection procedures.

All of this discussion relies on the idea that personality and/or other measurable psychological attributes are very important in determining what kinds of career you should pursue. As we have already seen when looking at matching theories, this is not universally agreed upon. The career theorist Bill Law threw up his hands in frustration at the *'worksheets, checklists, computer programs, psychometrics, data bases, inventories and frameworks'* that had come to comprise careers work and called for *'fewer lists, more stories'* as a way forwards.[2] And when we start to think about practice, it is important to consider further what we think the role of the career development professional is. A focus on these kinds of measurement instruments can often leave the professional in the role of just administering the test and informing the person as to what their score is (test and tell). This is a rather limited conception of what career development professionals do, so it is important, even if you do use career assessments, to view them as a starting point for an intervention rather than the intervention itself.

References

There is a lot written about MBTI and almost any basic book will give you an insight into the theory. Isabel Briggs Myers' *Introduction to Type* is as good a place as any to start. If you want a more objective discussion of its strengths and weaknesses, then King and Mason's discussion in *The Wiley Encyclopaedia of Personality and Individual Differences* is very helpful.

If you want to learn about the 'big 5' then Daniel Nettle's book *Personality* is very good.

The shift to narrative

The critique of lists and quantification in career development was made most powerfully by Mark Savickas and others who joined with him to propose the new paradigm of *life design*. They argued that major social shifts meant that the concentration on the measurement and description of personality was no longer the most useful way to understand careers or help people to manage them. These theorists viewed the self as always being under a process of active creation. The most important thing is for the individual to create a life story which provides them with meaning in an uncertain world.

Life design draws heavily on Savickas' earlier theory of *career construction*. Both of these theories move away from attempts to describe personality and align it with the environment. Career construction concentrates on '*identity rather than personality, adaptability rather than maturity, intentionality rather than decidedness, and stories rather than scores.*'[3] Life design takes this further, arguing that we bring our realities into existence through the telling of stories. It is this process of storytelling that both comprises the self and offers individuals the best way to get what they want from their careers. People can create themselves and influence what they want to happen in their lives by getting better at telling stories.

Life design is a postmodern theory that can be understood alongside postmodern theories that have emerged in other fields. Postmodernism rejects concepts like rationality, objectivity and universal truth and emphasises the diversity of human experience and the importance of narrative and discourse. This kind of approach can be seen in many ways as the polar opposite of John Holland's idea that you can scientifically describe a person and match them to the perfect career. Using this kind of matching approach is unlikely to guarantee you much happiness; instead, you need to recognise that life is what you make of it.

The idea that your career is a story that you can learn to tell differently is a very appealing one. It puts the individual in control of their life and gives career development professionals a major role in helping people become better (self) storytellers. But, others argue that this ignores the big structural 'grand narratives' that shape our lives and massively overestimate the capacity of the individual to retell their story, when so much of this story is determined by economic and organisational position, politics and luck.[4] The debate about how far someone is in control of their future and how far their future is shaped by the forces around them is sometimes known as the debate between structure and agency.

References

Various kinds of narrative career theory have been very popular for the past 30 years. Mary McMahon's *Career Counselling: Constructivist Approaches* is a very useful introduction to this. Jerome Rossier and his colleagues' chapter 'The Narrative Turn in Career Development Theories: An Integrative Perspective' also offers a good overview.

The chapter entitled 'Career Construction Theory and Practice' by Mark Savickas is a good place to start on this theory. You can follow this up by looking at what was essentially a manifesto for the life-design movement written by Savickas and others in 2009, entitled 'Life Designing: A Paradigm for Career Construction in the 21st Century'.

If you want to get your head around postmodernism, then Christopher Butler's *Postmodernism: A Very Short Introduction* is a good place to start.

How careers develop

Another important theoretical strand is developmental psychology, which examines how people develop their personalities and ultimately their careers. This is important for career development professionals because it can help them tailor the way that they work with people to the age and stage that these individuals are at.

Early development theorists viewed career development as an element of child development and so focused on the stages that people moved through as they achieved maturity. For example, Ginzberg and colleagues argue that young people begin life by thinking about careers in a fantastical way ('I want to be a dragon!'). Then, from 11 to 17 they begin to form tentative interests in different careers and areas. By the age of 17, young people become more realistic, engaging in more exploration and gradually crystallising their interests.

The idea that as people age, and as they learn more about their career, they achieve a state which is sometimes called 'career maturity' remains influential. For example, Flouri and Buchanan measure career maturity based on five statements which ask young people whether they have a career plan, know what they need to do to get training and a job that interests them, whether they can see the steps that are needed to make a career decision, and whether they know themselves well enough.[5] Those who answer positively to all of these statements are judged to be more 'career mature'.

The idea of career maturity raises an important question for developmental theories. Do we change our relationship to our career through a process of 'normal' physiological and psychological development, or is career development a process of learning and experience? To put it another way, is it is inevitable that we achieve career maturity, or will this maturity only emerge under certain circumstances?

Donald Super is another theorist who was interested in how people's careers develop, but he thought about this across the whole lifecourse rather than just thinking about how young people reach adulthood. Super ultimately developed the idea of the life/career rainbow in which he argued that life and career go through a series of different stages, which he describes as follows (see Figure 6.2).

Super views *growth* as taking place in childhood, *exploration* in adolescence, *establishment* in early to mid-adulthood, *maintenance* in middle age and *decline* at the end of working life and into retirement. He also discusses the way in which our careers are not just made up of our role as a worker, but also combine a range of other roles. As life unfolds, we can trace the varying importance that we give to each of these roles. Super also explores the transitions between stages that we make in relation to these roles in a process

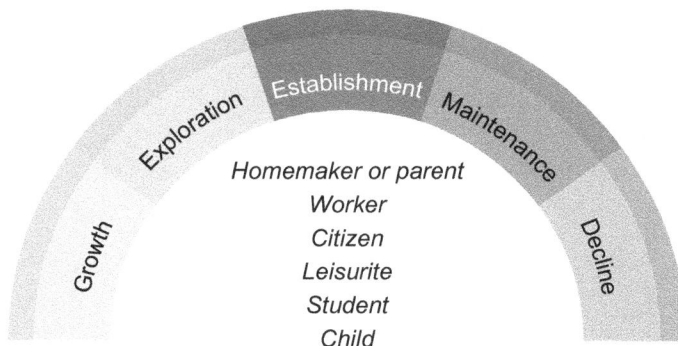

Figure 6.2. Super's life/career rainbow

he calls 'mini-cycles' and the tasks that support these transitions are where career development work can usefully focus.

Super's theory has a lot to recommend it. Its understanding of life and career as a multi-faceted endeavour in which people combine a variety of roles broadened thinking about what a career is to the kind of definition that we discussed in Chapter 1. However, his work is also extremely normative: it posits an idealised version of how careers work that undoubtedly made sense to Super (an educated man working in a Western industrialised, rich and democratic (WEIRD) society), but other theorists have pointed out that this kind of life and career trajectory is not afforded to everyone.

Mary Sue Richardson emphasises the ways in which careers are gendered, not just in terms of the different occupations that men and women do, but in the different ways that careers are structured and conceived. While Super acknowledges the different roles that people play through life, he still accords the organising role to paid work. In contrast, Richardson gives equal weight to market work (paid work), personal care work (caring for yourself and others), personal relationships (friendships, romantic and familial relationship), and market work relationships (relationships with people within work and other professional contexts). Each of these contexts shapes how career is experienced with women in many contemporary WEIRD (and other) contexts often required to spend more time in care and relationships than their male counterparts, meaning that their careers unfold in different ways.

Another developmental perspective that foregrounds gender issues is Linda Gottfredson, whose theory of circumscription and compromise suggests that young people develop their career identities through four stages: from 3 to 5 years, children recognise that adults have careers and begin to perceive some differences between them; from 6 to 8 years, they start to recognise that these roles are gendered and that men and women do different jobs; from 9 to 13 years, they recognise that different jobs are accorded different social value; finally, around the age of 14, young people start to think about their own interests and capabilities and how these might influence their future career. Gottfredson views this as a process by which potential careers for consideration are gradually reduced (circumscription), and then young people select between options depending on their accessibility (compromise). This process is strongly influenced by social norms as well as by the interests and capabilities of the individual.

Developmentalism can be useful in identifying how careers develop at different ages and stages, but they struggle to account for careers which do not follow a 'normal' trajectory. This is particularly problematic where assumptions about development have strong cultural elements which may not apply to all people in all circumstances equally. Nonetheless, it is important not to ignore the idea of social, psychological and physical development as an important element in how people's careers work.

Resources

Ginzberg and colleagues' book *Occupational Choice* is a good place to start exploring the relationship between developmental theories and career theories. Meanwhile, Super sets out his life-career rainbow in his article 'A Life-Span, Life-Space Approach to Career Development'.

Mary Sue Richardson summarises a lot of her ideas about the gendered nature of careers in her article 'Counseling for Work and Relationship' which also draws out many of the implications of this theory for career counselling. While Linda Gottfredson reviews her theory in 'Using Gottfredson's Theory of Circumscription and Compromise in Career Guidance and Counseling'.

These career theories might also be complemented by looking at a broader book on developmental psychology, like Thornton and Gliga's *Understanding Developmental Psychology*.

Reflection

Think about your own career and consider what role your personality, interests, capabilities and desires have played in the development of your career.

How far do you think you have found the perfect career for you? Was this inevitable, or were there other possibilities that could have made you equally (or even more) happy?

How malleable do you feel your personality is? Can you change yourself? If so, what are the implications of this for your career?

The world

The theories discussed in the last section all focus on the individual and ask what it is about us that suits, drives and enables us to pursue different careers. Inevitably, these theories continually run up against the problem that careers are not wholly, or even mainly, a psychological process. Our careers are influenced by schools, exams, interviews, employers, promotions and demotions, families, friends and many other factors. And all of this takes place in a world where the economy cycles through boom and bust, where governments come and go, wars happen and the environment moves ever towards crisis. Given all of this, we might argue that it is all very well looking at your wants, needs and interests, but if we are going to understand how your career operates, we might be much better to look at what is on offer.

A lot of the theorists who focus on the world rather than the self come from the discipline of sociology rather than psychology. This is one of the jarring things about career theory: you've just got familiar with a set of psychological ideas like 'traits', 'personality' and 'person-environment fit', and all of a sudden you are looking at theorists who aren't interested in any of those things. Career theory is international and interdisciplinary and uses multiple research approaches. This can make it feel less like a conversation and more like a series of different discussions happening in different rooms.

Careers in society

Sociological theorists are interested in how societies work and in considering what structures, processes and institutions are important. Work, education, employment and career are all important social institutions. Many sociologists and anthropologists (yet another discipline) have been interested in investigating how people are allocated to particular jobs. These investigations generally report that societies are not organised on a rational basis in which interests and talents are matched to opportunities; rather, that opportunities are unequally distributed, and there is a tendency for people to follow in their father's or mother's footsteps (social reproduction). As Paul Willis puts it in his ethnography of working-class boys, understanding careers is really a process of understanding *how working class kids get working class jobs*. Other similar studies have also found that gender, race, religion and disability structure access to careers. Once you get into employment, these factors also structure who has access to opportunities through the creation of sticky floors (which mean that it is more difficult to get promoted out of entry-level jobs for some people) and glass (and class) ceilings (which create barriers to getting to the highest level in occupations and society).

In the 1970s Ken Roberts put a name to this way of thinking about careers: *opportunity structures*. Careers, from this perspective, are not a process of choosing between or managing opportunities but rather a process of interacting with opportunity structures. These opportunity structures are formed through the inter-relationship between family backgrounds, educational experiences, labour market processes and employers' recruitment practices. This typically leaves people choosing between similar types of options, so working-class kids choose between different minimum-wage jobs, while the children of the elite follow their parents into the elite professions. Choice does exist, but many choices lead you to similar outcomes.

Other theorists have built on this thinking to explore the place of work in people's lives and how careers develop through working life. David Blustein's psychology of working theory is important here as it recognises that work can be organised in many different ways which have varying effects on individuals and their careers. He also highlights the way in which our psychology bridges our working life and our wider life so that problems of work organisation need to be understood as integral to psychological well-being. Blustein asks why people work and identifies three main reasons: first, to survive and gain access to power and opportunity, second, to connect socially with others (work and career as a collective as well as individual endeavour) and third as a way of shaping yourself and the world around you.

While Roberts sees social and economic structures as primarily shaping individuals, for Blustein this is a more dynamic relationship. The theorist Pierre Bourdieu also addresses these questions about the relationship between individuals and their environment. He argues that environments are not just external things with which people interact, but rather something that we internalise. So, we no more notice the unfairness of an opportunity structure than a fish notices the water around it. In a process similar to that described by Gottfredson, we become socialised into thinking about our careers within what we understand to be realistic possibilities for us. Bourdieu calls our internalised assumptions *habitus,* as it describes the social space that we inhabit.

Hodkinson and Sparkes draw on the ideas of Bourdieu and apply them to career theory. They develop the idea of 'careership' which thinks about how a person's habitus and the opportunities that are available create *horizons for action* that people perceive within their careers. They emphasise that people make 'pragmatically rational' career decisions and perceive themselves to be taking meaningful action to change their own lives but recognise that these actions happen within socially and psychologically constructed horizons and environmental contexts, which limit what is possible. They also explore how personal and career changes occur, noting that people usually spend a lot of time in *routines* where they don't examine their life and career trajectory closely. However, periodically, people experience *turning points,* which could be as banal as a bad day at work or as existential as a life-threatening injury. These turning points have the potential to shake people out of their routines and make changes, sometimes even to the extent of shifting their horizons for action.

Bourdieu also offers another very important theoretical concept that has been used in career theories: that of capitals. This starts from the sociological observation that we have already discussed, which states that those who have more money (*financial capital*) tend to do better in life and career than those who have less. However, this is not a simple relationship; otherwise, there would never be any social mobility. Money matters, but so do other things. Bourdieu says that this can be understood by recognising that there are other forms of capital, which can substitute for money in some circumstances. So, knowing a lot of people, particularly powerful and successful people (*social capital*) can provide people with resources that allow them to develop their lives and careers. Similarly, *cultural capital* describes how our tastes in things like music, cinema or arts, and our hobbies, values or preferences can help us to get ahead in certain contexts. For instance, someone who listens to Motörhead and eats with their hands might struggle to become a barrister, even if they have a great legal brain.

One role for career development professionals is to help people think about these issues and to recognise both the structures they face and the agency they have. In some cases, this might be about encouraging people to recognise what they need to do in order to get the most out of the structures within which they are operating, while at other times, it might be about thinking about challenging or changing these structures.

💡 Resources

There is a rich tradition of school ethnographies that explore how people's career identity is formed. Paul Willis's *Learning to Labour* is the classic of this genre, but there are many others to explore, including Christine Griffin's *Typical Girls,* which explores the school-to-work transitions of young women. An interesting counterpoint to this is Friedman and Laurison's *The Class Ceiling: Why It Pays to Be Privileged* which explores how class and other aspects of privilege continue to matter once you go to work. Meanwhile, David Blustein outlines his theory in the book *The Psychology of Working*.

Ken Roberts theorises these processes through the concept of opportunity structures, which he discusses in 'Opportunity structures then and now'. Alternative theorisations are offered by Bourdieu in books like *Reproduction in Education, Society and Culture* and in his chapter on 'The Forms of Capital'. This is picked up and given a more careers-focused twist in Hodkinson and Sparkes' work on 'Careership'.

Family, community and culture

Moving on from the kinds of structuralist approaches outlined above, there is also a wide array of work which looks at how careers are shaped and formed by relationships and culture.

Lots of career theorists have noted the way in which careers are formed and supported within families. This research has looked at how parents and extended families both shape the career horizons of individuals and provide them with resources to develop their careers. Perhaps the most prominent theorist in this area is Richard Young, who has looked extensively at how parents engage with their children's careers in both positive and negative ways. He talks about adolescents' careers as a 'family project' in which other family members have a stake in the career of the individual. Other work has looked at how couples' careers develop in relation to each other, how being a parent might change the way that you interact with your own career (referring back to Super's life-career rainbow) or how family connections can offer career opportunities (referring back to Bourdieu's point about the importance of social capital). All of this work reminds us that while careers can often feel very individual, they are actually pursued in social and familial contexts.

A similar point can be made about the development of careers within communities. It is not just your immediate family who shape your thinking and provide you with support, but also the people around you. Bill Law's community interaction theory provides an account of these processes. He looks at groups like parents, extended family, neighbours, your peer group, your ethnic group and your school and asks how each of these groups interacts with you through expectations, feedback, support, modelling and the provision of information. He argues that tracing these community interactions typically provides a lot of clues as to how individuals choose and develop their careers.

In *Career Guidance in Communities* and associated work, Rie Thomsen builds on this interest in communities to ask where and how career guidance fits into it. She argues that career guidance practitioners need to not only understand the way in which communities are influencing people's careers but also actively engage with those communities and activate their power to support and develop people's careers. This positions both careers and career guidance as collective practices rather than just individual projects. Using 'career' as a verb, we could say we career together and support each other as we do so, and so it is important to make the most of these networks of mutual support as we develop people's careers.

Resources

There is a lot of work that explores the way in which relationships, parents and families impact people's careers. Young and Friesen's article 'The Intentions of Parents in Influencing the Career Development of Their Children' is one good starting place. There is also a lot of interesting work on 'dual careers,' which look at how couples manage their life and work in relation to each other. Clarke's 'Dual Careers: The New Norm for Gen Y Professionals?' provides a good entry point to this literature.

Bill Law wrote extensively about career theory. Much of his thinking is collected in an archive on the NICEC website (https://www.nicec.org/pages

/4-the-bill-law-archive). His original article 'Community Interaction: A "Mid-Range" Focus for Theories of Career Development in Young Adults' remains as essential reading. Rie Thomsen picks up many of these ideas around the importance of community in her book *Career Guidance for Communities* and then sets out her model in a paper called 'Career Guidance in Communities: A Model for Reflexive Practice'.

Luck, chance and chaos

If the sociological theories emphasise social and economic structures, and the community-focused theories emphasise relationships, the next group of theories focus on luck. They note that an awful lot of what happens in your career comes down not to your personality or the structures in which you live, but just to chance. Why did you happen to bump into an old friend and go for a coffee, only to find out that they have heard about a job in their company that would be perfect for you? Why did no one else apply for a particular job, meaning that you got it even though you were barely qualified? Why did you break your leg while walking the dog, meaning that you couldn't go to the company away day, only to find out that your rival got offered a promotion shortly after? All of these situations are very possible to imagine, but it is difficult to feel that either psychological theories of personality or sociological theories about the social environment provide a particularly good explanation of why they come about or what to do about it.

Chaos theory represents an attempt to wrestle with these problems of chance and uncertainty in careers. This does not mean that everything is 'chaotic' in the popular sense of the word, but rather that we need to understand careers as being part of complex, dynamic systems, which it is difficult for individuals to fully understand or predict. Robert Pryor and Jim Bright, the leading proponents of the chaos theory of careers, have borrowed from wider 'chaos theory' thinking in the natural sciences to develop their theory. They emphasise that careers are non-linear, which means that actions, even small actions, do not always result in logical or predictable outcomes. This was first discussed in terms of weather systems, with the famous idea that a butterfly flapping its wings in Tokyo can cause a typhoon in Los Angeles. The point is not that the butterfly has some enormous power, but rather that it is part of a complex system and that interactions with this system can have surprising consequences.

In terms of a career, this means that small decisions, like whether to go to a university in one town or another, can have big effects. Perhaps in one town, you meet your life partner and start the process of building a happy family life; in another you make a friend who becomes your business partner and together you build a multi-million-pound business. Or perhaps you and that friend go out one night and fall off a roof while engaged in some high-spirited student antics. It is difficult to predict these kinds of effects, and none of the theories that we have looked at so far help us to understand or respond to them, but they are clearly a very real part of career development.

Bright and Pryor provide a language to understand and analyse these chaotic patterns in our careers. They talk about *attractors* which describe the different processes that careers go through, variously following routines and hitting periods of change, experiencing continuity and predictability, but also moments of change and shift. They also use the metaphor of the *fractal* as a pattern that continues to repeat and change in small ways, but also forms larger patterns that can sometimes be very different. This provides a completely new way of thinking about careers, which they argue is capable of explaining experience much more clearly than previous theories.

This focus on luck and unpredictability might feel unsettling. If nothing can be predicted, how can we choose, plan and develop our careers? Bright and Pryor argue that it is not impossible, but that you have to focus on a different set of approaches. Principal among these is the idea of *luck readiness*, which emphasises flexibility, optimism, openness to risk, curiosity, persistence, strategy, efficacy and luckiness as a series of ways of thinking that the individual can adopt to make the most of unexpected opportunities and be more resilient to unexpected setbacks. A very similar idea has been popularised by Kathleen Mitchell, Al Levin and John Krumboltz, who argue that 'luck is no accident' and develop a theory of planned happenstance that emphasises preparation for and openness to unplanned events. They argue that it is most important to focus on

- **curiosity.** Exploring new learning opportunities;
- **persistence.** Exerting effort despite setbacks;
- **flexibility.** Changing attitudes and circumstances;
- **optimism.** Viewing new opportunities as possible and attainable; and
- **risk taking.** Taking action in the face of uncertain outcomes.

This kind of thinking refocuses the aims of career development work towards learning and the development of skills and personal capabilities. We are now a long way from where we started with the matching theories within their focus on the moment of decision-making and the dream of making the *right* decision.

⚡ Resources

For a general introduction to chaos theory, read John Gribbin's *Deep Simplicity*. The work of Pryor and Bright is central to the way that these ideas have moved into the careers field. Their article 'The Chaos Theory of Careers (CTC): Ten Years On and Only Just Begun' provides a short introduction, but it might also be worth looking at their book *The Chaos Theory of Careers*. The *Luck Readiness Index Manual* is also worth looking at to better understand their concept of luck readiness.

Planned happenstance was originally outlined in an article by Mitchell, Levin and Krumboltz called 'Planned Happenstance: Constructing Unexpected Career Opportunities'. A deeper and more practical discussion of this theory can be found in Krumboltz and Levin's book *Luck Is No Accident*.

⚙️ Reflection

Consider some of the ways in which the external world has shaped the careers of you and your students and clients. How do some of these theories help you understand the challenges and opportunities that have been important?

What are the implications of these theories for career development work? What can you do to support your clients in addressing these kinds of big picture issues?

The relationship between the self and the world

As we have seen, careers exist in a world of complexity. Both the individual and the world are dynamic and complex. What is more, there are considerable challenges in thinking about how we bring the self and the world together. First, how do we understand the relationship that exists between the outside world and the internal thought processes of the individual? Second, what does this mean for career development professionals? How can you meaningfully intervene in career development processes that are at once psychological and socio-political? So in this section of the chapter, we are going to look at theories that have tried to bring these different elements together, and recognise the fact that there are many different ways to do this.

Balancing through good decision-making

The first way that you can see the relationship between the self and the world is to view it as something that should be in balance. This is not to deny that there are tensions within this relationship, but rather to view the job of the individual and then of the career development professional as bringing these into balance in a way that allows the individual's career to progress.

This chapter began with the matching theories, which have a very neat way of bringing the self and the world into balance, described as *person-environment fit*. This is closely associated with an economic theory called rational choice theory. This theory argues that we can understand the economy by recognising that everyone will try to act in their own best self-interest and that they will do this by making rational choices based on the best information available to them. As we have already seen in this chapter, life is a bit more complex than this, with many of the theorists we have looked at outlining a range of factors that get in the way of people making rational choices, not least the difficulty of agreeing on what constitutes the individual's self-interest. For example, is someone's self-interest best served by getting a high-paying job in an oil company or by making choices that will enable them to remain on a liveable planet? Rational choice-making looks easy if you only think about one thing (e.g. money), but as soon as you start to factor in other aspects like interests, relationships with others and values, it all gets very complicated.

More recently, a body of theory has developed which combines psychology and economics to examine the gaps that exist between what rational choice theory would say is the best option in any particular situation and what people are most likely to do. Unsurprisingly, they find that people often behave in non-rational ways, for example staying in a job they don't like because finding a new job would require more effort in the short term. Behavioural economists are interested in how you can nudge people to make more rational choices. One way to think about career development work is exactly as this kind of nudging intervention, which is designed to make people gather more information and think more carefully about their choices. However, even with access to career guidance, the challenges about what constitutes self-interest remain difficult to solve, meaning that it may not be possible to find a way to hold the self and the world in perfect balance.

Bimrose and Barnes go further and argue that it is possible that different people make career decisions in different ways. They identify four styles which they describe as *evaluative* (thoughtful and reflective), *strategic* (logical, proactive and goal orientated), *aspirational* (long-term and hopeful) and *opportunistic* (reactive and willing to take risks). This theory suggests that career development professionals need to be much more focused on the approaches taken by their clients rather than assuming that there is a perfect and singular approach to career decision-making.

> ### 💡 Resources
>
> People interested in finding out more about theories of choice-making might find Michael Allingham's *Choice Theory: A Very Short Introduction* a useful starting point. Daniel Kahneman's *Thinking Fast and Slow* and Richard Thaler and Cass Sunstein's *Nudge* then explore the contribution that behavioural economics can make. Dave Redekopp makes the connection between behavioural economics and career development in his article 'Irrational Career Decision-Making'. Bimrose and Barnes set out their theory in an article called 'Styles of Career Decision-Making'.

Changing yourself through adaptation and learning

If achieving balance between the self and the world is difficult, one option is to recognise that the self is the more malleable of the two and to think about how we can change it. Such theories argue that it is difficult or impossible for individuals, even with the help of career development professionals, to change the world, and so the main question of career development becomes 'how can we best live within this world'. This kind of approach leads people to emphasise qualities that enable them to succeed and build careers.

We've already briefly discussed Bandura's concept of *self-efficacy* as one quality that is likely to be important in building your career. It is undoubtedly the case that people who have a lot of self-belief and confidence in their abilities are likely to do better in life. A lot of careers research, particularly from researchers based in psychology, seeks to develop greater clarity about what qualities really allow people to succeed. Key qualities highlighted in the literature and well supported by evidence include

- the capacity to build relationships and networks;
- career adaptability;
- the ability to set goals;
- proactivity/career self-directedness; and
- resilience and the ability to bounce back from setbacks.

In learning theories, these kinds of qualities become transformed into learning outcomes (often called career management skills). We will discuss these further in Chapter 8.

Critics highlight that there are problems in expecting people to endlessly transform themselves just to keep up. While it is undoubtedly a good idea for everyone to be proactive, networkers who can manage their careers, adapt to change and bounce back following challenges, it is worth asking why this is needed and whether it is really realistic that everyone can exhibit this level of psychological capacity and flexibility. Ronald Sultana argues that these kinds of concepts (he focuses on the terms *'vulnerability'*, *'resilience'*, *'employability'* and *'activation'* but also discusses *'agility'*, *'adaptability'* and *'flexibility'*) are *'dirty words'* and that *'encourage us to view systemic problems as if they were shortcomings of individuals'*.[6] So, while adaptability and related concepts might offer one way to bring the self and the world into alignment, it is not without its challenges.

There are a range of theories that consider how we can learn about career development and develop our capacity to interact with the world more effectively. We will come back to career learning theories in Chapter 8, but it is worth noting the importance of John Krumboltz and his colleagues' social learning theories of career selection, as they are so directly addressed to the question of how an individual learns to navigate the world.

Krumboltz argues that all career development is a process of learning and that this learning happens when the individual engages with the world through having experiences and receiving feedback of various kinds. In this theory, the individual is learning about themselves and their capabilities, as well as about the world and the opportunities that it offers. Gradually, through this process of learning, they are able to find a place in the world. It is worth noting the similarities to Gottfredson's circumscription and compromise theory and Bourdieu's concept of habitus, but Krumboltz frames this much more positively. It is not a process of accommodation to constraints but rather a process of discovery of the world and a growing awareness of how to thrive and build a career within it. Krumboltz also builds on these theories in his work on planned happenstance, which explores further what needs to be learnt in order to thrive in a happenstance world.

We have already looked briefly at Law's community interaction theory in an earlier section of this chapter. This has many similarities with Krumboltz's theories and particularly highlights the role of family and community in forming one's understanding of a career through processes like modelling, feedback and advice. Law also identifies four processes that he argues comprise career learning in a later article entitled 'A career learning theory'. In this he argues that individuals learn about their career through processes of *understanding* (anticipating consequences and developing explanations), *focusing* (taking one's own point of view), *sifting* (using concepts and making comparisons) and *sensing* (assembling sequences and gathering information). The theories of Krumboltz and Law view individuals as in a dynamic relationship with their world and describe how the accommodation that is forged through the two comes about through active learning processes.

⚲ Resources

There is a wide range of work investigating the qualities that support individuals in building good careers. Some good starting points include Eby and colleagues' 'Predictors of Success in the Era of the Boundaryless Career', Abele and Spurk's 'How Do Objective and Subjective Career Success Interrelate Over Time?' as well as more specific work from writers like Mishra and McDonald on 'career resilience', Savickas on 'career adaptability' and De Vos and Soens on 'self-management'.

Krumboltz and colleagues set out their learning theory in 'A Social Learning Theory of Career Selection' while Law sets out his theory in 'A Career Learning Theory'.

Changing the world

The previous section focused on how individuals can change themselves through learning and adaptation to bring themselves into alignment with what the world needs and make a good match. In this section, we focus on critical theories which seek to bring social change into the frame of what career development addresses. So, rather than seeking to fit individuals into the world, they ask whether it is the individual or the world that needs to change.

The idea of 'critical theory' originated with the 'Frankfurt School' in Germany in the 1930s as a group of theorists who drew on Hegel and Marx explore culture, modernity and society. However, Thomsen and colleagues argue that the term is now used more widely to describe a range of social and political theories which

- imagine different a kind of society;
- pay attention to power and how it works to shape society;
- unmask ideology by analysing phenomena and systems and clarifying how they work;
- understand individuals to be in a two-way relationship with the world in which they live; and
- view human beings as having the capacity to change their lives and the world around them (even if this is often difficult).

This kind of approach inevitably moves career development work into a more political space. However, Tony Watts argues that the question is not whether career development adopts a political position, but rather what kind of political position it adopts. He says that all forms of career development work have to take a position on whether they focus on the individual (the

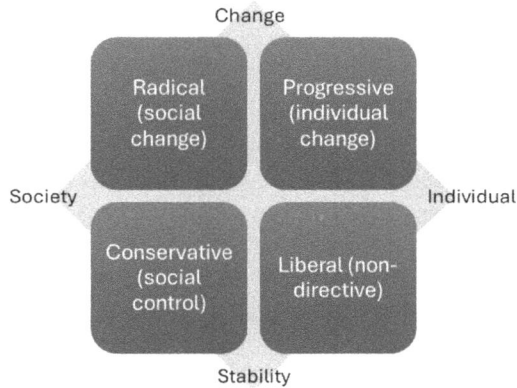

Figure 6.3. Watts socio-political ideologies of guidance

self) or society (the world) and whether they seek to keep things the same or encourage change. This led him to create four socio-political ideologies of guidance (see Figure 6.3).

Liberal approaches are highly client-centred and have no interest in changing the client beyond the client's own aspirations. *Progressive* approaches also focus on the individual, but in this case, they are keen to expand their horizons and encourage them to consider new opportunities outside their current frame of reference. *Conservative* approaches focus on social needs (e.g. skills shortages in scientific fields) and seek to steer the individual towards these social needs. Finally, *radical* approaches seek to empower clients to challenge barriers and change the world if necessary.

In recent years theorists have increasingly engaged with these radical approaches to career guidance and created the 'career guidance for social justice' movement. This theory argues that career guidance has the potential to support people in taking control of their world and changing it for the better. This movement brings together a wide range of theorists drawing on different traditions, including Marxism and socialism, feminism and queer theory, poststructuralism and post-colonialism, as well as a range of other critical theories. Inevitably, each of these theorists stresses different things, but some core ideas have been brought together into the 'five signposts to a socially just approach for career guidance', which argues that career guidance should do the following things to support social justice.

1. **Build critical consciousness** by helping people understand the world in which they live and how they can act on it.

2. **Name oppression** and help students and clients understand it and what to do about it.

3. **Question what is normal** and encourage people to think about other ways to live, work and career.

4. **Encourage people to work together** to help each other, provide support and take action collectively.

5. **Work at a range of levels** from the individual to the global to increase career opportunities and make a better world.

This theory remains emergent and contested by many, but it potentially points the way to a very different approach to career development work.

💡 Resources

Tony Watts set out his typology in 'Socio-Political Ideologies in Guidance'. Rie Thomsen and her colleagues explore critical theory in their article 'Critical Perspectives on Agency and Social Justice in Transitions and Career Development'.

A good place to begin engaging with the career guidance for social justice is the website https://careerguidancesocialjustice.wordpress.com/. Beyond that, you may want to look at Hooley, Sultana and Thomsen's two collections, *Career Guidance for Social Justice* and *Career Guidance for Emancipation* or their article on the 'five signposts'.

🧠 Reflection

Is it possible for individuals or career development practitioners to change the world? What examples can you think of where career development activities have made a difference in the wider world?

What are the structures and issues that make you wish that the world was different?

How can you avoid career development work becoming politicised and caught up in culture wars if it starts taking a more obvious stance?

Metatheoretical frameworks

Some theorists have tried to bring the different issues and insights from other theories together into a metatheoretical framework. What this means is that they have stood back and looked at all of the theories and tried to come up with a theory of theories. Perhaps the most successful attempt at this is Wendy

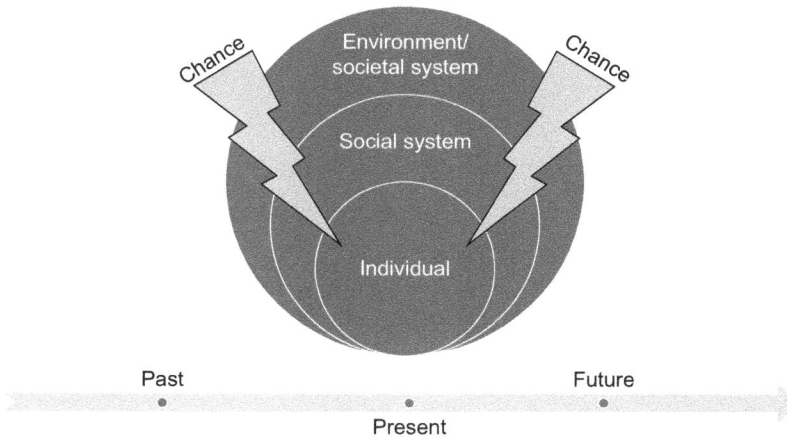

Figure 6.4. Patton and McMahon's system theory of careers

Patton and Mary McMahon's *systems theory framework of career development*. This theory sees careers as emerging out of a series of interconnected systems which represent most of the things that we have talked about in this chapter already, for example, the individual, their family, their community and society. Each of these can be understood as systems in their own right, with some nested inside others. So, our personality is a system made up of a lot of different processes and influences, and then we are an actor within the system of our family, both being influenced by it and influencing it (see Figure 6.4).

Patton and McMahon also highlight the importance of chance occurrences that cut across these different systems, leading them to interact in new and unpredictable ways. They discuss the way that time acts on these systems. For example, your relationship with the school system changes as you get older and ultimately leave education and move into work. This does not mean that the school system has ceased to exist, or to influence your career, but time and position within the system change the way that this works. One of the roles of the career development professional is to help people think about which systems are most critical to the development of their career and how, and then to develop a narrative which helps them to move their life forwards (which may often involve shifting focus from one system to another).

The challenge with this theory and other similar theories and metatheoretical frameworks is that they throw a lot of issues into the pot and do not necessarily give us a way to simplify this complexity. So if we go back to Einstein's definition of theory, these kinds of approaches do a better job of representing reality, but a worse job of simplifying reality to make it manageable.

Resources

Patton and McMahon have written a lot about systems theory. Their article 'The Systems Theory Framework of Career Development: 20 Years of Contribution to Theory and Practice' provides a good overview of their work and others who have adopted the framework. It is also worth looking at their book *Career Development and Systems Theory*.

There are also other similar approaches to systems theory and the creation of metatheoretical frameworks in careers that are worth looking at. Audrey Collins' article 'The Systems Approach to Career' offers a different way of thinking about systems theory, while Julia Yates' 'Metatheoretical Framework for Career Development Professionals' creates a framework from the perspective of practice.

CASE STUDY

Shona remembers learning about a lot of different theories during her training. At the time, it felt almost impossible to make sense of. There were a lot of interesting ideas, but it was like swallowing an encyclopedia.

But now that she is back in practice, ideas from the theory module keep popping back into her head. So, she recognises that Petr's story about his career journey from Poland to the UK is a narrative. He's got used to telling it as a tale of failure, but she can use career construction theory and life design to talk explicitly about the way he is creating this narrative and then encourage him to experiment with talking about his life differently. Most importantly, she uses this to help him focus on the future and design his life by building a new kind of (more positive and optimistic) narrative about the future.

Yesterday she met Orla, who was desperate for another job because she was feeling really uncomfortable at her current workplace. Rather than starting to focus on matching Orla to another job, Shona drew on ideas from career guidance for social justice and talked about how Orla might be able to challenge her sexist and bullying boss. She encouraged her to recognise her oppression and join together with others to challenge this. Orla went away resolved to stay and fight (at least for now) rather than being pushed out of a job that she likes just because her boss is a creep.

And when Mohammed told her that he couldn't possibly go back to college, she talked about what his horizons for action were and where those came from. When she put it like that, he was keen to try and stretch them a bit. So, they then started talking about the ideas of self-efficacy, self-belief and self-confidence and reflected on what he would need to do in order to get himself into a place where he was ready to step out of his comfort zone.

While she was studying, the theories seemed abstract, but now that she has learnt about them, she keeps recognising things in real life and finding the theories helpful in unlocking both what her clients are experiencing and what things to try in helping them move forwards.

In a nutshell

This (epic) chapter has discussed the main career theories. It has argued that

- theories seek to make the world simpler, without over-simplifying. This is often a tricky balancing act;

- the matching theory is at the heart of much thinking in career development, but many other theorists have argued that this is an oversimplification;

- some theories focus on the individual asking how we can understand someone's personality, capabilities and interests in ways that help to understand their career;

- other theorists focus on the world and try to understand what kind of environment this offers for careering; and

- finally, still more theorists are concerned with the question of how we bring the individual and the world together in a way that helps people to understand and develop their career.

Chapter 7
Career coaching and counselling

Introduction

In this chapter we are going to look at one-to-one practices for supporting and facilitating an individual's career learning. We will consider why we work in this way and some of the underpinning principles about our clients having autonomy over their own lives and what this means for one-to-one work. We will also address potentially confusing terminology, such as counselling, coaching and guidance, and go on to look at the foundational skills needed to work in this way. Finally, we will consider some of the possible models you can draw on in this work and consider how it connects with the things we cover in other chapters.

We have called this chapter 'career coaching and counselling' but there is a range of terms that could be used to describe this activity. As we discussed in Chapter 3, there is a lot of different language that is used to describe careers professionals and careers work. When people talk about one-to-one work, they often use the term 'guidance', often paired with 'information' and 'advice' as an alternative to terms like coaching and counselling. It is our view that the terms usually mean broadly the same thing, albeit with different histories and resonance. For a book like this, a focus on what they have in common seems more productive than spending a lot of time teasing out differences. This is not to say that there aren't different traditions of one-to-one work that emphasise different approaches, and we will try to draw on a range of these traditions and introduce you to them in this chapter.

Why we work with people one-to-one

There are three main reasons why we work with people one-to-one: its effectiveness, its potential to personalise the learning and the private nature of the interaction (Table 7.1).

Table 7.1. Rationales for one-to-one work

Personalisation	Working with one person at a time enables the practitioner to tailor their approach to the individual. This includes shaping the interview to focus on the issue that they present with and the ability to respond to the unfolding discussion. When so much of career development depends on the individual's characteristics and context (as the theories discussed in Chapter 6 show us), it stands to reason that everyone will need different things from their one-to-one encounter with a practitioner.
Privacy	The bond that a practitioner can build with a single client enables them to show empathy and build a relationship such that the person is more likely to be open about their career needs and concerns. In private, clients are more likely to disclose sensitive personal issues; just the sort of things that can have a big impact on career development.
Effectiveness	It works. Compared with group-based learning and the provision of information services alone, one-to-one work has been shown to be the most effective at supporting career development. That said, defining 'effectiveness' is a complex area, and it is undoubtedly true that one-to-one work isn't the best approach for all clients in all situations.

Resources

Susan Whiston's chapter 'Career Counselling Effectiveness and Contributing Factors' provides further details about the efficacy of one-to-one careers work and how this compares to other forms of career work.

Client-centredness

A focus on client-centredness is common to most forms of one-to-one work. This idea (sometimes referred to as 'person-centredness') draws on theoretical ideas that come from the field of therapeutic counselling, particularly the work of Carl Rogers. These theories assume that all individuals have the personal resources to move themselves in a positive direction and that the counsellor's role is to encourage the individual to make use of these resources. This suggests that if we focus on supporting a client to develop autonomy and agency, they will be able to develop more effectively than if we give them instructions, suggestions and advice. This leads the counsellor to take a 'nondirective' stance and not to tell clients what to do, instead respecting their choice to act as they wish.

Reflection

To demonstrate the value of nondirective and client-centred approaches, we would like you to engage in a silent (self) coaching activity.

Take a pen and a piece of paper into a quiet space where you can think about your answers to a series of questions. Next, identify a problem or challenge you are facing in your life. With that in mind, work through these 19 questions, writing down your answers in turn.

1. What are you trying to achieve?
2. Imagine that you have successfully addressed your issue. What does success look and feel like?
3. What do you really, really want?
4. What is going on that makes this an issue for you?
5. Who is involved?
6. What are the key features of the situation?
7. What assumptions are you making?
8. What – if anything – have you already done to address the situation?
9. And what has been the effect of what you have done so far?
10. What options do you have?
11. What else might you do?
12. If you had absolutely no constraints – of time or money or power or health – what would you do?
13. If you had a really wise friend, what would they do in your shoes?
14. You have just generated a set of options. Looking back at these options, rate them quickly on a scale of 1 to 10 on how practical they seem (where 10 means completely practical).
15. Looking over your list of options, which options will you actually pursue?
16. For each chosen option, what specifically will you do?
17. What help or support do you need?
18. What deadlines will you set for yourself?
19. What is the first step that you will take?

Congratulations – you have just coached yourself! Hopefully, you can see here that without any additional information or intervention from a professional, providing some space to think and a series of structured questions has the power to help people determine their best way forwards. Someone could ask these questions without even knowing what your problem is.

Carl Rogers would argue that the job of the counsellor is to provide this kind of space and structure to enable clients to think. He proposed that this kind of client-centred approach requires the counsellor to adopt three core conditions: empathy (understanding the feelings and experiences of the client), congruence (being genuine and real with the client) and unconditional positive regard (being positive and unjudgemental about the client). Experiencing these core conditions, he proposed, allows a person to grow and to heal.

Rogers' approach to client-centredness is appealing, but in career development work, it can be quite difficult to operationalise in a pure way. A key challenge is that person-centred counselling would often take place over an extended period, sometimes years, whereas in careers work, practitioners rarely have this luxury. Also, the kinds of career dilemmas that people face often require a relatively quick decision. We have spent a lot of time in this book talking about the labour market, the education system, how people learn and how careers work, and the incorporation of this into our practice might well render it wholly distinct from counselling. As careers professionals, we might need to be relatively proactive and introduce people to new information, provide them with options, help them to judge options, focus their actions and follow up on their plans.

After all, Tony Watt's ideas about socio-political ideologies that we covered in chapter six show us that a focus on the individual, which is who we are working with directly in one-to-one work, is just one aspect of career development work. Ultimately, we are working with individuals in a societal context, and it is important to hold both dimensions in tension through our work.

⠿ Resources

The opening chapter of Julia Yates' *The Career Coaching Handbook* examines some of these issues, and the rest of the book also provides valuable resources for thinking about one-to-one careers work. Jenny Kidd's chapter 'The Career Counselling Interview' discusses a range of different approaches, including alternatives to client-centred approaches.

Carl Rogers' *Client Centred Therapy* and *On Becoming a Person* are essential readings for people wanting to understand the theories that underpin much one-to-one careers work. Ross Crisp's article, 'A Person-Centred Perspective to Counselling in Educational and Vocational Agencies' provides some useful discussion of how this has been translated into use in career development work. Meanwhile, Barbara Bassot's chapter, 'Client-Centred Career Development Practice: A Critical Review', provides a more critical discussion on client-centredness.

Counselling and coaching skills

Career development practitioners use a range of specific interpersonal skills to manage one-to-one conversations with their clients, according to the context in which they work. In this section, we will unpick these skills and then consider how they fit together, and how you can develop them.

Establishing a relationship

It is important to create a rapport with a client that puts them at ease and enables them to talk about their career hopes and difficulties openly. This requires the careful use of interpersonal skills. Much of this is instinct: we use eye contact, smile, remember people's names, and show an interest in them. We should consider how we build rapport when we reflect on our own practice or give feedback to a colleague on theirs, in order to build our 'conscious competence' (see Chapter 2). As we will see, this rapport creates the trust that is pivotal to overall effectiveness.

In the research literature, this process of relationship building is sometimes referred to as the 'working alliance'. The idea of the working alliance goes beyond just building rapport (the *bonds* between the counsellor and the clients) and also includes more practical issues such as: what is the purpose of this relationship (the *goals*) and how you are going to work together (the *tasks*). Research suggests that the establishment of an effective working alliance is critical to the effectiveness of career counselling and coaching.

💡 Resources

Susan Whiston and colleagues' article 'The Working Alliance in Career Counseling: A Systematic Overview' provides a detailed discussion of the evidence around the working alliance.

Listening

There are different types of listening that Bob Thomson argues we can consider as a ladder (Figure 7.1).

How do you know when a person isn't really listening to you? They don't look at you; they interrupt you; what they say bears no relation to what you have said. They might even yawn! Not being listened to can make you feel uncomfortable and lead you to stop talking.

In turn, how do you know when someone is listening? In an extension of those rapport-building skills, they are attentive and use their body language

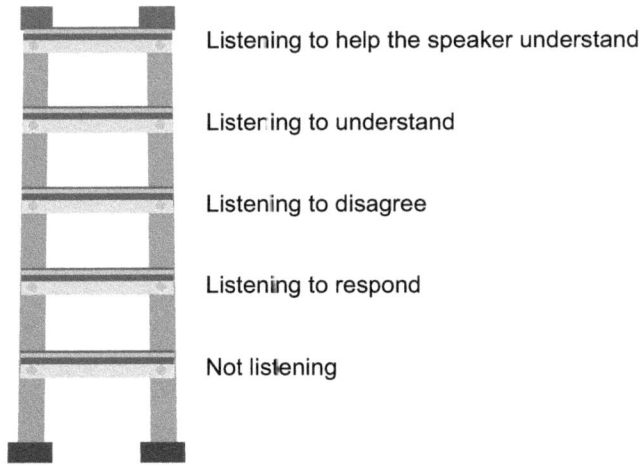

Listening to help the speaker understand

Listening to understand

Listening to disagree

Listening to respond

Not listening

Figure 7.1. Thomson's listening ladder

to show their interest in you. But sometimes listeners are really talkers-in-waiting, *listening to respond*. They might interrupt you too; they'll jump in as soon as you finish because it is their turn.

In media interviews, we can be exposed to a lot of *listening to disagree* – where the listener is only listening because they want to get their point of view across. They are listening so they can jump in if there is a weak point in what you are saying. With an 'I win, you lose' mentality, they simply want an argument.

Better listening is *listening to understand*. Here, the listener starts to be able to see the world as it appears through the client's eyes. It is key to developing empathy needed for a relationship and helps the career development professional to ask better and more useful questions. It is part of your process of 'reading' someone's career development using the range of theoretical lenses we discussed in Chapter 6.

An even further level is *listening to help the other understand*. This might involve holding a period of silence so the client can listen to themselves too, becoming more aware and taking responsibility for their actions.

When working one-to-one with clients, we are listening to lots of things. We are listening to the facts that clients tell us and the stories they present themselves in. We can hear what they say about their feelings but also the feelings that show in other ways. This listening can tell us about the values, assumptions and beliefs they really hold about their situation. By also listening to what is unsaid, we can get a picture of the whole issue, going beyond what the client has said.

With practice, you can develop your listening skills to progress up this ladder of listening. Don't worry if at first you are panicking about what you will say next; remember the development of conscious competence we looked at in Chapter 2 and keep practising.

Another part of our development as listeners is listening to ourselves. Our felt responses and reactions to what we hear can be very revealing food for thought. They can help us to identify values and beliefs that are key to our professional identity, as well as unconscious biases and blind spots that we need to surface and challenge through reflective practice.

Questioning

As you build on the rapport you have with your client, you will want to provide some structure to the interview and encourage them to talk about the issues that matter for their career development. The way we phrase and pose questions guides the client through the process.

A good question will provoke thinking in the client, raise their self-awareness and help them to be truthful. It is not so much about finding out for ourselves about the person in front of us but creating a space where they can learn about themselves and their options. A good question is often quite short and simple. By sticking closely to what the client wants to talk about, questions can trigger considerable learning for the client, giving them the motivation they need to act.

The best way to get someone talking in a conversation is to ask them open questions: questions beginning with words like What? When? How? Where? Who? Why? (although 'why' questions can come across as very challenging and so should perhaps be reserved until greater rapport is built. See the skills pyramid section below).

These are the opposite of closed questions, which can be answered with a simple *Yes* or *No*. These do have some value – with unfocused and talkative clients, or when you want to elicit an immediate reaction to a forced choice, so that a client hears themselves express a preference. Sometimes you might also ask a direct or closed question to clarify a person's story or to gain simple factual information.

In the spirit of 'listening to help the client understand', good questions stimulate thinking by asking clients to tell you more about something. As the silent coaching showed, 'what else?' can be quite effective. However, good questions can lead to silence while that thinking takes place. Don't be afraid of silence; keep the rapport going and it can be very helpful.

Some of the pitfalls we see as students learn to ask good questions are things like:

- **Hidden suggestions.** Sometimes a question is actually a suggestion or a direction, for example, 'Have you thought about applying to university?' Even if it isn't meant as such, clients will often focus on the suggestion rather than the question. Suggestions have their place, as we will discuss later, but should be used sparingly and purposefully.

- **Long or complex questions.** Good questions are short questions. Take your time and phrase questions concisely and carefully.

- **Multiple questions.** Ask questions one at a time. Asking more than one question can confuse a client and leave them unsure about which one to answer.

To help you generate questions, it can be worth revisiting some of the theories we covered in Chapter 6 and using those to come up with some theoretically informed questions. These might initially be framed as questions you ask yourself as you are thinking about the client – but can then be developed into questions *for* the client. Some examples are given in Table 7.2, deliberately crafted to relate to different types of clients. Try and think of some more for yourself.

Table 7.2. Example questions

Self-reflection questions	Client questions
What role might be a good fit for this person's personality?	What do you enjoy doing?
How does this person see themselves?	How would your friends describe your strengths?
How are this person's life stage and roles affecting their career challenge?	What have been the most significant steps in your career journey to date?
What are the limits of this person's horizons for action?	What are your main career ambitions? Have these changed? What were they in the past? What options immediately spring to mind? What jobs have you had a chance to learn about from the people around you?
How is this person's family or community influencing them?	What else is going on in your life that is relevant to the choices you are making right now?
What does this person need to learn to take advantage of career opportunities?	What would taking a risk look like to you?
What structural barriers might be facing this client, e.g., discrimination or harassment?	What if any challenges do you think you might face in pursuing that goal? Let's look at them and consider ways to address them.

Other conversational skills

Of course, we don't just bombard our clients with questions; it's more of a conversation in which we might summarise, paraphrase or share some insights of our own. Other skills that are important in interviews include the following.

- **Paying attention to the language that a client uses** and mirroring it where appropriate. This might even involve reflecting a person's language back to them. For example, if a client says, 'I am feeling totally overwhelmed right now', you might simply respond, 'overwhelmed?'. This helps to keep the focus on them and what they need from the conversation.

- **Summarising** keeps a conversation moving, either to check your own understanding or to help a client develop their own understanding. It can be useful when you need time to think, or when the client has given you a long story or explanation. It can also be useful at different stages of the intervention – for example, summarising is often used towards the end of a session or part of a session.

- **Paraphrasing** is similar to summarising, but where summarising condenses a lot of discussion into a short summary, a paraphrase involves using your own words to explore what a client is saying in more detail, '*It sounds like you are saying . . . is that right?*' This can help check your own understanding of a client's story, give clients a language to express an idea they are struggling with or even help a client see something differently. Paraphrasing is a very useful skill, especially at the beginning of a session when a practitioner needs to spend time understanding a client's situation and their needs.

- **Reframing** is restating something to enable a client to see it differently. This might involve acknowledging the client's perspective but then asking something like, 'Is there another way to look at that?' 'How would someone else see this situation?' or 'What are some other possible reasons that this could have happened?'

- **Immediacy** means drawing attention to the immediate environment. You might reflect back to someone that their face or body language changed when they spoke about different options and ask if they have thoughts about what this means. You might comment that they seem angry or upset about something as a way of helping them move through their emotional responses.

- **Suggestions, information and advice** also have a place in our career development conversations, and we explore how we work with information in Chapter 9. Sometimes we provide information directly or refer to other sources, always with the goal of helping the client use information independently in the future. Sometimes our own professional knowledge will make a particular course of action seem to us to be the best way for the client to proceed. We can suggest this course of action to a client, but the process of them gaining ownership and building commitment to the action is critical to whether they will do it or not. One way of doing this is by making a clear suggestion: beginning by labelling it as such, offering the idea and then inviting the client to respond to it.

Integrating counselling and coaching skills

In their book, *A Counselling Approach to Career Guidance*, Lynda Ali and Barbara Graham represent these skills as a pyramid (see Figure 7.2).

Their premise is that active listening skills are the foundation of the pyramid and allow for the development of an empathic relationship between career development practitioner and client, where the client knows the career professional is on their side. Understanding skills build on this and help the relationship develop. In turn, the career development professional's influence becomes greater. At the peak of the pyramid are the higher-level skills of interpretation, where we might challenge a client or draw their attention to how they are presenting. Interestingly, providing information is up here as a higher-level skill, demonstrating that providing information needs to be done in a careful and considered way – something we will delve into in more depth in Chapter 9.

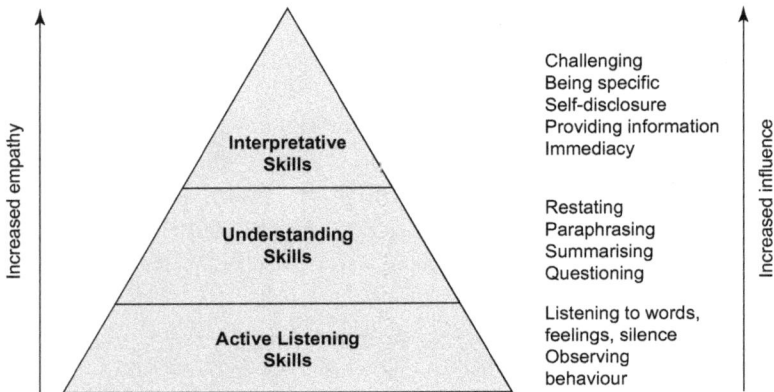

Figure 7.2. Ali and Graham's skills pyramid

CASE STUDY

Karl is supporting John, who has recently found out he is 'at risk' of redundancy from his role as a maintenance manager in a local authority. Karl introduces himself and asks John to say a little about what he would like to cover in the session. John says he wants to focus on interview skills, as he will soon be interviewed for a new role as part of a restructure in the council and has very little experience of putting himself over well.

Karl says they can discuss interviews, but first of all, it would be helpful to get a better sense of John's skills, and John agrees that they should start there. Karl asks a series of open questions about his work and what he has learnt, summarising for him the skills he can hear. John describes his current tasks and the challenge of keeping an eye on the work of his team, and Karl rephrases it as 'setting up systems for monitoring and tracking progress'.

Karl then moves to a discussion of interviews, prior experience with them, and how John has prepared. Karl senses John's resentment about having to be interviewed, so gently raises this, and John reveals his anger at the situation. From here, Karl can ask if he really wants to continue working in the restructured team. Karl shows John some local job vacancy information to help him consider whether he might prefer to take the redundancy payment and take his skills to a different employer. John agrees to speak to some contacts and explore his options before they meet again.

Structuring counselling and coaching sessions

The case study of Karl and John not only shows the skills the practitioner uses but also reveals how Karl structures the conversation to create and manage a working relationship. In this section, we look at a basic three-stage approach to a career coaching or counselling conversation.

Beginning

Career counselling and coaching sessions should begin with the process of 'contracting' as a way of establishing a 'working alliance' for the session or sessions.

The idea of a contract borrows legal language to describe a process where the client and the career development professional agree on what they are meeting for, what is and isn't acceptable within this encounter, and what some of the rights and responsibilities are. This kind of contract isn't normally written down, although there are occasions where this is done, but usually takes the form of a conversation.

This contract begins to be negotiated prior to the meeting, for example, through the marketing information that is put out about the interview and the form that the invitation and confirmation of the appointment takes. It is commonplace for the career development professional to then take some time at the beginning of a session to cover some important features of how they work and their boundaries, including a summary of some of the basic features of the session such as how long it will be, whether there will be a possibility for a follow-up, and an explanation of and reassurance about confidentiality. This may be followed with some broad opening questions to explore the client's agenda such as *'what are you hoping to get out of our conversation today?'* or *'what would be the most useful way to use our time together today?'* These kinds of questions can be useful to help get the client talking and may be used to discuss a focus for the session, and clarify how the session is going to work, building on both what the client wants and the approach and constraints that the career development professional is working within.

Don't rush this stage; spend time with the client finding out what you need to know to agree on a focus for your conversation. This might involve challenging a client's assumptions or expectations – such as delivering information directly (*'I might not be able to answer all your questions, but I can show you places to look after we have spoken'*) or providing directive advice (*'It's not my role to tell you what to do, but I can help you work out for yourself your best option'*)

Middle

In the middle of the session, you are seeking to address whatever has been agreed upon as the goal and purpose of the conversation. It is likely to begin with additional exploration of the background to a client's concerns and what they have already done, before moving on to explore different possibilities for action. This section should be an opportunity to continue to build the working alliance and ensure that you and the client are aligned in what you are doing.

In the middle stage, you work actively with your client. This might mean providing feedback or information to your client, engaging in different kinds of activities, or using different tools or resources (see chapter 9) to help them gain new perspectives on their situation and choices. You need to keep an eye on the time of the session, and you may check in with your client about how they feel the session is going. If a number of concerns are unearthed in this process, you may need to discuss with your client how to use your time together and return to your contract to agree what you will focus on. This stage might also include referral to some information resources and generate ideas for future actions your client could take.

End

As the session draws to a close, it is time to consider what your client has learnt and what action they are willing to take as a result. Moving into this stage can be signalled by reminding the client what was agreed upon at the start of the session. A useful way to check a client's understanding and motivation to take their next steps is to ask them to summarise what has been covered and go on to put into their own words what they will do next. In some cases, this can take the form of a written action plan that can be referred to by both the client and the careers professional after the session.

Discussion about how to summarise and record the session can be a good basis for any record-keeping that you do and enables you to remind them about how their data will be stored. Checking in about how sure they feel, further support that they need, and offering encouragement can all increase the likelihood of the agreed actions being taken. At this stage, you also need to confirm any follow-up activities you might engage in with them, such as a follow-up appointment or phone call. After the client has left, time to tidy and store records can also help you reflect on the conversation and how you handled it.

Using career counselling and coaching models

In the section above, we have described a basic three-stage model for a one-to-one session. However, there is a wide range of other career counselling and coaching models that offer more detailed approaches to delivering a one-to-one session or sessions. We cannot cover the full range of possibilities in detail here, but offer a handful of examples in this section for you to explore further.

Different models are underpinned by different theories and assumptions. It is also very likely that different approaches will be more or less useful in different contexts and with different types of participants. The important thing is to be able to *critically evaluate* their value for the client you are with at the time and flex your approach in the most effective way. Many models lay down a process for you to follow as you go through the conversation. The 'GROW' model is used extensively by people drawing on the coaching tradition, and offers a four-stage approach to thinking about working with clients (Figure 7.3).

The acronym stands for Goal, Reality, Options, Will, and is the basis for the coaching questions we asked you in the exercise earlier. It maps onto the

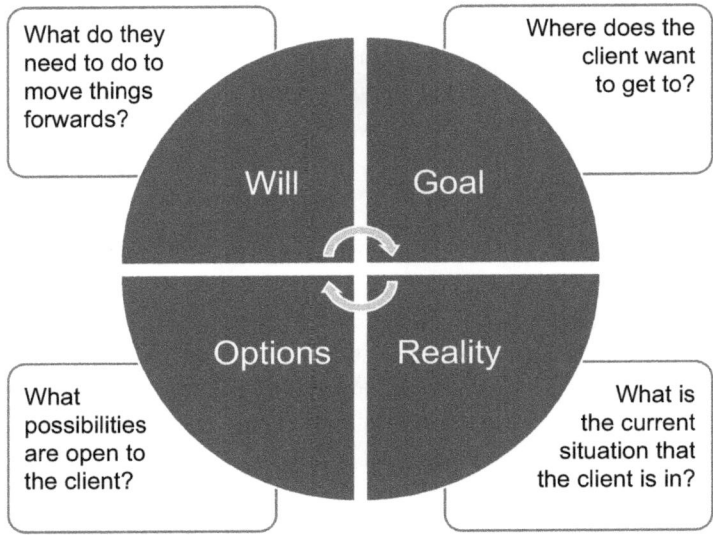

Figure 7.3. The GROW model

three stages we outlined above, with a goal at the outset, reality and options in the middle and what the client will do, or their actions, at the end. Its critics point out that it requires a client to be able to articulate a goal and to be quite self-aware and decisive – arguably the sort of high-functioning person who might well get where they want to go without help. What do you think?

Robert Reese and Gerard Egan's book *The Skilled Helper* offers another model for one-to-one work. This process flips the order in which Reality and Goal are addressed in the GROW model, starting by exploring a client's current situation before looking at alternatives and the future. This is designed to provide more support to the client in working out where they want to go (Figure 7.4).

Another model was laid out by Ali and Graham. This builds on the three stages of beginning, middle and end, but extends the middle section into two sequential stages of exploring and evaluating to reflect the increasing depth and challenge involved. Ali and Graham's model has also been revised by Hooley, who repurposed it to actively address social justice concerns.

As this discussion shows, there are a lot of detailed models for one-to-one career interviewing. The list above only scratches the surface of what is available. But, as you will see, many of them have a lot of similarities and can best be thought of as refinements of the basic three-stage model that we began this section with. Others do approach interviewing from a different direction, and we would encourage you to experiment with some of these.

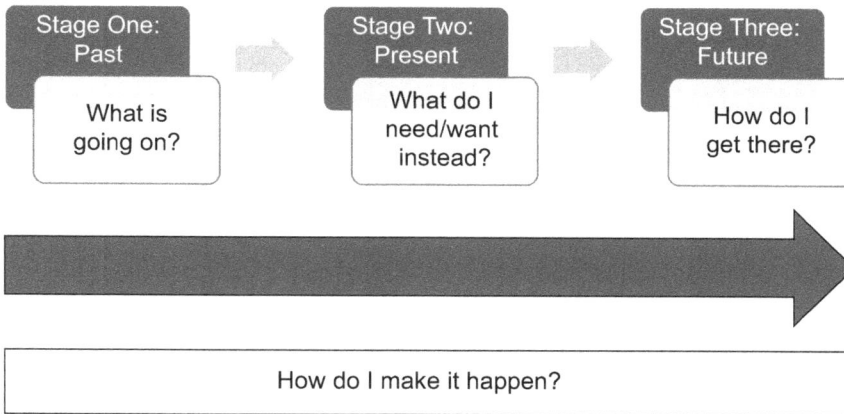

Figure 7.4. Reese and Egan's skilled helper model

But always remember that it is possible to combine different approaches as you develop your own approach to practice.

Reflection

Which of these models appeals to you most and why?

Which can you see as suiting different types of clients?

What are the pros and cons of different approaches?

Resources

Julia Yates' *The Career Coaching Handbook* and the accompanying volume *The Career Coaching Toolkit* provide more detailed summaries of the array of different approaches and tools that are available.

John Whitmore and Tiffany Gaskell's *Coaching for Performance* sets out the GROW model in some detail.

Other models can be found in Reese and Egan's book *The Skilled Helper*, Ali and Graham's book *The Counselling Approach to Career Guidance* (with Hooley's revision of their model in his article 'Building a Radical Career Imaginary').

Developing your approach to career counselling and coaching

In this final section, we set out some developments that have emerged from career counselling and coaching approaches that you may wish to think about more as you develop your practice.

Working on the telephone and online

While the traditional image of a career coaching session tends to be a face-to-face encounter in a private room, recent years have seen a rapid rise in such conversations happening via telephone or online. While undoubtedly accelerated by the Covid-19 pandemic, the trend was already evident due to greater convenience, reach and choice. Telephone counselling has been an approach used for many years, but in recent times there have been a range of possibilities for online career counselling or coaching, which include the use of videoconference tools like Zoom or Teams, in which the encounter is fairly similar to face-to-face work, but also the use of text-based approaches such as synchronous 'live chat' features and asynchronous approaches such as the use of email or text messaging, which means that the interview may go on over a number of days or weeks. Indeed, as new technologies develop, they offer a wide range of opportunities to move career coaching and counselling online and often encourage us to explore new ways of working, which combine career counselling or coaching and career education (see Chapter 8).

Working online creates some additional considerations for us and for those we are working with. We need to think about digital access for those we are trying to reach, not just in terms of equipment and connectivity, but also clients' capacity to use online tools and whether they have access to appropriate spaces to participate in career coaching or counselling. Preparing clients in advance so they can engage in the conversation in private and without interruption, as well as configuring our own work environment, needs some thought.

Building rapport and interacting online and via the telephone can require new skills as well, as some possibilities like eye contact and body language carry less weight and new opportunities emerge for example, providing links in chat or sharing your screen. You need to be confident about the use of the equipment and tools that you are using to facilitate the session and also take efforts to minimise background noise, think about data protection issues and how to incorporate appropriate tools and information resources into your counselling. You will also want to build into your contracting issues such as technological failure. If your work primarily involves online or telephone interventions, then you will also want to engage in additional CPD to ensure that you are appropriately skilled to work in these contexts.

> ## 💡 Resources
>
> Kate Dunn has produced a useful factsheet called *Working Online in the Counselling Professions* that raises a range of important issues in relation to online work, while Jones and Stokes' *Online Counselling* and Maxine Rosenfield's *Telephone Counselling* offer deeper investigations of these issues.
>
> There is also an emergent literature which focuses specifically on career counselling online, such as Jenny Bimrose's chapter 'Constructivism in Online Career Counselling' or Claudia Deniers' article 'Experiences of Receiving Career Coaching via Skype'. Broader discussions of online careers practice can also be found in Tanis Goddard's PhD thesis *Online Career Learning* and Ingrid Bårdsdatter Bakke and Tristram Hooley's chapter 'Neither Online, nor Face-to-Face, but Integrated Career Guidance'.

Group counselling and coaching

So far, we have focused primarily on individual career coaching and counselling, but it is important to note that there is also a long tradition of group and collective forms of coaching and counselling. Some of these merge into the kind of career learning that we will discuss in Chapter 8, but there are also approaches that draw on counselling and coaching models and apply them to work with groups.

Delivering counselling and coaching to groups can increase the efficiency of the interaction as you can speak to a larger number of clients in a single session, but it also changes it in important ways. Many of the advantages that we began this chapter with around personalisation and privacy have to be renegotiated in group settings. This can result in contracting becoming more complex as it ceases to be purely a contract between the career development professional and the client and becomes a process of setting collective ground rules for the group. Group settings offer new opportunities for peer support, the sharing of experiences, and the generation of individual and collective solutions. As such, it is better viewed as a new modality of counselling and coaching rather than simply an expansion of one-to-one approaches to encompass more people.

> ## 💡 Resources
>
> There is a range of books and resources available to support group career counselling and coaching. K. Richard Pyle and Seth Hayden's *Group Career Counselling* is a good starting point, while Susan Meldrum's article 'Group Career Coaching' provides a recent review of the area and some practical examples.

Dealing with varied contexts and constraints

Career counselling and coaching can take place in a wide variety of contexts, and each of these has its own challenges and opportunities. Depending on the context of your practice, you are likely to find that things like the environment in which you are practising, the length of the interview and the typical number of sessions vary. Different contexts will also require different approaches to record-keeping for follow up and usage monitoring and compliance with local data protection legislation.

We have not said much yet about how long one-to-one conversations take, how appointments are made, or how clients invited to prepare. There is probably a gold standard answer to these questions, which would argue that interviews should be at least 45–50 minutes long, based on the 'therapeutic hour' common in personal counselling. This 45-minute minimum is recommended by the CDI in the UK and is also picked up in the Statutory Guidance for Schools in England.

Ideally, clients would have access to multiple sessions and have the opportunity to research and reflect in between sessions before returning for their next session with new ideas. In this kind of environment, the stages in the models that we set out earlier in this chapter would happen in each session, but there would also be an overarching process that might take place over multiple sessions. However, much career development practice does not have this kind of resourcing, and so we often have to deliver services in more concise and creative ways.

There is a range of strategies that are used to manage the delivery of career counselling and coaching in resource-constrained settings. These include some of the following approaches.

- **Single sessions.** The default model of practice in many settings is focused around single sessions to help manage resources. Sessions can vary in length. Ideally, the option for multiple sessions remains available for those that need it. Clients may not be offered follow-up appointments as standard, but options for telephone follow-up or email may be introduced.

- **Reducing session length.** Short sessions, or 'drop-ins', may be a way of reaching more clients. In some settings, reducing the standard length of sessions may be a way of offering multiple interventions – so, for example, rather than offering a one-off one-hour session, offering two half-hour sessions may offer some benefits.

- **Blending with online and self-help resources.** Some services integrate their one-to-one contact with a career development professional with the use of self-help resources in order to maximise the potential for a client's career development learning.

- **Telephone and online counselling.** Delivering career sessions online can reduce travel times for career development professionals as well as clients and allow more sessions to be conducted.

- **Targeting.** Services may target one-to-one services at particular clients who are judged to be most in need of them. However, this requires the careful development of targeting criteria and consideration of what is available for those who fall outside of it.

- **Triage.** To balance the availability of practitioners with demand, it is common for triage systems to be put in place to assess need and then to direct clients to appropriate services. In many cases this may not include seeing a career development professional practitioner one-to-one, but rather a group session or access to information resources.

- **Charging for services.** This approach obviously limits access to those who can pay and also requires a whole other set of considerations about how services are advertised, contracted and evaluated.

All these approaches require careful implementation and monitoring to avoid unintended consequences. The fact remains that one-to-one career coaching is a very effective activity, and service users will often want as much of it as they can access. Trying to assess who needs it most and who has the most to gain from it is a perennial concern of service managers.

Reflection

Is it appropriate for a year group of school students to all have access to at least one career counselling or coaching session in a year? If so, what would be the most practical and useful way of organising this? And how could you make the case to your managers for the resources to deliver such a service?

How could you establish a career counselling or coaching service in a college or university in a way which allowed students to book appointments on demand? What will the service offer be? How can you avoid ending up with a small group of super-users, while most students just ignore the service?

Getting better

Developing and honing your ability to conduct one-to-one career coaching sessions is something that never stops. Remembering the process we considered in Chapter 2, of moving from a starting point of unconscious incompetence through to unconscious competence, means a learning curve of practising, reflecting, getting feedback from peers and more experienced colleagues, and building confidence. But once careers practice does become second nature, there remains an important process of keeping the saw sharp

– our clients face new barriers, our unconscious biases need constant review, there are new techniques and ideas to try. Every client deserves our full attention and our skills in helping them to learn about their career.

There is a range of approaches to ensuring continuous improvement in your practice. These include reading, participating in CPD, and reflecting on your practice. But it is also worth noting two established approaches to practice improvement that are commonly used in a variety of one-to-one settings. Firstly, there is value in having a mentor (in counselling this role is often filled by a supervisor) whom you can talk over your practice with and discuss particularly challenging experiences. Secondly, there can be value in practice circles where you and your colleagues talk over current cases (respecting confidentiality) and identify new and innovative solutions.

In a nutshell

This chapter has broken down career counselling and coaching practice and considered the fundamental underpinning assumptions as well as the skills and structures that will enable you to provide one-to-one support. It has argued that

- there is a strong rationale for working with people one-to-one to help them develop their careers;

- effective one-to-one work relies on a range of skills, including the ability to contract, establish a relationship, listen and question;

- there is a range of models and approaches that allow you to structure counselling and coaching sessions in different ways; and

- once you have mastered the basics, you will likely need to engage with tools, online approaches, group approaches and dealing with a variety of different contexts and constraints.

Chapter 8
Career education

Career development is an act of learning. Throughout our early lives, we become aware of the world around us and recognise that we will have a part to play in it. Gradually, we start to explore different possibilities, try things out, receive feedback and change our strategies and directions. These processes of career exploration, development and management are all learning processes.

A lot of career learning will happen regardless of education and certainly of formal (career) education. Many people build successful lives and careers despite never having attended a careers lesson, gained access to a mentor or participated in any kind of educational work experience. Learning is central to what we are as human beings and so it has a way of just happening whenever we encounter the world and the other people who live in it.

But this recognition that learning, and indeed career learning, is a natural part of being human does not mean that there is no point in helping people to learn. Career education is designed to help people learn more quickly and deeply than they otherwise would have done. It also hopes to ensure some equity in what people learn. While we all learn about careers through our everyday experiences, because we have different experiences, some people are more likely to learn about professional careers than others, while others are more likely to have the opportunity to try things out and experiment with different possibilities. Career education tries to build on these informal kinds of learning and fill some of the gaps that individuals face in their experience and learning. It aims to ensure that we all get the opportunity to think deeply, broadly and hopefully critically about the world and our place in it.

How we learn about careers

The question of how human beings learn about the world has been a source of wonder and enquiry for thousands of years. Some early learning theorists sought to reduce it to its most basic elements and isolate the inputs and outputs that made up the learning process. So, the psychologist Burrhus Frederic Skinner taught rats to press buttons by rewarding them with food pellets, concluding that learning was a behaviour that could be brought about by the application of an appropriate reward structure. His theory is often called *behaviourism*.

However, other learning theorists argued that learning is a more complex process. It is not just a process of learning behaviours by rote, we can also think about what is happening to us (*cognition*) and even think about how we learn and how we could learn better (*metacognition*). Still, others noted that we learn differently, and often more effectively, in groups and with other people and that different approaches to teaching can elicit different kinds of results. Differences between learners have also been discussed and how people are affected by things like their background, the learning environment and their motivation.

One of the most important general learning theories that is used a lot in career learning is Kolb's theory of experiential learning. Kolb argues that experience is central to the way in which we learn but makes the important distinction that learning does not just happen through experiences, it is also the way that we reflect on and learn from these experiences that matters. Kolb's model views learning as cyclical and based on four stages as set out in Figure 8.1.

The learning experience begins with someone having a *concrete experience* like visiting a business and hearing about what that organisation does. They then *reflect* on this experience and consider what they saw and heard. They then try and make some sense of it (*conceptualisation*) and consider what its wider applicability might be to their life or their understanding of the world (*abstraction*), finally they put their learning into practice in some way (*active experimentation*).

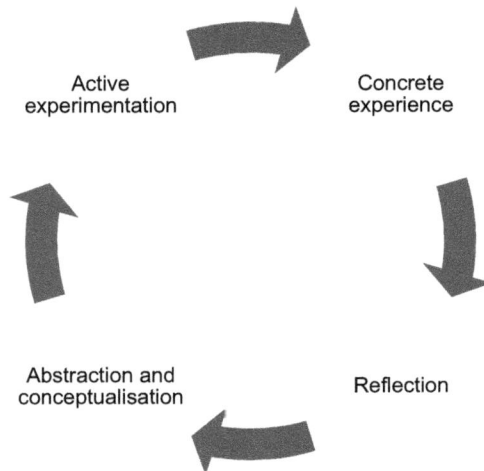

Figure 8.1. Kolb's experiential learning model

CASE STUDY

Petr decides to try working some temp shifts in different kinds of organisation to see whether he enjoys other kinds of work more than his normal role in a kitchen. The first temp job he gets is a day's labouring work for a construction firm. He spends the day basically carrying heavy tools around and trying to learn the names of all the different materials and equipment. At the end of the day he *reflects* on his *experience* and concludes that it was interesting and different. He thinks about all the different roles that he saw working on the site (electricians, brick layers and surveyors) and considers whether this sector offers more opportunities (*conceptualisation*) and thinks about whether he fits into it (*abstraction*). He isn't sure but resolves to continue his *experiment* and try a few more shifts within this sector. Petr recognises that he has learnt something about construction, but that he still has a lot more to learn. Maybe he should talk about it more with the careers adviser to help him to deepen his thinking about his experiences and what he should do about them.

These kinds of general learning theories have been very influential on career learning theories. A career learning theory is one which tries to focus on how people particularly learn about careers.

The American theorist John Krumboltz and the British theorist Bill Law (both of whom we have already met in Chapter 6) offer theories of career learning which have a lot of similarities. They both argue that we learn about careers from engaging in self-reflection and increasing our self-awareness, but also note that this must be balanced by engaging in the world. We can learn from reading information and participating in lessons, but career learning is often strongest when it is social and experiential. So, we learn a lot from talking to people about their careers, through watching others (*career models*) and through trying things out. As with other learning, it is also important to get feedback on our ideas, as we develop them, and on our capabilities. This kind of feedback often comes from careers educators, but it can also come from peers, employers and family. Indeed, Law highlights that our engagement with our immediate family and community is a powerful resource for career learning, suggesting that we are often particularly influenced by the people who are closest to us.

> ## 💡 Resources
>
> There are lots of good general texts on learning theory out there. An appealing starting point is Bob Bates' *Learning Theories Simplified*, which breaks lots of theories down to their basics and considers how these can be applied. If you want to look at Kolb in more detail, he set out his theory in a book called *Experiential Learning*.
>
> For career learning theories, have a look at Bill Law's article 'Community Interaction' and his chapter entitled 'A Career Learning Theory'. For Krumboltz have a look at the article that he and his colleagues wrote entitled 'A Social Learning Theory of Career Selection'.

Where career learning happens

As we've started to discuss career learning, we keep coming back to the idea that it is valuable to think about how we can purposefully intervene in an individual's career learning to help them learn faster, more deeply and more completely. In Chapter 5, we've already discussed the main contexts where career development work takes place. When we are thinking about career learning, it is useful to make distinctions between *formal, non-formal* or *informal* learning.

Formal learning takes place in organisations like schools, vocational educational institutions (including colleges and training providers) and universities. It is typically structured, written down, includes elements of compulsion and often leads towards some kind of qualification. Organisations that deliver formal learning often exist primarily to support people in learning, although they may have varying degrees of interest and engagement in career learning. The fact of being in a learning organisation, surrounded by education professionals, creates an important context for career learning. Perhaps because of this, learning organisations are the most common place where careers education is formally constituted and given time and resources.

It is worth noting that a wide variety of terminology is used to describe what are essentially careers learning programmes in all types of educational institutions. For example, the terminology of 'employability' is often used in higher education (with 'work-integrated learning' being another common term). In vocational contexts, this might be labelled as 'professional practice', while in special education, this might be described as 'life skills' or 'transition learning'. There are strengths and weaknesses to each of these terminologies, and some of them do not map exactly onto careers education, but it is important to be a bit flexible and to work to understand the institutional cultures, terminologies and expectations as you develop and deliver career education programmes in your work.

Non-formal learning takes place in a wide range of organisations including the kinds of learning organisations discussed above as well as voluntary and community groups, employers and trade unions and professional associations. Non-formal learning still aims to foster learning, but it is typically more loosely structured, more voluntaristic and is less likely to lead to a qualification. For example, young people may learn how to light fires, camp and use a map in the Scouts or Guides, but such activities are understood, managed and delivered very differently from how they would be at school. Similarly, a business may offer employees an opportunity to participate in a personal development programme or conference to help them develop their skills and aptitudes. Such non-formal learning often addresses career development, for example, by developing skills, confidence or networks, but is rarely labelled as a 'careers education programme'. This raises questions about how career development professionals relate to it.

Informal learning can take place anywhere, including on your own, in families and in any of the contexts that we have discussed already. It describes any opportunity that people have to learn about anything and therefore covers a huge range of human experience. Many people don't recognise that they are involved in informal learning as it is usually embedded into their wider experience. For example, a conversation with your aunt at a family party may involve you finding out about her profession, asking questions about how she got there, thinking about whether this is right for you and making a decision to follow up with her to access more help. In such a case a lot of career learning has taken place, but there is no teacher, nor student, nor whiteboard, homework or anything else that we normally associate with career education.

It is worth highlighting a couple of particularly important contexts for informal learning that career development professionals should think about. First, people do a lot of informal learning about their careers via films, TV, newspapers and increasingly social media. Helping people to think about what they have seen and sort out fact from fiction and fake from real news is a really important role that career development professionals can play. Second, the workplace itself, including when it is accessed through forms of work experience, is a very important site for career learning. We probably figure out most of what we know about careers once we are actually in the workplace, and so as a careers professional it can be useful to help people to think about this informal learning and reflect on what it really means.

As a career development professional, it is your job to encourage people to engage in career learning. This does not mean that you always have to be involved in developing and delivering formal career education programmes. Sometimes it is about recognising the learning that people are involved in and encouraging them to engage more deeply in it, perhaps by encouraging them to reflect on their experiences as part of a one-to-one guidance session (see Chapter 7).

💡 Resources

Martin Johnson and Dominika Majewska have a very useful paper called *Formal, Non-formal, and Informal Learning: What Are They, and How Can We Research Them?* which provides a lot of clarity about these different types of learning.

There are lots of books that discuss the delivery of career education in formal settings. Some of the more practical volumes focus on schools (Andrews and Hooley's *The Careers Leader Handbook*, Daubney's *Careers Education to Demystify Employability*, or Bernard's *The Ladder*); vocational education and lifelong learning (Gravells' *Delivering Employability Skills in the Lifelong Learning Sector*) and higher education (Fallows and Steven's *Integrating Key Skills in Higher Education*).

There is much more limited literature that looks at career learning in non-formal and informal settings. We're not aware of any really definitive accounts of these processes, but articles like Ali Abadi and colleagues' 'Informal Learning and Career Identity Formation', Monique Bernadette van Rijn and colleagues' 'Understanding Employees' Informal Workplace Learning' or Vela and colleagues' 'Improving Perceptions of STEM Careers through Informal Learning Environments' all explore these processes in interesting ways.

Career learning and career education

In the sections above, we have discussed career learning as a process that arguably covers all forms of career interventions: people learn through career counselling and coaching, through information, and through engaging in education programmes. In this next section, we turn to career education specifically. Here we understand career education as a structured intervention delivered to a group of individuals, with an educational purpose. It is distinct from other kinds of roles that you might hold as a career development professional, involving different skills and approaches than, for example, you might use in one-to-one work.

Pedagogy and how to design careers education

The idea of career education, regardless of what setting you might deliver it in, opens big questions about how and what you are going to teach. We are going to come to the nuts and bolts of teaching later in this chapter, but first we need to think about what teaching is and how it is best organised. In this chapter we refer to 'pedagogy' which basically means how we approach the method and practice of teaching.

Within the educational community there are lots of different ideas and approaches about teaching and how it is best organised. Sometimes these debates get simplified into 'are you focused on content (what to teach) or process (how you teach)', but there are many different ideas out there about what constitutes effective teaching and learning. If you thought that Chapter 6 on career theories was complicated, rest assured that there are a lot more people writing about educational theory and a lot more opinions. We aren't going to try and cover all of this in this chapter, but we are going to prompt you to think about your career pedagogy and argue that the way that you teach career education needs to be carefully thought through.

Your career education pedagogy is a description of the way in which you see career education happening. It describes your philosophy of how and why people learn and also sets out how you are going to go about translating this into practice. Complete the following reflection to help you to clarify your pedagogic position.

Reflection: Developing your pedagogic stance

Spend some time reflecting on the following four questions about your pedagogic stance. There are different schools of thought on what the 'right' answer is to each of these questions, but it is also important to think about yourself, your values and your context as you answer them.[1]

- *How do you see your professional role in the learning process?* Are you the learners' main source of knowledge, a guide on their learning journey or are you co-careering alongside the learners? How do you want the learners to see you?

- *What theory and evidence do you base your approach on?* How have you drawn on career theories and evidence of the kinds that are set out in Chapter 6? What other pedagogical theories and evidence have you engaged with? What does this tell you about how to approach careers education?

- *How do you see the student?* Do you want them to sit quietly and listen to what you say or spend most of their time talking and acting? How should they relate to you, for example, do you want them to call you by your first name, put their hand up before they speak or lead some of the learning activities? How do you want the students to interact with each other?

- *How will you make the most of your personality, strengths and capabilities?* Every teacher brings some unique qualities to their teaching. What is it that you bring that is uniquely you? How are you going to use this in careers education? What are you going to share and not share with the groups that you are teaching?

> ### 💡 Resources
>
> There are many resources that can help you to think about your pedagogic stance and how you want to approach careers education.
>
> A good place to start is with a general introduction to teaching and learning, such as Alex Moore's *Teaching and Learning*. This covers a lot of important basics as well as gives an overview of some of the main pedagogic theories.
>
> A more practical discussion of these issues can be found in Mike Sharples' *Practical Pedagogy*, which looks at a variety of pedagogically informed approaches and explores how they can be put into practice as part of learning and teaching.

Learning outcomes and objectives

Alongside developing your pedagogic stance, you are also going to need to decide what you are actually trying to educate people about. One of the most common tools that people use to do this is the development of a learning outcome or objective. This states what it is that you want to achieve from the career education and will usually include some kind of description of what the outcome for the learner will be.

Learning objectives can be articulated at a variety of levels. So, you could design learning outcomes for a year's worth of activities or for a 15-minute intervention. Some people believe that learning outcomes should be very specific and highly measurable, while others prefer the statement of looser goals which recognise that different learners are likely to get different things out of participating in learning and that sometimes some of the most interesting learning crops up unexpectedly.

Learning outcomes are an important aspect of integrating into any kind of curriculum as they communicate what the purpose of any educational activity is and create a common language between educators. This is particularly important if you are working in formal learning environments like schools or universities where courses have published and identified learning outcomes. In such cases, it is possible to look through these learning outcomes and identify where there may be possibilities for careers educators to support the achievement of these aims, as well as meeting our own career-related learning outcomes. Table 8.1, for example, sets out some of the learning outcomes from the GCSE in English language.[2] The second column gives some ideas about how career education activities could be linked to those learning outcomes, which we will return to later.

Table 8.1. Mapping GCSE English to careers

Learning outcome	Where career education could contribute
Identify and interpret explicit and implicit information and ideas. Select and synthesise evidence from different texts.	Show young people a range of labour market information and job descriptions. Encourage them to think about issues like bias and persuasive writing in these kinds of texts and use them to create a picture of a particular occupation or sector.
Communicate clearly, effectively and imaginatively, selecting and adapting tone, style and register for different forms, purposes and audiences. Organise information and ideas, using structural and grammatical features to support coherence and cohesion of texts.	Encourage students to write career-relevant communications in a range of forms, e.g., an email to a colleague, a letter to a client, a job application. Discuss the structure of these kinds of writings and emphasise and demonstrate the importance of spelling, punctuation and grammar to employers and in professional settings.
Demonstrate presentation skills in a formal setting.	Get students to develop and deliver a professional presentation, e.g. for use in a job interview or as part of a pitch to a client.
Listen and respond appropriately to spoken language, including questions and feedback to presentations.	Engage students in preparing for, participating in and receiving feedback on mock interview performances.

This process of careful mapping of learning outcomes and looking for opportunities to intervene is a very important skill for career development professionals who are looking to contribute to wider student experiences.

CASE STUDY

Shona has noticed that many of the people that she works with in one-to-one careers interviews have similar concerns. Lots of her clients are working in low-skilled jobs or jobs with limited prospects and are keen to explore the idea of moving sectors. So, she decides that she is going to put on a one-day 'boot camp' on the topic.

After some thinking about her pedagogic stance, she decides that this should be a very practical, discussion-based day in which all of the students are encouraged to share their experiences and aspirations. But she is also keen to make sure that they come away with some new knowledge about the labour market and some new career management skills.

Before she starts designing activities for the day, and long before she starts putting PowerPoint slides together, Shona sits down and thinks about what the high-level aims of the day are. By the end of the 'boot camp' she would like the participants to be able to

- reflect on their current employment situation and decide what they like and don't like about it;
- identify a range of alternative employment opportunities and gain insight into what each of these might offer;
- articulate transferable skills in writing (e.g. in a CV) and speech (e.g. during an interview)
- develop an action plan about how to move their career forwards.

She shows these outcomes to a couple of colleagues and clients, and everyone is enthusiastic about the idea. So, she resolves to develop a series of specific activities that will deliver these outcomes.

Setting learning outcomes is important because they help educators plan and design a session and evaluate the effectiveness of activities. When planning a session, it is useful to ask yourself how the learning outcomes will be met, and whether your activities could be better designed. At the end of a session, you might also collect feedback or other evidence from participants to check whether the outcomes have been achieved.

It is worth noting that you do not always have to generate learning outcomes from nothing. There has been a lot of work across many countries to develop frameworks for what are variously called 'career management skills', 'career competencies' or 'employability skills'. Where such frameworks exist, they will often provide some indications of how they can be translated into learning outcomes.

For example, in England, the Career Development Institute has developed the Career Development Framework, which argues that to be successful in your career, you need to be able to

- **Grow throughout life** by learning and reflecting on yourself, your background, and your strengths.
- **Explore the full range of possibilities** open to you, including learning about recruitment processes and the culture of different workplaces.
- **Manage your career actively**, making the most of opportunities and learning from setbacks.

- **Create opportunities** by being proactive and building positive relationships with others.
- **Balance life and work** by focusing on your well-being, other interests and your involvement with your family and community.
- **See the big picture** by paying attention to how the economy, politics and society connect with your own life and career.

These high-level career management skills are designed to serve as the foundation of career development programmes at all levels. The CDI has gone further by looking at how these might be implemented across a range of different contexts and then developing detailed learning outcomes for each of them. So, the CDI suggests that for the first area (grow throughout life) young people aged 11–14 should be

- aware of the sources of help and support available and responding positively to feedback;
- aware that learning, skills and qualifications are important for career;
- willing to challenge themselves and try new things;
- recording their achievements; and
- aware of their heritage, identity and values.

This means that in many cases you have a well-thought-out starting point that you can draw upon to use as a basis for your learning outcomes.

💡 Resources

You will find a range of resources out there to help you in writing and working with learning outcomes. Books like Simon Paul Atkinson's *Writing Good Learning Outcomes and Objectives* can be very helpful if this is a major part of your job.

In the careers field, people normally talk about career management skills (or career development skills or competencies) when they are thinking about the development of learning outcomes. There is lots of academic work looking at this, such as Ronald Sultana's 'Learning Career Management Skills in Europe' or Tristram Hooley and colleagues' article 'The "Blueprint" Framework for Career Management Skills'.

If you want to look at a practical example of a career management skills framework, then the CDI framework in England (https://www.thecdi.net/resources/cdi-framework) provides a well-worked example with detailed learning outcomes for different ages and stages. But, you should look in your country and sector to see what other frameworks exist that you can use.

Teaching tips and tools

It is worth looking at some of the practical approaches that are used in delivering careers education. Here are our top ten tips or tools that you will find useful in classroom settings.

1. **Write a lesson plan.** Never go to the classroom without a plan that connects to your learning outcomes. You should always plan what you are going to do and think about how it fits with the time available. It is important that learning activities run to time, so think about what content and activities you could cut if you aren't going fast enough and additional things that you could add if you burn through content too quickly.

2. **Co-teach.** You do not have to do everything alone. Especially when you are starting, it can be good to team teach with someone else, for example, a subject specialist or form tutor. Team teaching allows you to share the work and learn from each other but does require careful organisation.

3. **Learn people's names.** It is a lot easier to teach people if you can learn their names. If you are working with them for more than one session, this is essential. So, take the time at the start to learn as many names as possible. If you are delivering a one-off session, think about using name tags, or at least having access to a class register.

4. **Deal with behavioural issues.** A classroom, or other group learning environment, needs to have some rules to function effectively. You need to think about those rules before you start, for example, do you want people to put their hands up before they speak? Are people allowed to leave the room if they want to get a drink? How should people treat other people in the group and so on? Once you are clear on these rules, make them clear to the class at the beginning of the session and then call people out when they are not adhered to. This is a very equivalent process to the process of contracting that Chapter 7 described in relation to career counselling and coaching. This contract is the basis of all behaviour management as well as a wider statement of what you want to achieve as part of the intervention. If you are taking a lesson in a school, consider having a teacher present who can support with behaviour management if necessary.

5. **Vary your delivery approach.** Avoid just talking to people for hours and boring them with PowerPoint slides. Good teaching will usually include a mix of activities. These can include listening to lectures, reading, watching videos, individual reflection, group

work, experiential activities and hearing from other people, for example, employers.

6. **Design activities carefully.** Learning activities include a variety of different approaches; they can include games, simulations, discussions, debates, research tasks, projects and so on. The purpose of these activities is to get students to encounter new information and ideas, think about it, and work with it. It is not just to give people a break from listening to your presentation. So, activities need to be designed carefully, linked to the learning outcomes that you have identified and managed actively while they are running.

7. **Use the class as a resource.** You are not the only person in the room who has something valuable to say. Give students a chance to talk and a chance to interact with each other. Students can learn a lot both from hearing what other students know and from having the chance to express themselves.

8. **Use pyramiding.** Pyramiding is a technique to build students' knowledge and facilitate class discussions. To pyramid, you start by presenting students with some information. You then give them silent time to think about it on their own. They are then paired up with a partner to discuss and check understanding, and then put into groups (and usually given a new task which builds on the previous one). Finally, you can bring together the whole class into a discussion which everyone has had time to prepare for.

9. **Homework.** Depending on the situation, you may be able to set students homework or preparatory work for the next session. This can help to raise the level of knowledge and skill in the classroom and encourage students to take ideas out of the classroom into their lives. Homework can include things like students visiting organisations they are interested in, applying for jobs or courses or interviewing people working in the jobs that interest them.

10. **Review what worked.** After every lesson and at the end of every course, spend some time thinking about what worked (and what didn't). This should include reflecting on whether your learners met the learning outcomes, something we will discuss further in relation to assessment later in this chapter. You might also like to refer back to Chapter 2, where we discussed reflective practice, to help with your reflections. Remember, don't beat yourself up about the things that went wrong, but try and develop strategies to improve them. And really notice what went well and make sure that you remember to do it again.

💡 Resources

There are loads of practical sites and resources designed to help teachers. The first thing to do is check if your employer offers example lesson plans and/or if your colleagues have lesson plans that you can use or adapt.

Have a look at resources available through Google (https://edu.google.com /intl/ALL_uk/teaching-resources/), the BBC (https://www.bbc.co.uk/teach) and Oak National Academy (https://www.thenational.academy/#teachers) for general resources for teachers.

The BusinessBalls site (https://www.businessballs.com/) is also hugely useful for career and professional learning and has lots of simple explanations of learning theories and tools.

There are also a range of sites that offer resources specifically for careers education, such as Youth Employment UK (https://www.youthemployment .org.uk/teachers-resources/), The Careers & Enterprise Company (https:// resources.careersandenterprise.co.uk/explore/all-resources-all-one-place) or MyFuture (https://myfuture.edu.au/assist-others).

A good example of all of these issues being brought together in practice can be found in Gill Frigerio's and colleagues' *Re-designing Work-Related Learning*.

Careers and the wider curriculum

Once you get involved in careers education, you will hear the term 'curriculum' used a lot. In general, curriculum is used to mean two things. First, a programme of learning of the kind described in the last section. So, in a *careers curriculum,* you are likely to set out what you are doing and why, how it is going to be delivered, and what it will lead to. But, when you are working in a formal learning environment, you are also likely to discuss how careers can be integrated into the *wider curriculum*.

While career development is a strong motivator for participation in many learning programmes, students are rarely enrolled to study a careers education programme. Instead, they will be studying English literature, chemistry, electronics, plumbing, teaching or business and often a number of these subjects together. This subject will be where most of the learning organisation's resources go and where students spend most of their time. Each subject will have its own learning outcomes, programme of content and learning activities, and all of these elements will be drawn together and organised into a curriculum which may either be formally written down or implied.

Careers education within formal learning settings can relate to the mainstream curriculum in three main ways.

- **Curricular.** Delivered as part of the mainstream curriculum, embedded within subjects or afforded a formal curricular status as a subject in its own right.
- **Co-curricular.** Delivered alongside curriculum subjects in ways that reference and support them but are not fully embedded. So, for example, you may organise an employer talk by a chemical company and promote it to the Chemistry students.
- **Extra-curricular.** Organised outside of the mainstream curriculum, without any direct reference to it. For example, you may organise an opportunity for students to learn about recruitment processes without any reference to the subject that they are studying.

In our GCSE English example above, we have already looked at how learning outcomes offer you one way to engage with wider curricula by looking at what learning they hope to foster and then supporting them to achieve these learning outcomes in ways that use careers content. We have found that there are very few subjects or topics that a careers perspective cannot enrich.

However, intervening in the wider curriculum is about more than just seeing opportunities and developing career-relevant content. Inserting career learning into the curriculum is a complex process of negotiation and collaboration. You will need to convince your colleagues that career learning is important and that it can enrich their programme.

Collins and Barnes set out a series of factors that enable career education to be embedded into the curriculum.

- **Vision and leadership.** Embedding careers content into the curriculum works best if it is done in a purposeful way and guided by an overall vision for the learning organisation and the curriculum.
- **A well-designed curriculum.** Activities cannot just be dropped into the curriculum at random, the curriculum needs to be well organised with appropriate time allocated to careers content.
- **A strong focus on the learning process.** Approaches based on reflection, dialogue, practice and inquiry and supported by good quality learning resources have the most impact.
- **Professional staff.** Careers content needs to be delivered by people who understand it and value it, rather than just handing out materials to all teaching staff with no training. This means that as the careers specialist, you either have to be directly involved in the delivery of the content or support other teaching staff to deliver it.
- **Engagement of partners and career informants.** Careers education works best when it engages a wide range of stakeholders,

including parents, employers, other education providers and the curriculum in the delivery.

- **Progressive and regular.** Curriculum interventions cannot be a one-off, but instead have to provide ongoing learning opportunities which build on each other.

Finally, it is important to think about how career learning can be assessed. It is not common for students to sit a careers exam, but this doesn't mean that there is no assessment. Assessment can be used for a variety of purposes to strengthen learning. We can think about assessment in three different ways:

- **Assessment of learning.** Tests what has been learnt and is sometimes linked to the provision of a final grade.
- **Assessment for learning.** Uses assessment to provide feedback to learners, helping them to understand what they have learnt and where they need to focus their efforts going forwards.
- **Assessment as learning.** Drives learning through the assessment process. For example, it requires students to engage in research and discovery as part of their assessment.

When delivering careers education, it is worth thinking about how you use assessment in your practice. This does not always need to take the form of a final exam. In fact, teachers are assessing students all the time as part of teaching. Every time you ask a question, listen to what a student asks, set a classroom task or just watch the class interact, you are engaging in assessment. The setting of more formal assessments just extends this process and allows more precision about what is being assessed and how feedback is given.

CASE STUDY

Shona's one-day 'boot camp' for helping people to move sectors is going really well. One of the things that has been working well is that she has set participants a lot of practical exercises. She gets them to give short presentations, work in groups and revise their CVs. As they do this, she forms an increasingly clear picture of who is ready to start their transition to a new sector (assessment of learning). She is also able to identify who is struggling to understand the different tasks that she has set, and this helps her to direct more feedback, help and support to them (assessment for learning). Finally, she chooses to offer a final assessment for students, and because her assessment tasks are well chosen, the students actually use them to drive their learning. So, the CV writing assessment sees students checking information online, sharing information around the class and experimenting (assessment as learning).

At the end of the day Shona issues all students a certificate saying that they have attended the Sectors Transition Bootcamp. She reflects that while no one has received anything like a grade or a qualification, she has used a lot of assessment during the day.

Resources

Collins and Barnes' paper *Careers in the Curriculum* looks at the evidence behind how careers education can be delivered in schools.

There are plenty of texts that look at approaches to assessment with Ian Smith's *Assessment and Learning Pocketbook* being a practical introductory text.

Designing career programmes

As we covered at the beginning of this chapter, career learning can take place in a variety of ways, not just through career education delivered in classroom settings. As well as being involved in the development and delivery of workshops, lessons or other teaching activities, you will also want to think more widely about the ways that career learning takes place. One way to think about what you are doing is to put yourself in the role of a *learning designer*. As a designer, you do not have to deliver everything, but you might think strategically about the kinds and range of activities that your clients have access to and how they work together to provide opportunities for career learning. This is to think in terms perhaps of developing a 'career programme' where you think carefully about what you are trying to achieve and plan or map activities to allow you to deliver it.

In some cases, you might have a ready-made design to use. The Gatsby Benchmarks are a well-disseminated framework in both England and a range of other countries for delivering a career learning programme in schools, colleges and other educational settings.[3] They set out that a career learning programme should have eight main elements, which are as follows:

1. A stable careers programme;

2. Learning from career and labour market information;

3. Addressing the needs of each pupil;

4. Linking curriculum learning to careers;

5. Encounters with employers and employees;

6. Experiences of workplaces;

7. Encounters with further and higher education;

8. Personal guidance.

From a higher education perspective, the Advance HE *Framework for Embedding Employability in Higher Education*[4] serves a similar purpose and provides a basis for developing an institution-specific framework by articulating student attributes and competences to be developed, linking these to the educational practices of programme teams and creating links with overall strategic drivers.

If you have a framework like this in your context, it can be very useful as it sets out what you or others should do and often specifies things like when things should be done, in what order, and how frequently. Where individual career education sessions will be guided by learning outcomes, a career programme may also be guided by overall learning outcomes. Just as with individual career education sessions, it is important to reflect on the links between the programme learning outcomes and the delivery framework to ask whether the activities in your programme will lead to your students or clients achieving the learning outcomes that you want.

Reflection: Thinking through your learning design

What do our students need? It is important to start by thinking through what your students need. What issues are they facing? Do you have any feedback from last year? Can you talk to any of them?

What learning outcomes do you want to achieve? We have discussed learning outcomes above, and these should be at the heart of the design of your career education programme.

- *What activities will you offer to enable the achievement of these learning outcomes?* What combination of group-based activities, employer talks or visits, career coaching and other learning activities will support these outcomes?

- *How do you want to scaffold learning?* This is about thinking through the order of your activities. For example, people need to have an experience before they can reflect on it. Simple concepts might need to be covered before they can be broken down and discussed more critically.

- *What kind of assessment will you use?* How will you assess the learning that has taken place?

If, on the other hand, you do not have a framework to work with, you might want to reflect on whether you, your managers, and the stakeholders you work with might benefit from designing your own programme. Working through the following questions will help you to do this.

💡 Resources

There are a lot of books and resources that discuss how people learn and how you should respond to this as a teacher. Some of them use the language of 'learning design' or 'instructional design' to encourage you to think about the creation of a learning programme as a design problem. Books like Julie Dirksen's *Design for How People Learn* or Neelen and Kirshchner's *Evidence-Informed Learning Design* are good starting points.

For more specifically career development-focused approaches, you might want to look at Anthony Barnes and colleagues' book *An Introduction to Career Learning and Development 11–19* or its follow-up by Bassot, Barnes and Chant *A Practical Guide to Career Learning and Development: Innovation in Careers Education 11–19.*

🐿️ In a nutshell

This chapter has argued that

- career is fundamentally about learning (about ourselves and the world);

- there are a range of theories that help us to understand how career learning works;

- career education is a critical part of supporting people's career learning, which can take place in a range of contexts and through a range of different approaches;

- as a careers professional it is important to develop your pedagogic stance as you think about delivering careers education; and

- that we should use learning outcomes to guide the development and delivery of careers education programmes and our intervention into the wider curriculum.

Chapter 9
Using career information, resources and tools

Introduction

Career development, as we have explored in this book, is a process that is shaped by the education and working contexts around us. Understanding the kinds of opportunities that are available, the training and development routes in different professions, and the demands of different careers in relation to our own skills, capacities and interests are all key to making effective career decisions.

As a career development professional, then, alongside being able to use listening and coaching skills to facilitate career conversations with clients and deliver career learning, it is also important to be able to provide information about the world of work to clients or to help them source their own information. In this chapter, we explore the kinds of information and other resources or tools you might use, and how you might use these to support your work.

The kinds of tools and resources that are important

The tools and resources that are useful in your work can be grouped into three main categories.

- Career and labour market information
- Career assessments
- Other tools such as activities or exercises

We will explore each of these areas in this chapter.

Career and labour market information
In your training, you will almost certainly come across the phrase 'labour market information' or the acronym LMI as something that is important for careers professionals (we have already discussed this in Chapter 4 and

returned to it in several of the other chapters). You might also come across the terms 'career information' or 'career and labour market information' (CLMI). All of these terms relate to information about the world of work that might be useful for clients in making career decisions. The exact terms differ slightly in meaning:

- **Labour market information** is a phrase that is often used by policymakers and is often understood as relating primarily to statistical information (sometimes called 'quantitative data') about the labour market. It might include things like whether an industry is growing or shrinking, what proportion of people in an industry are women or men, what proportion are approaching retirement and so on. It can be used to predict levels of demand in a profession in the future. Sometimes the term 'labour market intelligence' is also used, and this typically means labour market information that has been interpreted by a career development professional or via a dedicated career development resource to make it more useful to individuals in their career decision-making.

- **Career and labour market information** and **career information** are terms that are a little broader. These terms are more likely to include information about education and training routes, the kinds of skills or other qualities that are valuable in a profession and so on. Career information might also include insights about professions or industries shared through case studies, videos or employer talks and so on. These kinds of personal insights are sometimes called 'qualitative data'.

When policymakers are thinking about career services, they are often concerned with funding services that are going to support the economy and are therefore more likely to think in relatively restricted terms of 'labour market information'. However, for clients, statistical information about the labour market can be difficult to make sense of. Instead, clients often require help with interpreting statistical data in ways that are meaningful to them. They may also prefer qualitative data, case studies and stories, and 'insights' rather than information in helping them to imagine their future careers.[1] Being able to help identify the kinds of information that a client might need and helping them to access and interpret this information is a key part of being a professional career development professional.

Career assessments

Alongside information resources, other tools that you might use in your work are career assessments, which are tools that help to assess a client's suitability for different kinds of career pathways.

One form of assessment is a psychometric assessment of an individual's personality. In Chapter 6 we discussed 'matching' theories that focus on how an individual's personal traits match the requirements of different jobs. One of the most well-known matching theories is Holland's theory of vocational personalities and work environments, which categorises people and jobs across six dimensions: realistic, investigative, artistic, social, enterprising and conventional (RIASEC). Following this theory, it is possible for individuals to undertake a test to determine their RIASEC code and then explore the careers that match this code. Following on from Holland's work and the early matching theories, several other kinds of matching tests have been developed.

Another popular resource, which we also discussed in Chapter 6, is the Myers-Briggs Type Indicator (MBTI). This assesses people's personalities and preferences across four dimensions: extraversion versus introversion, sensing versus intuition, thinking versus feeling, and judging versus perceiving. As an outcome of the assessment, people are given a four-letter code to represent their personality type across these dimensions such as INFJ, ESTP and so on. To undertake the full assessment requires input from a trained professional and is often costly; however, the MBTI has also been the basis for the development of several other shorter tests that people can undertake free of charge. The MBTI is something that might be used to help make career decisions but is also often used by employers to facilitate employee development and understanding of teams. A further recent development is *strengths-based assessments*, which aim to identify your inbuilt strengths rather than your learned skills and so provide another perspective for people exploring what might suit them. There has been a trend towards 'strengths-based recruitment' in some sectors, particularly in graduate recruitment, with employers seeking the strengths that successful employees demonstrate and looking for those in new hires.

Alongside psychometric tests, you may also use skills assessments or interest inventories. These are typically computer-based tests where an individual indicates the kinds of work or activities that interests them and/or the skills that they have and like to use. As a result of answering these questions, the computer programme then recommends several career options that may be suitable.

The assessments we have discussed so far typically involve individuals answering a series of questions and being given a score or result at the end. They can be thought of as *quantitative* assessments based on analysing people against predetermined sets of criteria. However, personality, skills and interests can also be assessed through *qualitative* means. Qualitative assessments typically involve systematically discussing interests or vocational personalities with a client, through which the client and career development professional can come to an assessment of where they might fit in the workplace. An interest in qualitative career assessments is associated with constructivist and narrative career theories (see Chapter 6). These theories propose that rather than it being possible to objectively assess vocational personality, interests or skills, the stories that people tell about themselves and their subjective interpretations of who they are, are more important.

Savickas' career construction interview is a good example of a qualitative career assessment. Using this interview means asking a series of six questions that focus on a person's interests, goals and story, including

1. How can I be useful to you as you construct your career?

2. Whom did you admire when you were growing up? Tell me about them.

3. What are your favourite magazines, TV shows or websites? What do you like about them?

4. What is your current favourite book or movie? Tell me the story.

5. Tell me your favourite saying or motto.

6. What are your earliest recollections? I am interested in hearing three stories about things you recall happening to you when you were three to six years old or as early as you can remember.

Savickas then provides guidance for how career development professionals should interpret and respond to the kinds of answers that people give to these questions, to help them to develop their story and their career.

Other kinds of assessments or mapping exercises might also be used to identify client skills, interests or priorities and sometimes your employer will have tools or activities that they recommend or endorse. This might include things like:

- **Career management skills assessments:** mapping or assessing people against a list of career management skills to identify their needs or priorities.

- **Life mapping exercises:** which might include mapping client needs against a list of predetermined kinds of life priorities.

- **Timeline exercises:** where you ask people to draw or describe their career timeline to understand more about their skills, interests and histories.

- **Card sorts:** providing people with a series of cards with skills, interests, images or other content on them, and asking them to prioritise these according to their interests or needs.

- **Visualisation or visual exercises:** where you ask people to visualise their futures and use these to identify goals or priorities.

💡 Resources

Many careers websites offer some form of career assessment tool. You might like to look at the following:

- If you are in England, the skills and assessment tools offered by the National Careers Service: https://nationalcareers.service.gov.uk/skills-assessment
- If you are in Scotland, the *Tools and Quizzes* page on MyWorldofWork: https://www.myworldofwork.co.uk/tools-and-quizzes/
- If you are in Wales, the career match quiz from Careers Wales: https://careerswales.gov.wales/career-match-quiz
- And in Northern Ireland, the career matching tool: https://www.nidirect.gov.uk/articles/careers-online-support

You may also find it useful to look at other tools, such as the Career Planner or job match assessment on the 'Prospects' website, which is run by the UK higher education sector with support from the Association of Graduate Careers Advisory Services (AGCAS) and designed specifically for university graduates: https://www.prospects.ac.uk/planner

Peter McIlveen and colleagues offer an overview of the use of assessment tools in their chapter 'Career Assessment'. For an overview of qualitative career assessments, Susan Whiston and Daryn Rahardja's article on 'Qualitative Career Assessment: An Overview and Analysis' is a good place to start. You can find out more about the Career Construction Interview in Mark Savickas' work, including his chapter 'Career Construction Theory and Practice' and in Hartung's chapter on 'The Career Construction Interview'.

Other tools

Alongside information and career assessments, other kinds of tools might be useful for helping individuals overcome barriers or blocks that are preventing them from moving forwards with their careers. A good example of this is that even when a person has all the information they need and knows where they want to get to with their career, they might still struggle to actually make changes in their lives. Sometimes this is about a lack of confidence or motivation, or it could be due to do with other kinds of blocks or barriers. Another example is a client who might know that they need to speak to an employer about the possibility of changing their work but does not know how to do this. If you identify that a client has particular barriers or blocks, you might use different kinds of tools to help them address these. These might include

- **Visualisation exercises.** Visualising where a client wants to get to can help build motivation. Visualising experiencing and overcoming barriers can also help a client build resources for overcoming their challenges.

- **Role play.** Role-playing a scenario can help a client to prepare for it and develop the skills and confidence they need.
- **Planning tools.** Helping individuals understand how to set and achieve goals can be helpful. This might involve helping them clarify and specify clear goals perhaps using 'SMART' targets.

There are many different kinds of activities you might use depending on the needs of the client.

💡 Resources

For an overview of different kinds of techniques that can be used with clients facing different kinds of barriers or blocks, Julia Yates' *The Career Coaching Toolkit* is a good place to start.

Accessing information and resources

Although information and tools can be helpful in careers practice, you might find yourself confronted with a bewildering array of options. In particular, the development of the internet has led to significant growth in the quantity and range of career information tools and resources that are available. However, with the internet also comes significant challenges – how can you or your clients understand which sources of information to trust? How can you prevent risks of accessing misinformation? And with tools and resources, how do you know that the assessments or other tools you are accessing are reliable, valid and ethical to use? In this section of the chapter, we explore how you can identify sources and resources.

National websites

One important source of information, and often of tools and resources, is national career websites or occupational databases. These websites typically offer a searchable database of different occupationas and then provide information about these in terms of the nature of the work, entry requirements, training routes and so on. Sometimes these websites combine statistical information with written or video case studies. Websites will also sometimes include general information about things like job searching, writing CVs and applications, career management skills (CMS) and so on. They also sometimes include interactive tools or resources that individuals can engage with, and the ability for individual users to develop a profile or store resources that interest them.

The advantage of national careers websites is that if they are supported by a government agency or professional body, they are normally reliable sources of information. In some countries, there might be multiple websites for different kinds of clients. For example, in the UK there are national careers websites in Scotland, England, Wales and Northern Ireland, as well as a website for university students supported by the Association of Graduate Careers Advisory Services (AGCAS).

Although national websites are a good place to start, they will not always be able to offer all the information you need. Typically, you will find that these national websites offer links to further sources of information. This might include links to industry bodies or professional organisations some of which provide additional information and resources relevant to people in, or seeking to enter, certain professions. This includes organisations like the NHS, for example.

Finding other resources

In your training, you will be introduced to different kinds of resources. Continuous Professional Development (CPD) is also an important way to find out about and stay up to date with new tools and resources.

Asking colleagues for ideas about the resources they use when working with clients with particular needs or barriers, or when preparing certain kinds of learning activities, is also a useful thing to do. There are a lot of communities of practice active through various kinds of social media such as LinkedIn and Facebook. It is worth spending some time to find an active community of careers professionals doing a similar job to you. Once you have found this kind of online community, you will see a lot of ideas and resources being exchanged (as well as gossip and the occasional heated debate).

When you have identified a useful resource, storing it for future reference is important. You might do this through using bookmarks for internet resources, and digital or paper-based filing systems for tools or resources you find offline.

Using generative AI

Recently, a range of new resources have been developed which are usually described as 'generative artificial intelligence (AI)'. These resources claim to be able to synthesise existing information to produce new resources, often in a very short time. For example, you may see a client who is interested in working as a goat herder or some other very niche occupation. You are unable to find any resources, so you visit a site like Chat GPT and ask it to generate a careers fact sheet for aspiring goat herders. This quickly produces a resource which you can provide the client with, and everyone goes away happy.

This kind of opportunity probably sounds too good to be true, especially given that a range of generative AI services are available for free. While generative AI is an amazing resource and definitely something to watch, there are a range of reasons to be somewhat sceptical. We'd encourage you to at least think about the following issues.

- **Be careful what you ask.** Generative AI tools will respond precisely to what you ask them to do. So, spend time crafting your prompt. Specifying which country you want information from, setting thresholds of quality and stipulating the time period that you are interested in will all improve what you get out. 'Can you draft a careers factsheet on careers in goat herding and other agricultural animal care careers in the UK over the last ten years?' will get you a much better outcome than 'Tell me about goat herding'.

- **Ask follow-up questions.** You can refine the outputs that you get from generative AI by asking more questions. These can be specific questions like 'Can you tell me more about this career in Wales?' or evaluative questions to help you to make a judgement about whether to trust the information, for example 'Can you tell me where this information came from?'

- **Treat this information as sceptically as you would any other information.** The next section focuses on assessing the quality of resources. Everything in generative AI tools has come from somewhere. Until you know where, or can corroborate it from another source, it can be difficult to be clear on how to value the information.

- **Pay attention to the purpose of the tool and developments in generative AI.** It is important to understand the context of the tool that you are using. Who developed it, how does it work and why are they giving it to you for free? How does it fit into the overall landscape of generative AI? The more you know the answers to these questions, the better you will be able to make appropriate decisions about their use.

💡 Resources

There are lots of useful resources available out there on making the most of this new technology which we would advise you to look at. These are changing all the time, so it is worth doing some searching (and even asking generative AI to make some suggestions). However, some useful starting points might be:

Harvard's Mignone Centre for Career Success offers an excellent primer on using AI for careers at https://careerservices.fas.harvard.edu/channels/ai-for-professional-development-and-exploration/

Newcastle University's resource on Using AI for your Career https://www.ncl.ac.uk/careers/support-and-resources/using-ai/

More advanced thinking on this can be found in Graham Atwell's blog about AI and career counselling https://aipioneers.org/ai-and-career-counseling-advice-and-guidance/

Assessing the quality of resources

Whenever you find an information resource or a tool, it is important to be able to assess it in terms of its quality. Recommendations from other professionals are a good way to start finding tools and resources. However, even if a resource is recommended to you, it is sensible to do your own quality check of the resource to make sure it is suitable and appropriate for use.

Quality means thinking about how reliable or valid the information is, and how useful it is for clients. In some countries, there are quality awards for career resources (in the UK, for example, the Career Assured Award is available from the Career Development Institute), and where a resource is branded with this award, it is a useful signal that the resource has met an external quality standard. However, in other cases, you will need to be able to assess the value of the resources you find yourself.

Assessing careers and labour market information

Beyond national careers websites, there are a huge number of different sources of information about careers available. You will find national statistical datasets, information on professional or company websites, YouTube videos and TED talks, personal blogs and vlogs, social media content and reviews of companies (on platforms like Glassdoor). When assessing the quality and value of information, you might find it useful to ask yourself the following questions:

1. **Who has produced the information?** When looking at a website, for example, check who has written the website. If it is an organisation's website, check what the organisation does. This will help you to determine whether the information is likely to be reliable and impartial, or if it might be biased: being presented in a certain way to meet the purposes of an organisation.

2. **What does the information relate to?** When identifying information, make sure you know which geographical territory it relates to. Information about career progression and the labour market that is produced by American websites, for example, is unlikely to be useful in a British context. In the UK, training routes are different in some professions between England and Scotland, and so it is important to be very careful using English sources in Scotland and vice versa.

3. **How has the information been sourced?** When it comes to statistical information, try to make sure you understand how the information has been collected. Was it a survey of ten people working in one organisation, or a survey of 30,000 people across an industry? Understanding this will help you work out how generalisable the information is, and whether or not it is likely to be

valid. If 60% of 10 people have reported something, it is likely to be less reliable than if 60% of 100,000 people have said something. Bear in mind that how a survey collects data (what exact questions are asked, to whom and by whom) can impact the results.

4. **How current is the information?** You should check when the information was gathered: for statistical information, this would include when a survey was conducted; for written information and video case studies, it would be the date of collection.

When you are working with information resources with clients, it is also valuable to help your clients understand some of these issues of quality. Quite often, people have heard about different career pathways from friends or family, or they have watched TV programmes about certain professions. Such sources can provide useful information, but it is important to consider it alongside other sources. Helping clients to explore different sources can be helpful in correcting misinformation that they may have accessed and show them how to find reliable information. When working with clients, it can be helpful to highlight the sources of information and navigate resources together: 'this is the national careers website', or 'this is the NHS careers website'. You might indicate or refer to personal stories and insights from employers or employees working in certain industries, especially as quite often clients find this kind of information very helpful indeed, but it can be useful to point out that these are subjective perspectives that represent one person's specific experiences.

Reflection

You are working with a young woman who is interested in careers in construction. What might be the advantages and disadvantages of the following sources of information:

- A career overview on a national careers website of pathways into construction.
- Statistical data are provided by a national organisation on the gender balance in the construction industry.
- Information from a sector-specific organisation (in this case, the Construction Industry Training Board) about routes in construction.
- A video case study of a young woman in construction from the construction industry website.
- The website of a local construction firm, advertising for employees.
- A blog from a young woman exposing her experiences of working in construction and issues of gender discrimination in the workplace.

Assessing assessments and other tools

When accessing assessments or other tools, you will also want to understand something about the quality of these tools. An important term that you will come across is whether tools are 'evidence-based' – that is, whether there is evidence to support their validity and their utility.

In the case of personality tests, some of these have been developed by psychologists and scientifically tested and validated. In contrast, other tests might have no scientific basis at all and may be no better than the kinds of quizzes you might find in a magazine or on social media. To understand how valid a measure or a test is, it is useful to check who has developed it and how. It is also important to recognise that even the most quantitative test is still underpinned by a range of assumptions and biases. Tests are linked to career theories, and it is important to reflect on how you feel about what the test is trying to do and whether that is something that fits with your approach. For example, instruments like MBTI and RIASEC have a lot of research evidence to support them, but there are also a lot of well-researched scientific articles that challenge them and question their value as both summaries of personalities and tools to use in careers practice. Becoming familiar with these discussions and debates is useful and can help you to use career assessments in a reflective way.

In the case of activities or other tools you might use with clients, it is useful to consider what the evidence is for their impact or value – is there evidence that they have been useful with other clients, for example? Some exercises might have been tested and supported through research evidence, but other exercises or tools might have less evidence supporting them. One way of understanding the potential value of different exercises is to collect your own evidence through your practice. By asking clients how useful they have found an activity, or through your own self-reflection, you might identify which kinds of exercises are particularly useful in your practice, and for what kinds of situations. Your colleagues may also offer insights into the kinds of activities, lesson plans or resources that, in their experience, have been useful for different kinds of clients or circumstances. When thinking about the use of different exercises, it is also important to consider the ethics of using different kinds of tools and how you might use them, something we turn to in the next section.

Integrating tools into practice

In this last section of the chapter, we explore how to integrate information and resources into your practice as a career development professional.

Understanding a client's needs

The most important point is that the use of tools and information should be guided by your client's needs and should be used purposefully to support the objectives of a session or intervention, rather than being the primary focus of a session themselves. Undertaking a personality assessment, for example, might be interesting but is likely to be more useful for someone reflecting on which career might suit them, than for a client looking for help with making a job application. Similarly, statistical information about pay gaps and potential growth areas of industries might be interesting but may not be particularly useful unless it is relevant to a client, and they can understand what the information means for their decisions. It is the job of a career professional to make decisions about what kinds of tools or information might be useful to a client, and when and how to use this in the most meaningful ways.

Before you introduce information or a tool or exercise, then, it is important to spend enough time in understanding a client's situation, why they are accessing career services, and come to some conclusions about what a client needs. In many cases, you will find that a client comes to a career development session with a 'presenting problem'. This is the initial need that they present with, such as 'I came because I just don't know what I'm doing with my career' or 'I need to get a CV'. Often there is a temptation to answer the presenting problem directly, so in the examples above, we might suggest someone does a career assessment to identify a suitable career path or suggest accessing CV resources. But a better first step is often to explore what is behind this problem – asking someone what they have already done to explore their options, or what they already know about CVs, for example, before suggesting specific tools or resources, or offering information. Finding out what a client already knows, or what they feel they need is important to avoid providing duplicated information or information that is not particularly useful. It is also a good way of assessing a client's understanding of the world of work and identifying any misunderstandings they have or misinformation that they may have accessed.

Supporting client ownership and autonomy

We talked about the aspiration for careers work to be 'client-centred' in Chapter 7. Given this, it is important to understand that suggesting an activity or an exercise, or providing information can feel challenging to a client. Not every client is comfortable drawing, visualising or role-playing. And providing information can be challenging if it contradicts what a client thinks they already know or have already been told, or if it suggests that a certain career route is going to be difficult for a client to follow. Providing information or suggesting use of a tool or resource, therefore, needs to be done with care.

When providing information or using a resource or activity, it is good practice to ask a client whether they would like to try an exercise, or if they would mind you sharing some information with them before you do it. This gives a client a chance to have some autonomy and say-so in the process.

When offering information, it is also good practice to present information tentatively and carefully, and it is often advisable to explore information resources together with a client, so that the client can access and process the information with you. When suggesting an exercise, it can be useful to explain what the exercise involves, how long it might take, and the purpose of the exercise before asking a client if they wish to proceed. Once you have provided information (or explored information together) and once you have undertaken an exercise, it is also good practice to ask a client about their thoughts or experience of the exercise or resources. This can help you to check what impact the information or exercise has had and to intervene or correct any misunderstandings.

An alternative to undertaking an exercise in a session or accessing information and resources is to encourage a client to engage in these activities outside of a session. However, it is useful to reflect on the fact that sometimes clients will not do these activities, and sometimes they need support to make sense of the activities or information they engage in. Therefore, if you suggest activities to be completed outside of a session, it is often useful to arrange to follow up with the client, either through a subsequent appointment or a telephone call, to find out how they have progressed.

Ethical practice

Ensuring a client has a sense of autonomy or control in how information or resources are used in careers practice is part of ethical practice. There are also further ethical considerations when using information and resources, some of which are:

- **The limits of your own knowledge:** it is important to ensure that you are giving accurate information. If you do not know for certain that the information you are providing is correct, you should not provide it. It is better to acknowledge that you are unsure, and then look up information together with a client in a session or offer to do some research for a client and arrange a follow-up meeting than to provide incorrect information.

- **The limits of your experience or competence:** it is important not to undertake an exercise or activity that falls outside of your competence. For some psychometric tests, you need to have a particular qualification to be able to conduct them. More simply, it is wise to only undertake activities that you feel confident with. Before trying an exercise for the first time, it is valuable to ensure that you have read about it, run through it in your own mind, and maybe tried it out in a professional development session or watched it being done through shadowing another professional.

- **The appropriateness of information or an activity:** always consider what is appropriate for your client group and the potential impacts of activities. If you are working with adults approaching retirement, facing redundancy or young people leaving school, different forms of activity or information are likely to be useful. Ensuring that information is accessible and understandable according to the age and educational level of a client is also important.

Developing your own model of practice

A final point when it comes to integrating tools into practice is that how you do this will vary according to your own developing professional model of practice and the contexts in which you work. As you develop as a career development professional, reflecting on the best ways to use information and resources that suit you, your professional identity and your professional context will be valuable.

To demonstrate the ways that you might use information and resources differently according to your model of professional practice, you might want to reflect on Chapter 6 where we explored different theoretical understandings of career development. For example, if a career development professional is influenced by the 'matching' theories, then they might think about their purpose as a professional primarily in terms of diagnosing client personalities and matching them to a career role. From this perspective, career assessments might be viewed as diagnostic tools. However, if we consider the constructivist theories, which propose that career identities are more fluid and influenced by the ways that we think and speak about ourselves, then career assessments are also likely to be understood as relatively fluid or flexible. And if we think about career development in terms of the learning theories, then undertaking a career assessment might be understood as a tool for reflection and learning.

It is also useful to consider the models of one-to-one practice we explored in Chapter 7. As different practitioners follow slightly different models of practice, this might then impact how tools or resources are used. So, for example, a professional utilising a highly non-directive approach might focus on facilitating individuals to access information and resources themselves, with multiple follow-up sessions to explore with clients the information they have found. Other practitioners may follow a more directive model or be in settings where multiple sessions are not possible, and this might mean they have more of a focus on directly providing information.

Similarly, it can be useful to think about how you might incorporate information, assessments and resources into career education approaches (see Chapter 8). Career education can offer opportunities to encourage students to explore information in groups and to do so critically, perhaps by exploring or preparing different kinds of information that address the same career. Career education activities also benefit from creative resources that allow students to work together and explore a particular topic.

In recent times a growing movement around career guidance for social justice has also started to think critically about the ways that information is used in career development practice. Scholarship in this area has raised the fact that a lot of labour market information and other resources are produced by governments, private companies and other organisations with a clear stake in the career decision-making of individuals. This raises an important question about whose interests such tools are working in and how we address this in career development practice. An interest in social justice, then, might influence how practitioners approach and utilise resources. In terms of information, for example, providing information might be a way of raising awareness about issues of inequality and social injustice in the world of work.

Throughout this book, we have discussed the value of reflective practice in developing your own professional skills and identity (see especially Chapter 2). Continuing to reflect on how you provide information and the kinds of activities and tools you use is an important part of this.

Resources

A good starting point for an understanding of careers and labour market information and how it can be used by careers professionals is the report by Alexander, McCabe and De Backer (2022) *Careers and Labour Market Information*. Jenny Bimrose's chapter 'Labour Market Information for Career Development Practice' is also a useful summary of the evidence on the use of LMI.

More critical takes on the role of LMI can be found in Rosie Alexander's article 'Why LMI?' and Staunton and Rogosic's article 'Labour Market Information and Social Justice'.

CASE STUDY

Stuart works in a university career service. Joanna has booked an appointment with him for 'help with a CV'. When she arrives, Stuart asks what she wants to get out of the appointment, and Joanna says she just wants to know how to write her CV. Rather than straight away giving information about how to write a CV, Stuart explains that he can certainly help with that, but that first it would be useful to understand a little bit more about her and what she needs her CV for. By exploring the background to her question, Stuart aims to understand what Joanna already knows and what she would find useful.

Joanna explains that she is graduating in two months and wants a CV to apply for graduate jobs. Stuart asks what kinds of jobs Joanna will be looking for, and she says she is unsure; she just wants a 'graduate job'. With some additional discussion, Joanna volunteers that she actually feels really overwhelmed by the need to get a job and she just doesn't know where to start. Stuart provides a bit of information, explaining that although some jobs will require a CV, others will not. Stuart also explains how there are lots of different kinds of 'graduate job'. He suggests that it might be best to identify what kinds of jobs would suit her first and where to look for them. Joanna agrees that this would be helpful.

Stuart asks Joanna if she has used any careers websites before, and Joanna says she has briefly looked at something but 'didn't find it helpful'. Stuart asks if it would be useful to look at some resources together, and Joanna agrees. He shows her the national graduate website and how to navigate it to find information about different careers and to search for jobs. He shows her some online tools and where to find general information about graduate career options. He asks her what she thinks of the website and what she thinks would be useful to do next. Joanna says she thinks the website will be a really good start; she says she would like to do the online career test that it offers and see what it suggests. She also wants to look at some of the job adverts on the site in more detail. Stuart agrees that this sounds like a good plan and asks her if she would like to come back for a follow-up appointment to discuss how she gets on. Joanna thinks this is a great idea.

The following week, Joanna returns and discusses her research with Stuart. Working together over the next couple of weeks, Joanna gradually refines her interests and ideas and builds confidence in being able to use the website to find the information she needs. She applies for a number of different jobs, none of which require a CV.

In a nutshell

This chapter has explored the kinds of information, resources or tools that are important in the delivery of career development services. It has argued that:

- being able to use career and labour market information, along with a range of assessments and other tools, is a key part of career development practice. How these are used will vary according to context and professional identity;

- in order to effectively use information tools and resources, career development professionals need to be able to identify appropriate sources and to make judgements about their quality. National career websites are often a good starting point, but they are not the only source of information and are unlikely to be sufficient to cover the range of client needs and enquiries a career development professional handles;

- using information and resources in practice should be done with care, and in an ethical manner. This includes spending sufficient time understanding client needs before providing any form of intervention and engaging a client in decisions about when and how to access information and resources; and

- utilising tools and information effectively requires staying up to date with existing resources, effectively engaging with professional communities and CPD, and should be informed by ongoing critical and reflective practice.

Chapter 10
Working with organisations and systems to support career development

Introduction

Most career development professionals work within organisations and these organisations shape what they do and how they do it. Yet, most of what we have discussed so far in this book has focused on the *micro* level: the relationship between you and your clients. We have occasionally moved up to the *macro* level and talked about the big contexts that shape this work in terms of things like politics, the economy, the labour market and the organisation of the profession. But there is another important level to consider which lies in between these two levels. This is sometimes called the *meso* level and generally concerns how we work within organisations and other local systems.

The organisational level is important because it is where our work is framed, managed and directed. It is also where we interact with many other key stakeholders to support people's careers. Perhaps most importantly organisations provide a critical context for individuals to develop their careers. So, for young people, career is not something that they are going to start after they leave school, but rather something that they are already embedded in while studying *in school*. For employed adults, this is even more true, with their employers typically framing their career and providing them with barriers and opportunities for a range of different career pathways.

Thinking about the organisational level is important because it helps us to understand the circumstances within which our clients are operating and provides context for our own work and access to resources to help our clients and ourselves achieve our aims. It also provides a new type of practice that we can undertake (organisational and systems work), which is distinct from counselling and coaching (Chapter 7), education (Chapter 8) and the provision of information, assessments and resources (Chapter 9). Organisational and systems work involves working with others to seek to influence organisational structures, such as the design of the curriculum, the structures used for promotions, the access people have to personal development and training and the extent to which career development features as part of the organisational objectives.

Delivering career development in different kinds of organisations

Careers professionals can be found in a myriad of different contexts. These include schools, special schools, universities, vocational colleges, community centres, public employment services, the armed forces, employers, prisons and a whole host of other settings. In some cases, professionals are employed directly by these organisations, and in other cases, a professional might work for a standalone career service, or on a self-employed basis, and then be contracted by these organisations to deliver a service. Whether you are employed directly by an organisation or contracted in will change the nature of your relationship with these organisations considerably. But it remains the case that you should be aware of both of your own direct employment context and the organisational contexts that you work in, in order to decide how to work most effectively.

For the purpose of this chapter, we are going to discuss five main contexts for career guidance provision: education and training providers; employment services; career development services; employers and other settings. We recognise that within each category there are important differences (including size and complexity) between organisations, such as between a school and a university, but would argue that the function of an organisation is key to thinking about how we can work with it as career development professionals.

Education and training providers

As we have already discussed in Chapters 3, 5 and 8, a lot of careers work takes place within education and training providers such as schools, vocational colleges and universities. What unites all these organisations is that their primary purpose is to develop students' capacity to learn and to imbue them with new skills and knowledge. In theory this should be a good fit with careers work, as career development can be thought of in many ways as primarily a process of learning and development. However, there are some important tensions between the aims of education and training providers and those of the career development professionals who work within them.

Education and training providers typically focus on defined bodies of knowledge and skills (e.g. academic or technical subjects described through a curriculum) and on the assessment of these skills and knowledge through examinations. Organisations are also typically interested in (and often have targets relating to) the destinations of their students, meaning their education or employment outcome immediately after completion of a course. Although career development professionals can support students with their immediate steps after leaving an educational institution, their focus is often on the longer-term career pathways of students. They are also focused not just on whether a young person who leaves education is employed or continuing to study, but whether this job or course is suitable and rewarding for the young person in question. Similarly, although education institutions might want to ensure that students remain enrolled and turn up for classes, careers professionals are focused on their clients, supporting them to achieve the best outcomes for themselves, and sometimes these objectives can be in tension. For example, a career development professional might help students to reflect on their 'fit' to their courses, which in some cases may involve supporting a student to change course or provider or to follow a different pathway.

Within education and training organisations there are a wide range of different groups that you might interact with as a career development professional. These include teaching or lecturing staff, people in leadership roles (e.g. head teachers, governors or trustees, principals or deans) as well as other staff like librarians, administrators, psychologists and counsellors and a host of other roles. The complexity of these kinds of organisations requires careers professionals to make a series of judgements about who they should be working with, how they should be working with them and what proportion of their effort and time should be put into building these kinds of relationships.

Employment services

The second main organisational context within which careers professionals might work can be described as 'employment services'. This describes public employment services (such as the UK's Jobcentre Plus) and a host of other standalone organisations which are principally concerned with supporting people to engage with employment systems and, to a lesser extent, with the fields of education and training. This might include youth employment or employability services and a range of other variations. Some of these might be independent organisations, some part of government departments or local government structures, but still have a degree of autonomy, and some might be charities or private companies which seek funding for this kind of activity.

Career development professionals who work within an employment service will hopefully find that the organisation's objectives are closely aligned with their core professional purpose. So, if you are working in the public employment service, its main objective is likely to be supporting unemployed people, or people at risk of unemployment, into good, sustainable work. However, there can also be important differences in objectives, with governments and employment services typically more interested in the speed at which people return to work and in placing people in a paying job, while career development professionals are typically more interested in giving people a chance to identify what the right job is for them, which will lead them to more sustainable employment that can underpin their well-being.

In some cases, the work of employment services will be linked to the administration of the benefits system, with career development professionals asked to contribute to decisions about whether someone continues to receive employment benefits or gains access to funding for training. This can create some substantial ethical problems, and ideally, you should try and create clear boundaries between the services that you provide to individuals and any wider administrative responsibilities. This is an area where discussing issues with your colleagues and consulting with your professional body and trade union is likely to be critical.

Employment services are likely to have less diversity of roles than many other organisations where career development professionals work. However, they will still have leadership, administrative and support roles (e.g. information and systems management) and may offer different forms of services run by other staff (e.g. forms of training). It is important to build a picture of the professional landscape of the organisation within which you work.

Career development services

Some countries will have dedicated career services which are distinct from the education system and the public employment system. Such services are likely to be strongly aligned with the professional values of career development professionals and have a majority of staff who work in dedicated career-related roles. They may be funded by the government or required to seek funding, often from a mix of different kinds of sources.

Some career development services offer services for the general public, which typically include forms of career counselling and coaching and some forms of group work. Typically, such services are targeted to particular sections of the population but may also be open to all. In addition to these kinds of services, many career development services (such as Skills Development Scotland) will also work in a range of forms of partnership with educational providers and the public employment service. In such cases, it is important to consider not only the organisation where you work but also the organisation that you are working with.

Employers

The organisation where someone works is a critical site for their career development. All employers, other than very small ones, have some kind of human resource management (HRM) function which is designed to get the most out of their employees. In many cases, this is likely to be supplemented by developmental line management relationships in which managers are encouraged to think about how they can support the staff that they manage to do their jobs better, and potentially to develop their skills and support them to move into new roles (e.g. through promotion). Sometimes this takes the form of formal developmental meetings in which managers may even be required to discuss career development with their staff. In other words, there is often a lot of career development work going on in employing organisations, even in cases where there are no career development professionals to do it.

In some cases, employers may provide a formal career development service, which could be organised through the learning and development element of the HRM function, but on occasion might even include a dedicated organisational career service. Other employers might organise this on a more episodic basis, for example, by bringing in 'executive coaches' to support the development of those identified as 'high potential', who are ascending to the top tier of the organisation or perhaps bringing in 'career solutions specialists' (also known as 'outplacement advisers') to help people move on during times of redundancy or organisational restructuring. In some countries, trade unions and professional associations also play important roles in providing career development services within organisations.

As the discussion so far shows, career development work within employing organisations is highly varied and often very complex. Career development is relatively rarely a distinct function but rather interfaces with a wide range of other business functions such as HRM and learning and development. It can include work by careers professionals who are employed by the organisation or by people who are brought in to provide external consultancy. But, in all cases, it is operating within a context where the career development of workers is at best a secondary function for the employing organisation.

Although supporting staff development and, in cases of redundancy, redeployment, are aims that potentially align with career development work, there can be tensions for careers professionals working in these contexts. So, for example, an area of contention might be whether business leaders see career development as a useful contribution to the development of organisational skills and capacity, or whether they view it as dangerous and likely to lead to poorer organisational retention. In reality, people don't leave companies because they have talked to a career development professional, but rather for a wide range of other issues relating to pay, conditions, alignment with the organisational mission and so on, but as career conversations can be catalysts for change, this can be frightening for business leaders. This may be an area you need to discuss with senior leaders to reassure them that providing career development support for employees is ultimately likely to lead to a happier workforce, where skills and talents are better utilised and that it will serve both individual and organisational objectives. 'Three-way contracting' between you, your individual clients and the organisation is how this kind of stakeholder management is sometimes described.

For careers professionals operating in this kind of context, there are a bewildering array of functions and roles to get to grips with. Doing careers work within employing organisations requires a strong understanding of the organisations' internal labour market and of the kinds of roles that are contained within that organisation. Of particular importance are likely to be relationships with business leaders, HRM teams, learning and development specialists and line managers and mentors within the business.

💡 Resources

To understand career development within employing organisations it is important to learn more about HRM practices. A book like Nick Wilton's *An Introduction to Human Resource Management* might be helpful in this regard, or connecting with a professional association like the Chartered Institute of Personnel and Development (CIPD) at https://www.cipd.org/uk.

Building on that, it can be helpful to understand how learning and development structures are set up in organisation and a book like Thomas Garavan and colleagues' book *Learning and Development in Organisations* can be useful.

Reflection

It is important to consider the following questions regardless of the context in which you are working, but it becomes particularly important when you are working in a new context or a non-standard one.

● What are the main objectives of the organisation where you are working? How does career development fit into these objectives?

● What are the main opportunities that this context affords you? Why is it a good place to undertake career development work?

● What are the main barriers or challenges that this context poses? How can you overcome these barriers?

● Who are the key partners and stakeholders that you need to work with to achieve your objectives?

● In light of these reflections, what are your objectives for working in this context? What approaches to delivery might be particularly useful to you as you develop your work in this context?

Other organisational contexts

The four contexts discussed so far each represent distinct environments for careers work. But, as we discussed at the start of this chapter, there are also many other contexts where career development work takes place, such as community centres, migrant services, prisons and health and well-being contexts. In most cases, each of these contexts will have similarities with some of the contexts discussed above, but they are all likely to be distinct. Because of this, if you are working in any of these contexts, it is a good idea to spend some time reflecting on what kinds of aims and objectives might characterise the organisational context you are working in and how your work might align and/or sit in tension with these.

Working in organisations

In the discussion above, we have already highlighted the opportunities and challenges that you are likely to face as you develop your practice within different kinds of organisation. All of this reminds us of issues that we discussed in theory in Chapters 4 and 6; career development is not just shaped by the individual, but rather by the individual in their social context. Similarly, career development work is not just a question of you doing your job well, but rather a question of you making the most of the environment in which you work and the people around you.

Given this, the following skills and activities are likely to enable you to be effective within the organisational contexts that you work in.

- **Analysis of organisations.** Effective career development is context-specific. This means career development professionals should take time to analyse the contexts that they are in, build an understanding of an organisation's drivers and culture and then think about how to work effectively within this. For example, most organisations will publish a mission and vision statement, and it is useful to be familiar with this and able to describe the ways that good career development practice might support the achievement of these aims.

- **Building internal partnerships.** One of the most critical skills within organisations is the ability to build internal partnerships, networks and alliances. This involves mapping which employees are key to your students' or clients' career development and making sure that you have a way to dialogue with and engage this group. For example, in a university, this is likely to involve building relationships with academic staff, understanding the pressures that these staff are under and finding ways to engage them in the career development of their students.

- **Developing models of inter-professional working.** Engaging with employees in an organisation is only the first step towards building effective organisational careers work. To really make a difference, you will need to find ways to work with them on career development activities. This is likely to mean finding ways to draw together their skills and knowledge with yours. For example, in schools, careers professionals might co-teach a session with a subject teacher, building on the teacher's existing relationship with the students and their knowledge of the subject, and providing new information about the labour market and career possibilities related to that subject.

- **Referral.** We have already discussed referral in Chapter 3, but it is important to recognise that referral is a key part of organisational working. Effective career development professionals understand the range of other services that exist for their students and clients both within and outside the institution and make regular referrals. To support this, it is a good idea to have regular meetings with other professionals to whom you regularly refer clients and to include referral and dual support arrangements (i.e. where you are both working with the same student or client) as a regular item to discuss.

- **Promoting the value of career development and of your work.** By its nature, career development work exists on the periphery of most organisations. Career development supports people to think beyond their immediate circumstances, make transitions and move through education and work. This often means that career development is a secondary or subsidiary function within larger organisations such as schools or employers. Because of this, it is important for career development professionals to clearly articulate their purpose and actively communicate why it is important to the overall mission of the organisation.

Working on organisations

As we have seen in the last section, career development work relies on professionals who can build a strong understanding of the organisations and contexts within which they work, build alliances within them and find ways to articulate their value to these organisations. But career development professionals also have some other roles which involve helping students and clients to operate effectively within often imperfect organisational systems and even changing and developing organisations to make them better places for people to build their careers.

Given this, the following skills and activities are important for this kind of organisational work.

- **Advocacy.** Many of the approaches to careers work that we have discussed so far in this book have been about building the capacity of the individual to act on their own behalf. There are, however, occasions when individuals are not capable of dealing with the issues that they face alone. In such cases, you may decide that the best way for you to support their career development is to either accompany them to a meeting or to represent them in writing or in person. This could, for example, include calling an employer to discuss adaptations to the work environment that a particular student might need or discussing problems that have been communicated to you with a recruitment process that you have just supported a student through. Advocacy is a challenging area as it can often involve you getting close to your professional boundaries (see Chapter 3), but it is one of the tools that you have in your toolkit to help move people's lives and careers forwards.

- **Feeding back.** Careers professionals have access to a huge number of insights from their clients. Depending on the contexts in which you work, you have probably started to build up a picture of where the strengths and weaknesses are in an organisation in relation to career development: who the bullying managers are, which academics offer brilliant mentoring, where the sexist employers are and so on. These kinds of insights, especially if you can find a way to quantify them and draw them together from your colleagues, can give you a huge amount of power when you are trying to drive institutional change. Once you know what is wrong and where it is wrong, you can explain that to senior managers (while respecting confidentiality and the wishes of your clients) and exert pressure to change things that are going wrong for multiple people.

- **Organising and bringing people together.** Identifying problems and bringing them to the attention of senior managers can be a powerful way to change the context for career development, but unfortunately, it doesn't always work. In other cases, you may need to build a movement for change by working with your clients, partners and other stakeholders to think about how things can change. This could include things like organising meetings to discuss problems, speaking to key influencers, writing an open letter about a particular issue or liaising with the trade union or staff or student representatives.

- **System change.** The longer you work in an organisation the greater understanding you should have of how it works and what works well and not so well. As part of this growing understanding, you should try and develop some practical ideas about how things could work better. Most organisations will give you a variety of means to provide feedback, such as meetings, staff surveys and other forms of consultation. Take these chances to provide your ideas for how the systems should change in ways that will improve your life and the life of your clients.

The kinds of roles described above are quite a long way from the public perception of what career development work involves. When most people think about career development work, they think about what is often called Information, Advice and Guidance (IAG), which essentially describes many of the activities that we have covered in Chapters 7 and 9. But we have also added education as another activity in Chapter 8 (you may also have seen the acronym CEIAG, which stands for 'Careers, Education, Information, Advice and Guidance'). We are not big fans of these kinds of acronyms, both because they are confusing to those outside of the field and because they limit the possibilities for careers work. There are other definitions of career development work which include a far wider range of activities, including the ones discussed above.[1] Tristram Hooley and colleagues set out a broader definition in their chapter 'The Neoliberal Challenge to Career Guidance'.

> Career guidance supports individuals and groups to discover more about work, leisure and learning and to consider their place in the world and plan for their futures. Key to this is developing individual and community capacity to analyse and problematise assumptions and power relations, to network and build solidarity and to create new and shared opportunities. It empowers individuals and groups to struggle within the world as it is and to imagine the world as it could be. Career guidance can take a wide range of forms and draws on diverse theoretical traditions. But at its heart it is a purposeful learning opportunity which supports individuals and groups to consider and reconsider work, leisure and learning in the light of new information and experiences and to take both individual and collective action as a result of this.

This kind of thinking about what career development is encourages us to focus on the outcome that we want our students and clients to achieve, to recognise that they have a wide range of individual and collective resources to draw on in achieving these outcomes and then to use a wide range of career development techniques to achieve this.

Of course, we need to feel comfortable and competent in the approaches that we use to develop careers and organisations, but you should feel that you have permission to help people in the best way possible as long as it is within your professional boundaries, rather than just choosing from the limited menu of information, advice and guidance. Theorists who argue for career development professionals to engage with social justice often focus on things like collective action, advocacy and organisational work as key techniques (see Chapter 6). The logic is that it is very difficult for people to have great careers if they work for terrible organisations, or have limited support in the institutions they study in, so sometimes to move people's careers forwards, we have to try and improve how organisations and systems function. When you are engaged in this kind of work, you can face challenges and dilemmas, so making sure that you have appropriate support from your line manager, supervisor or wider team can be helpful in allowing you to work out the best ways forwards.

Working across organisations

As well as working within organisations, it is important to recognise that career development work sits on the edge of organisations and is often focused on helping people manage transitions between different organisations. This means that building partnerships within an organisation, you are also likely to need to build partnerships across organisations. This can include some of the following activities.

- **Networking.** Through your work, you will meet people working for different organisations and in different roles which are allied to your own. Asking them about their work, what they do and who they work with is good practice for building your own network. Gathering email addresses, telephone numbers or LinkedIn contacts can provide you with a network of individuals who can help you when you are looking for support for a client or need further information.

- **Attending or convening meetings or training sessions.** As part of your work, you will identify particular topics or areas that might be useful to work with other professionals to address. You might attend or set up meetings on relevant topics. For example, you might attend a local authority-run meeting looking at youth employment, or an NHS event on work and well-being. Attending meetings gives you a chance to build a network and develop opportunities to work together.

- **Employer and provider visits.** These might include visiting different kinds of services, or educational providers and employers, to get a better understanding of what different employers and providers are like, what services other organisations provide, and the experiences of people who engage in them.

- **Stakeholder mapping.** There are a lot of potentially interesting networks to be made and sustained, but in practice, you only have a limited amount of time. So, before you start to undertake any activities with other organisations it is important to build your awareness of what organisations are out there, to think about their interests and to make a judgement about whether they are a priority organisation to work with. This is best achieved through some kind of process of stakeholder mapping in which you systematically review the landscape and build a plan for engagement.

- **Promotion and raising awareness.** Career development provision is often not a top priority for the organisations you work in and between, and a key part of careers work is being able to raise awareness of your service and encourage employers, learning providers and other important stakeholders to recognise that you exist and your value. This might include a wide range of activities, from setting up meetings with key stakeholders, working on your service's website, establishing a regular newsletter, promoting your service through a variety of local channels or even seeking endorsements and support from former students and stakeholders.

- **Information exchange.** Encouraging agencies to provide you with regular updates, signing up for newsletters and providing updates of your own help to maintain awareness of your services and those of others.

- **Co-delivery of projects and programmes.** Finding out what other organisations exist and what they do will help to identify ways of collaborating. As a career development professional, you will have a key role in bringing partners together – for example, you might arrange for an employer to visit a school or support with work placement programmes or internships.

- **Collaborating with multiple professionals to support a client.** Depending on your context, you may have clients who have complex needs that require intervention from multiple agencies. For example, you may have a student with learning difficulties and family problems who is about to leave school. In such a case, it is important to work together as a team of professionals, including teachers, social workers, support workers and possibly other people like parents and employers. You might be a part of multi-agency meetings, and in some cases, you may convene these meetings. Such multi-agency working needs careful thought about who should be in the room, what information should be shared with whom, who has responsibility for different actions and how you balance the involvement of the client with their vulnerabilities. You also need to be clear on your own professional and legal responsibilities and boundaries.

As discussed already, all these approaches place you in a different kind of role. Rather than delivering career learning and support to an individual directly, you are engaged in building an environment where you can help a client access the support they need.

Resources

One particularly well-evidenced area for partnership working in careers is working with employers. Students and clients learn a lot from hearing from, visiting and engaging with employers and working people. Given this, these employer relationships are likely to be an important area for partnership building for you in your work. The Education & Employers research pages are an excellent place to start exploring this area: https://www.educationandemployers.org/research-main/

CASE STUDY

Shona is a career development professional working in a community centre. She has recently seen the number of migrants and refugees who are using her centre increase. Many of them access the centre to connect with other members of their community and to use childcare and English language services, but hardly any of them have found their way to ask for career development support yet. Shona starts talking to her colleagues who deliver English language tuition, encouraging them to co-deliver some career development activities for this group. One of the tutors is enthusiastic, and Shona co-delivers some sessions on career development for the group, combining career development and English language learning outcomes. The evaluations of the sessions are positive; however, Shona reflects that the impact of the sessions has not been as great as she would have liked because many of them face a range of complex legal issues which prevent them from studying or working. Others report prejudice from employers when they have applied for jobs.

Shona decides to create the Vanchester Migrant Support Forum and invites a range of different organisations that are working with migrants to meet together. She also decides that it is a good idea to invite some learning providers and the local Chamber of Commerce to become part of the group. Finally, she makes sure that there are some representatives of the migrant groups themselves in the Forum. At the first meeting, Shona describes what has led her to create the forum and seeks to secure the support of the members. In the following meetings, aims and objectives are agreed upon.

The Vanchester Migrant Support Forum starts to take shape. It really operates on two levels: first, a strategic one, liaising with local government, coordinating partnership working and campaigning on issues. Second, it provides an infrastructure for very practical inter-organisational working and cross-referral. With this infrastructure in place, it becomes much easier to help migrants. It even generates new types of practice where, for example, careers advisers and employment law advisers arrange to see clients together.

The end result is that Shona's work on establishing the Forum has made it much easier for migrants to access learning and work and to begin the development of their careers in the UK. It has also made her one-to-one and small group work with migrants much more effective as she is plugged into all the right networks. But, to achieve this, she has had to do a lot of organisational and systems work, which has inevitably taken up some of her professional time.

Effective partnership working

Lots of what we have discussed in this chapter is essentially about working with others either within your organisation or across different organisations. The ability to build partnerships for a range of different purposes is a key element of career development work. It offers you the possibility to increase the expertise, resources, reach and creativity that you have available to you.

Partnerships can take a wide variety of forms. These can range from an informal agreement between you and another professional to a detailed organisational agreement underpinned by a contract or memorandum of understanding (MOU). All partnerships, regardless of their formality, address the following issues.

- **Purpose.** Why are you partnering, what are you trying to achieve and what will a good outcome look like? It is important to remember that not everyone will have the same purpose, but through discussion, it will be possible to align your interests and agree on the purpose for the partnership.
- **Scale.** Who is involved in this partnership and at what level is it operating? Is it just a bilateral exchange between practitioners or does it involve multiple organisations? Figuring out these questions of scale is very important to making partnerships work effectively.
- **Degree.** How closely are you going to partner? What activities will be involved in the partnership? What is the depth of the relationship? Are you just exchanging information from time to time or integrating your organisations' strategic objectives?
- **Duration.** How long will the partnership endure? Is it a one-off or a long-term relationship? Is it open-ended or time-limited?

It is possible to view the different types of partnership as a staircase in which relationships become progressively deeper. While reaching one step does not mean that you have to move up the staircase, it is likely that deeper forms of collaboration move through a range of steps as they mature and become deeper (see Figure 10.1).

Reflection

What partnerships are important to your work?

How are these partnerships organised and managed?

How close are your partnerships? Would it be valuable for them to get closer?

How long do your partnerships last? When is the right time to review and evaluate them?

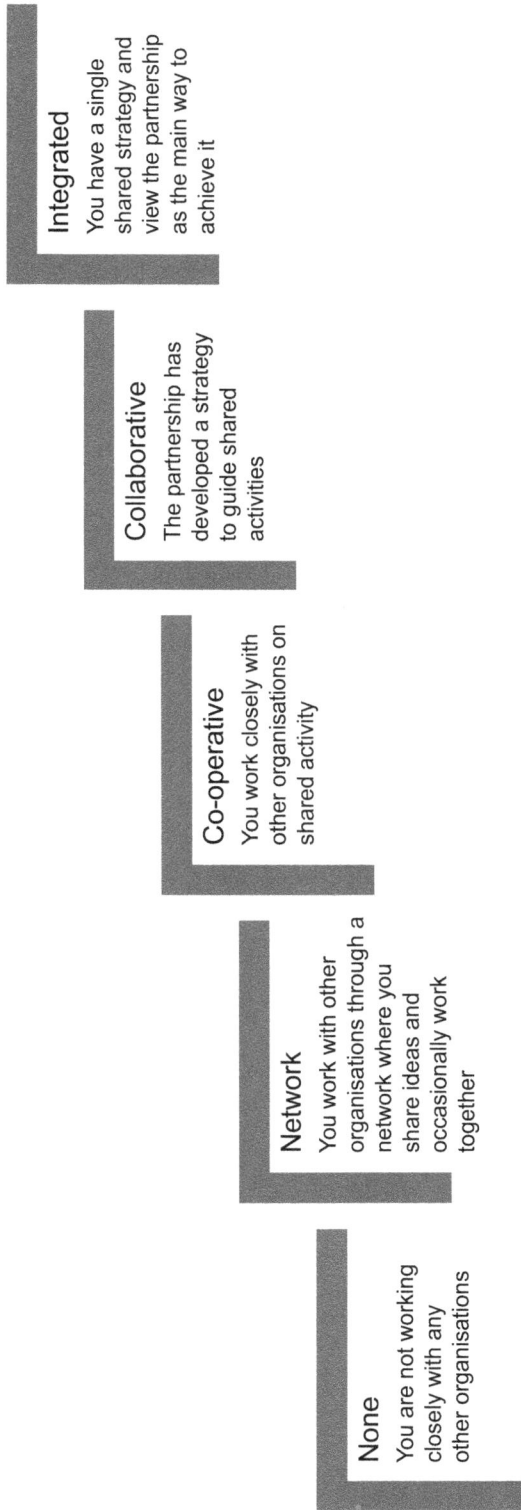

Integrated
You have a single shared strategy and view the partnership as the main way to achieve it

Collaborative
The partnership has developed a strategy to guide shared activities

Co-operative
You work closely with other organisations on shared activity

Network
You work with other organisations through a network where you share ideas and occasionally work together

None
You are not working closely with any other organisations

Figure 10.1. The partnership staircase

In a nutshell

This chapter has discussed career development work in organisations and systems. It has argued that

- all career development work takes place in organisations and system. Thinking about the nature of these organisations and systems is critical to your role as a career development professional;

- organisational and systems work is an important part of career development practice and should be viewed as another string to your bow alongside approaches like counselling and coaching, career education and the use of information;

- at the heart of lots of organisational work is building a deep understanding of the operation of your organisation and considering what tools, partners and opportunities it provides for supporting people's career;

- sometimes work within organisations and systems requires you to work on the organisation to make it a better place for people to develop their career;

- by its nature career development work sits on the edge of organisations and is interested in the relationship between organisations. Building connections and partnerships and supporting cross-organisational learning is a critical part of this; and

- the idea of partnership working sits at the heart of a lot of organisational and systems work. It is important to be reflective about the partnerships that you build and to attend to how they work and can work better.

Chapter 11
Leading career development services

Whether we work alone or alongside other career development professionals, we are all managers. We need to manage ourselves and our work and manage projects we are working on. Some of us might also manage people, supervising the work of others who are also involved in delivering career development services. Similarly, we all have a role in relation to leading career development services, whether it is responding to leaders in our workplace or contributing to the process of determining the vision and purpose of our services.

Recognising the big picture

When we talk about 'career development services', we are using this term to describe the management units in which career development support is organised. These might be standalone careers development services operating as individual companies, or they might be services which are parts of larger organisations – such as a career development service within a university.

Regardless of where they are situated, as you start to think about issues related to leadership and management, it is important to recognise the wider context within which career services operate and the drivers and barriers that they are negotiating. A career development service does not exist in isolation and does not have complete autonomy over what services to offer and how to deliver them. Instead, it is subject to wider forces which include

- **Public policy influences.** As we explored in Chapter 5, the majority of career services are publicly funded. This means that the public policy context can have a strong influence in directing what kinds of services are delivered, how and to whom. This might be direct, in the case of countries with a national career development service, where national career guidance policies or strategies have a strong influence. In other cases, the influences might be indirect or multiple. For example, in the case of services provided within schools or universities, educational as well as youth employment policies are likely to matter, shaping both the availability of funding and regulation.

- **Wider organisational goals.** Where services are provided within an organisation, wider organisational goals or objectives are also important. So, for example, a service within a university might be tasked with addressing the priorities that matter to that institution.

- **Professional requirements.** Services which employ career professionals need to ensure that they provide an environment that allows these individuals to work in line with their professional requirements and codes of practice. For example, an organisation employing career professionals must make sure that confidential spaces are provided for in-depth conversations.

- **Theoretical influences and evidence-based practice.** Exactly what is delivered by a career service is influenced by existing career development theory (see Chapter 6) and evidence about best practices in the delivery of different types of services (see Chapters 7–10). Career development professionals often have a key role in helping to shape the practices of a service through their ongoing CPD and learning about best practices.

- **Quality standards.** Services sometimes sign up for quality standards or join membership associations as a way of demonstrating the high standard of their services. In the UK, for example, career development services in universities can sign up to be members of AGCAS (the representative body for the career development services in higher education). Some services will also aim to achieve quality standards; for example schools in England, Northern Ireland, the Isle of Man and the Channel Islands can undertake the Quality in Careers Standard, while standalone career development services and those in colleges can seek the matrix Standard. Other quality awards include non-careers-specific awards such as Investors in People. Engaging with these kinds of frameworks and standards has implications for how services are organised, managed and delivered.

- **Changing labour market and economic conditions.** Changing economic and social conditions can result in shifting priorities for career development services. Sometimes these impact directly on services as they reorientate their priorities or indirectly through public policy or organisational responses to these circumstances. In recent years, for example, the Covid-19 pandemic and economic crises have been important factors.

The way that services are framed by public policy assumptions and organisational contexts highlights that the ways senior civil servants, school leaders and university leaders understand career services have a very significant influence on service delivery. It is worth remembering that although many of these individuals have a good understanding of career development services, not all do. For many, assumptions about what career developent services are 'for' and how they are delivered might be based on particular approaches to delivery (e.g. one-to-one counselling and coaching) or focused on narrow outcomes (e.g. finding people employment as quickly as possible). All career development professionals have a role in utilising their leadership skills to help address misconceptions and promote career services.

The forces that shape career development services are continually changing. As new political parties come into power, or a new university vice-chancellor or school head teacher is appointed, the priorities for career development services are likley to change. Developments in career theory and innovations in career practice can create an evidence base for supporting different forms of service organisation or delivery. As a career development professional, it is important to stay abreast of changing contexts and to be able to identify, promote and take forward potential service innovations.

💡 Resources

There are lots of resources to help you improve the quality of what you provide, including the Quality in Careers Standard (https://www .qualityincareers.org.uk/), the matrix Standard (https://matrixstandard.com/) and Investors in People (https://www.investorsinpeople.com/). It is important for you to find out more about the infrastructure that exists for quality assurance in your country.

Responding to technological innovations

A key source of innovation in recent years has been the advancement of technology. Developments in technology change the context for individuals' careers and the opportunities that exist for the provision of career support. In relation to service delivery, this can include initiatives such as the development of purpose-built national careers websites which support national career services and often include searchable databases of career information, as well as access to online self-guided tools and resources, and searchable course and job databases. Other innovations include Career Services Management Systems (CSMS) which can be purchased by organisations and used to manage career information, appointment bookings, job databases and events information. Other technological innovations which can be used include technologies that are not specific to career services, such as Customer Records Management (CRM) systems which help to securely store records relating to individual clients.

To date, a great deal of the technological innovations available have focused on providing access to information and databases (for clients) and managing service delivery and records (for services). However, increasingly, the development of more advanced internet technologies, the generation of large data sets (often called 'big data'), the technological innovations to handle this, as well as the possibilities offered by artificial intelligence are changing the role that technology can play. It is increasingly possible for services to track the ways in which clients interact with services, and to use this to identify and target specific services at specific clients. The use of chat-bots and interactive tools is also likely to increase, allowing for a greater range of services, at a greater level of personalisation, to be provided to clients.

The technological innovations in career services offer certain possibilities and risks and are changing the nature of the role and role(s) services invest in. For example, the capacity to understand and interpret big data sets has become a skill set that many services have sought to secure. For career development staff, the ability to support clients in accessing and utilising technology has also become an important skill set.

💡 Resources

Tristram Hooley and Tom Staunton's chapter 'The Role of Digital Technology in Career Development' sets out a framework for thinking about how new developments in technology might impact career development practice.

Fiona Cobb's article 'There's No Going Back' offers some insights into the ways that higher education career services are transforming their delivery through the use of big data and in response to a changing political landscape.

Considering innovation in service design

Alongside technological innovation, services are also often interested in practice innovations that might lead to more efficient or effective services. This is where career theory and practice come into play and where practitioners often have a key role in supporting service improvement. The newsletters and websites of professional associations and bodies are full of examples of practice innovations that have been led by careers professionals, including things like:

- the development and/or introduction of a new tool or resource for working with particular client groups;
- the development of new partnerships and co-delivery of career education interventions; and
- experimentation with different styles of interviewing or different models of interviewing.

Another type of innovation is in service design, with these innovations more often led by service managers. A good example of this is how within higher education there has been a great deal of interest in the most effective way to organise career development services. Some universities have pursued a central service that extends into academic contexts, whereas others have pursued a model whereby careers staff and the services they offer are embedded in departments across the institution. With all innovations, it is important that these are carefully planned, implemented and evaluated, something that requires strong leadership and management skills.

💡 Resources

For insights into practice and service innovations, take a look at recent professional newsletters and publications. In the UK, the Career Development Institute's publication *Career Matters* or the Association of Graduate Careers Advisory Services' (AGCAS) publication *Phoenix* both regularly report on innovations.

Mike Grey's article 'How to Cope with the Complexity of Career Service Leadership' also reflects on the mix of external pressures and internal design decisions that higher education career services make.

Leadership and management

Leadership and management can be understood as distinct, but linked, concepts. Leaders motivate people to work towards a vision for your service, and managers allocate resources and put things in place to make that vision a reality in practice. A vision and goals for your organisation won't necessarily make anything happen, but equally, it is hard to implement anything without a clearly communicated view of the purpose of the activity and why it is important.

Management

Services need managing – from initial design (such as determining how to allocate resources for one-to-one work as we discussed in Chapter 7 or considering how to embed careers education from Chapter 8) through to the continuous operation of an effective offer. Those resource allocation decisions need to be evaluated, feeding into a cycle of continuous improvement.

Management is often thought about in terms of people, projects and resources (Figure 11.1).

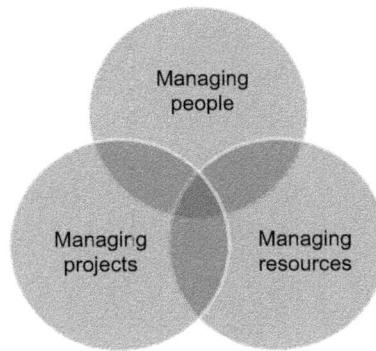

Figure 11.1. Domains of management

Managing people might involve being their line manager, with formal responsibility for agreeing on work objectives and being the formal interface between an employee and employer. Even if you do not have formal management responsibility, you are likely to be reliant on others for your ability to achieve your own goals at work and get done what you have agreed to do. Your communication and influencing skills with colleagues who might have more, or less, power than you in the workplace come into play here. Management is rarely about just telling people what to do and is more likely to be about discussing, consulting, negotiating and persuading. Sometimes, especially when you are in a line manager role, this can involve having difficult conversations. The skills you use in your one-to-one work are of course useful here: careful listening, clear explanation, effective challenge and agreeing actions are all in your toolkit.

From the outset of your work as a career development professional, you are likely to be *managing projects*: an event, a particular opportunity for clients or a new way of offering a service, for example. Simple project management tools can help you with this: being clear about objectives and success criteria, breaking tasks down into sequence and working out timelines, pinch points and key risks. Keeping things on track using timelines and documented workflows helps in monitoring progress and is especially useful if you are working in a team, as it helps motivate people towards shared goals and highlights your interdependence and accountabilities. At the end of the project, those success criteria can be carried forwards into evaluation and refinement in an 'action research' cycle.

There are many tools available for project management online which allow for varying degrees of complexity, but you can create a basic project plan effectively using a tool like Excel or free software such as Trello. Listing tasks on the left and a horizontal timeline allows for the plotting of project components and responsibilities, colour-coded for different actors or live status.

Finally, *managing resources* is worth highlighting as a particular aspect of people and projects. The primary resource at your disposal is your own time and energy, so finding ways of working that help you maintain focus and productivity to meet your goals and commitments is a key part of this. That said, remember that none of us are machines, and being a professional requires you to monitor your own well-being too and take care of yourself as well as your commitments to your employer or other stakeholders. Clear time management protocols can also help when you need to demonstrate if expectations have crept up beyond what is reasonable.

CASE STUDY

As part of her role as a career development professional in an English secondary school, Claire was asked by the senior management team to do something that demonstrated very clearly that sixth form wasn't the only option for year 11 students so that they could consider vocational options such as apprenticeships. She decided to create an 'Apprenticeship Week' to profile opportunities and get students and parents thinking.

Her Apprenticeship Week project plan included a timetable for communication to teaching staff to get their buy-in and ensure they promoted the event in classes and tutor groups. She negotiated class and assembly time throughout the week to convey key messages and organised an early evening event for parents and students. She secured an agreement that school administrative and technical staff would help with aspects of this event, liaising with employers and apprentices who would attend and ensuring it was recorded for those who couldn't attend. She even asked student leaders to meet and escort visiting speakers.

Her project plan was available on a shared drive so that even when her admin colleague was sick the week before the event, the office manager could clearly see what had been committed to and ensure the tasks were reallocated. After the event, her clear criteria enabled her to plan a light-touch evaluation using feedback from everyone involved to decide how effectively she had met the brief she had been given and plan improvements for future events.

Leadership

Leaders in our organisations and sector can be critical to inspiring our work, articulating and communicating a vision of what we are trying to achieve and maintaining our momentum towards it. Leaders do not necessarily have to have a formal position at the top of an organisational hierarchy, although this is often the case. People can lead by the brilliance of their ideas and their capacity to inform and inspire, as well as by their logistical competence and capacity to organise people and get things done. Leadership in organisations is often dispersed among a range of different people.

There are different understandings of leadership. Some contend that great leaders are born, not made, whereas others focus on how leaders can learn the traits or behaviours of a good leader and focus on defining what these technical, people and conceptual skills are. The recognition of leadership and management as an area of competence in its own right raises the possibility of being led by those who may have skills as managers but do not have training as career development professionals.

In addition to questions about what skills you might need as a leader or manager, it is also possible to recognise a range of different leadership styles. There are lots of different models of leadership, but perhaps the most famous is Lewin's and colleagues' model, which distinguishes between the following approaches.

- **Authoritarian leaders** provide clear direction and expectations but offer little opportunity for team members to input their ideas into the direction.
- **Democratic leaders** engage with their team and develop a common vision and approach. This is often viewed as the most effective approach to leadership (in most, but not all, situations), but it is also the most difficult to pull off.
- **Delegative leaders** let their teams do what they want and offer little direction. This can be effective when working with highly skilled and motivated teams, but it can also result in people losing focus and motivation.

Other approaches to leadership and management focus on dilemmas like whether to focus on the team or the task, what level of innovation, creativity and risk to encourage, how to manage uncertainty, stress and failure and how to balance short-term performance with long-term sustainability.

It is useful to reflect on your leadership style and to think about how you might need to flex this style as you work with different kinds of teams and address different tasks. The ability to adapt your approach to leadership to different team needs, contexts and tasks is often called situational leadership.

In situational leadership, you adapt your style to what people need in relation to balance between direction and support. Hersey and Blanchard, who developed situational leadership, suggest four main approaches to management, which managers and leaders should be able to switch between depending on the situation.

- **Telling** is focused on the task and giving instructions to ensure that the task is done.
- **Selling** is about engaging team members in the team and the task.
- **Participating** is about working with team members to develop a shared understanding of tasks and build an effective way of working across the team.
- **Delegating** is about giving up power and control to team members who are competent and engaged.

Some inexperienced or less engaged colleagues may need more of a focus on motivating or instructing, which could in turn be seen as unnecessary and intrusive by very skilled and committed colleagues. On the other hand, in leadership and management, a consistency of approach is needed for fairness, so there are some tensions to hold in balance here.

A more contemporary emphasis has been on leadership as a process, with all of us all playing varying times in the role of leader and follower, which we will look at in the next section.

💡 Resources

Lewin and colleagues' article 'Patterns of Aggressive Behavior in Experimentally Created "Social Climates"' sets out the basis of their theory. Ken Blanchard and Paul Hersey explore situational leadership in *Management of Organizational Behavior*.

As you move more into leadership and management, it is worth thinking more about these issues. Jon Bright's *Modern Management and Leadership* might be a good place to start. More specific books like Anthony Kelly's *Dynamic Management and Leadership in Education* or David Andrew and Tristram Hooley's *The Careers Leader Handbook* might also be useful.

Managing up and effective followership

Not all leadership and management in organisations are top down. People can exert forms of leadership from all sorts of places within an organisation. Technical expertise or being good at your job gives you some authority, and you can potentially use this to influence others and even the direction of the organisation itself.

Another source of power is your understanding of the organisational purpose, culture and politics. If you understand what the purpose of the organisation is, how leadership and management are structured within the organisation and who has responsibility for and authority over different areas, you are likely to be able to navigate your organisation more effectively and potentially influence things. Many of these processes build on the concepts we discussed in Chapter 10, such as undertaking organisational work within career development (e.g. engaging other staff in careers or integrating careers into the organisational vision) and shade into forms of leadership and management.

Barbara Kellerman argues that these forms of leadership from below are very important in understanding the success or otherwise of different organisations. She suggests that we have focused too much on the role of top-down leaders and neglected the obvious truth that there can be no leaders without followers. She refocuses the discussion on the role of followers, noting that how they behave in response to leaders makes all the difference. She argues that there are five different types of followers.

- **Isolates** try and do their job with as little interaction with their leaders, colleagues and the organisation as possible.
- **Bystanders** pay attention to what is going on in the organisation but try not to get involved in anything outside of their core jobs.
- **Participants** engage with the organisational mission and respond to their leaders and managers.
- **Activists** feel strongly about their work and their organisation and try and influence the direction, even if this means challenging their leaders.
- **Diehards** are committed to their cause or to their leaders and are willing to pursue this aim even if it creates problems and challenges for them and those around them.

Reflection

What type or types of follower have you been in the past?

What have been the advantages and disadvantages of the different positions that you have adopted?

How will this influence how you follow up in the future?

How would you deal with these different kinds of followers as a leader or manager?

It is also worth thinking about the strategies and approaches that are available to you when you are trying to influence things from below. These range from non-compliance, procrastination and active resistance to flattery, offering creative alternatives, enthusiastically supporting leaders that you agree with and asserting forms of individual and collective power. This might include refusing to do things because you believe that they are unethical or confronting your manager collectively, perhaps with the support of a trade union.

The process of trying to influence your manager in a variety of ways is often called 'managing up'. While it might sound like this is a hostile act, many organisations actively look for people who have the capability to manage their managers. Very few organisations want to put all their faith in top managers and just leave everyone else to act as drones. Organisations where there is a strong understanding of the organisation's purpose at all levels, and a willingness to speak up and challenge bad ideas, are usually stronger for it. So, it is important to think about what your manager is doing, why they are doing it and how you want to engage with it.

Managing up is a very subtle process where you have to think carefully about the best approach. Sometimes the right thing to do is to challenge a manager in a team meeting and set out a criticism or alternative approach. But usually, it is important to remember that you are not just discussing issues or processes, but also engaging as colleagues who both have feelings. Thinking about how to raise concerns in ways that are seen as supportive and productive is important. A little flattery will get you a long way, as will a willingness to take on tasks and develop leaders' ideas. You often have a lot of capacity to bend initially bad or poorly thought-out ideas into something more useful if you can do some of the development.

Ultimately, the key thing to remember here is that even if you have no formal leadership role, your decisions and actions matter, and so it is important to think about leadership even when it is not part of your job.

Resources

Barbara Kellerman's book *Followership* is an essential reading for both leaders and followers.

For ideas about how to manage up effectively, the Harvard Business Review's book *Managing Up* provides a concise and useful introduction.

Moving into leadership positions

When you move into a leadership or management position for the first time, it can be exciting and daunting in equal measure. In many cases you will have been picked for management at least partially because you are good at your current job, and so you are now being asked to manage other people who do that job. Your technical knowledge as a careers professional will be invaluable to you as you take up a management role, but remember that there are often lots of ways to do the same job, and just because your new team does not practise in the same way as you would, it doesn't necessarily mean that there is a problem.

If you are managing a career development team, you have an enormous head-start on becoming a good manager. Not only do you understand the job, but you also have a lot of experience in how you have been managed in this role. Given this, a good starting point is to reflect on what has worked well and not so well in managing you and your colleagues. This will probably give you some good ideas about what to do and what not to do.

The next step is to clarify your understanding of the organisational objectives and the scope of your role. If this is the first time you have taken up a management position, you are unlikely to find that you have unlimited power. Generally, you will be asked to manage within a specific framework. Start by meeting with your manager and ask them to talk you through what they think this role needs to do, what the key issues are and what success would look like. Managing up is a very important part of all management roles.

If you build on your existing expertise, reflect on your experience of being managed, and gain a clear understanding of the parameters of your role, you will have a good chance of making a successful move into management. Beyond this, we would offer the following five tips to help you get started.

- **Spend time listening and thinking before you act.** When you come into a team as a new manager, it is tempting to think that you have the answers. These will often be based on your previous experience and may not always fit the current situation. Give yourself time to listen to the expertise in your new team and think about how to approach any challenges. You will then know whether you need to make changes and be more confident that they are the right ones.

- **Focus on developing your staff.** It is much easier to manage competent, confident and engaged staff. In many cases, staff will be the main resource that you have to deliver your vision. So, spend time with staff, think about what their strengths and weaknesses are and how they can best be developed and deployed. Providing training, mentoring and directing are some of the most powerful tools that you have.

- **Trust people.** When you first become a manager, you may feel that you need to demonstrate your authority and prove that you are good enough. But, micromanaging and doing everything yourself is almost always a bad strategy. Trust your staff, delegate to them and be magnanimous in your praise of their contributions.

- **Give feedback and deal with problems.** Some members of your team will have weaknesses; others will make mistakes or perform badly. It is important that you set out the standards of performance you want and let people know when they are not being met. Setting aside time to give feedback and deal with various problems and issues is central. These conversations aren't always easy, but they are important.

- **Ask for feedback.** This is a new role for you; it is going to be a learning experience. Ask for feedback from your manager and from your staff. Try and find ways that both of these groups can give you positive and developmental feedback that you can act on. Find time to reflect on your own performance and try and find a mentor or a buddy to talk these things over with in a confidential fashion.

Resources

There are lots of books that discuss management and becoming a manager. Try Kate Minchin's *Always Time for Coffee: A Down-to-Earth Guide for Frontline Managers, Team Leaders and Supervisors* and Linda Hill's *Becoming a Manager.*

Effective planning

The first step in delivering quality services is to know what you want to achieve and how you want to achieve it. If you are delivering a career education programme, this is where you might want to think about learning outcomes (see Chapter 8). For other activities, you might develop different kinds of aims and objectives. Typically, a large project or programme might have quite a broad aim, for example, to improve transition rates of young people, reduce unemployment, or improve graduate outcomes. But to effectively address such a broad aim, it is important to break it down into a series of more specific objectives or steps towards achieving this aim. An objective articulates a concrete goal for a project or programme and offers more detail about how the aim is achieved.

Once you have identified your aims and objectives, you will need to develop a project plan. For simple projects or activities, this might be simply a case of listing the steps you will take and in what order. For a career education intervention, for example, your project plan would be your lesson plan. More complex projects are likely to involve a greater degree of planning. You might need to take some time to split your project into different workstreams or activities, and identify key milestones and indicators for each workstream. You might also plan how these will take place across a certain time period, making sure that the tasks are sequenced correctly. When you are undertaking this kind of project planning, using a tool like a Gantt chart or an online project planning tool can be helpful.

As part of your planning, it is also important to identify any resources you need and how you can secure these. When planning a lesson, it is good practice to make a note of the resources you will need for each part of your lesson plan, like handouts, post-it notes or pens and paper. The same is true for more complex projects, except here you might be thinking about resources such as which staff members might take on different tasks or workstreams, and what budget you might need for different activities. For complex projects, developing a separate budget plan might be necessary.

Whether you are planning a lesson, a project, or making an annual service plan, it is important to be realistic. It is a common problem that plans are too ambitious. If you are new to planning, then a good approach is to learn from a more experienced mentor – sharing a lesson plan, project plan or service plan with a trusted colleague will help you get feedback about whether your plan is realistic. It is also a good idea to draw up a basic risk assessment by trying to anticipate any potential risks to the achievement of your project goals and spending some time thinking about potential mitigation measures. Depending on the nature of your project, you may also want to engage in further planning processes; these can include things like stakeholder engagement plans and marketing plans.

Monitoring and evaluation

A good project plan makes the 'doing' of a project a great deal easier. With a good plan, you can ensure that projects are appropriately resourced and timed, and you can anticipate any major challenges and identify mitigation measures. However, for any kind of project, you may encounter unanticipated challenges. It is also possible that some of your activities may not have exactly the outcomes you anticipate, and this can then impact your planned subsequent activities. It is therefore important that you engage in ongoing monitoring of your project. If you are delivering a career education lesson or holding a one-to-one appointment, it is good practice to regularly reflect on how the session is going and whether you need to make any adaptations. In a larger project, monitoring includes regularly collecting data from different workstreams and activities, to check ongoing progress and to make adjustments where necessary.

At the end of a project or an activity, it is useful to engage in a wider review or evaluation of your activity. Project evaluation typically focuses on whether you achieved what you set out to achieve, and evaluation activities often form the basis of project or annual reports. The data that you have collected through monitoring your activities will provide you with some evidence about the effectiveness of the project, but it is also likely that you will want to collect additional data. For example, if you have been running a career education programme at your school, you might have gathered feedback forms from participants after each career education session, but at the end of the programme, you may also want to run a survey or focus group with participants to find out what they thought about the programme as a whole, and what the impact of the programme has been.

Effective monitoring and evaluation therefore means collecting multiple forms of data at different times. Carefully planning what kinds of data you will gather, when, and how right from the beginning of a project is useful, and you may do this through a monitoring and evaluation plan. Having a plan means that you avoid the traps of not having enough data, having too much data or not having the right data when it comes to completing project evaluations or final reports.

Theory-led evaluation

A particular kind of evaluation that is of growing popularity is theory-led evaluation. This approach seeks to understand not just whether or not an intervention or project 'worked' but asks how it works, in what circumstances, for which clients and to what extent?[1] This approach is therefore well suited to working with complex social interventions such as career development, and especially for facilitating ongoing exploration of how and why different forms of intervention might be valuable in different circumstances and for different client groups. Rather than concluding, for example, that 86% of people saw an improvement in their career management skills as a result of engaging in a programme, theory-led evaluations would be interested in how and why this group of 86% saw an improvement and also why the other 14% did not. It also helps to identify unintended outcomes of programmes or interventions.

The first step in theory-led evaluations is to develop a 'theory of change' for the project or programme you are working on. This involves starting from the overall programme or project aim and working backwards to articulate what needs to happen in order for this aim to be met. So, for example, if a service is aiming to improve employment rates of graduates, then it would be important to break down what might need to happen in order to address this aim. This means doing some thinking and background work to identify what is already known about the problem you are seeking to address: do you have data to suggest that particular graduates are more likely to be unemployed?

Do you know what the barriers might be to increasing employment rates? What does the evidence suggest might support employment rates? You then break down the steps that are necessary for achieving your overall aim, trying to identify all the conditions that have to be in place, how these relate to each other, and how they will be met in an overall model.

An example of this, relating to graduate employment, might present the theory of change as the following steps: graduates need to hold relevant skills for the workplace; then they need to have awareness of potential jobs; and then they need to have the confidence and skills to apply for these jobs. Once you have listed these conditions, you can design interventions to meet them. A theory of change also typically outlines the contextual factors and assumptions in a model. For example, graduate employment is going to be influenced by the contextual factor of the economy, and an assumption might be that all graduates want to work or are able to work. Normally, a theory of change is presented as a visual graphic that can be used with stakeholders. It can be a very good way of outlining the rationale behind a programme and raising awareness of the complexities at play. Evaluation activities can then be planned around a theory of change, with the purpose of testing and elaborating the theory and its assumptions.

Gathering data

What do we mean by the term 'data' and what kinds of data might we collect? Data here just means evidence about a project or an activity. Documentary evidence such as lesson plans and meeting minutes counts as data, as do records of how many clients have been engaged, or how many sessions have been run. But for career services, some of the most useful data is data that relates to outcomes for clients.

A useful model for thinking about the different kinds of data evaluating client outcomes is Kirkpatrick's four-level training evaluation model. This is a model widely used in education, but it can easily be applied to career learning. Kirkpatrick proposes that there are four levels of evaluation and that it is valuable to start with the first but build up through the other three should time and resources allow.

- **Level 1 Reaction:** this level focuses on the perspectives of participants who have been engaged in a project. Did they enjoy the activity? Did they find it useful? This kind of data can often be gathered through a feedback form at the end of an intervention (a careers appointment, or a careers lesson for example), or can be gathered through interactive polls or other activities. This provides useful information about participants' experiences, although it doesn't necessarily provide evidence of the effectiveness of an intervention – learning is probably more likely to have happened if someone has enjoyed a session, but if someone has enjoyed a session it does not necessarily follow that they will have learnt anything.

- **Level 2 Learning:** evaluation at this level is about identifying what participants have learnt from an activity. This might involve things like setting and assessing learning outcomes, or even pre- and post-testing, which is where you assess someone's knowledge or skills before undertaking an activity and then make the same assessment at the end to identify any changes.

- **Level 3 Behaviour:** the focus of evaluation at this level is on how far someone's behaviour changes as a result of undertaking an activity. After a job-searching workshop, for example, it might be interesting to explore whether participants actually apply for more jobs after taking part. This might be assessed through a follow-up survey with participants sometime after they have engaged in the activity, to find out what happened next. Alternatively, services might track the engagement of individual clients with different aspects of service delivery and be able to track changes in patterns of engagement after attending an activity, so perhaps after attending a careers workshop, people are more likely to log into the career service website.

- **Level 4 Results:** this level focuses on the overall success of a programme in achieving its aims. This is often at quite a high level and can involve tracking changes in the overall statistical outcomes of certain client groups, such as improved employment rates or improved retention rates.

Different kinds of data collection activities can be planned to gather this data, with activities like feedback forms, polls, surveys, focus groups and sometimes interviews as common means of collecting data.

Understanding data

Engaging in planning and monitoring and evaluation will help you to engage in continuous service improvement. However, it is important to take a judicious approach to data collection, taking care not to collect too much, too little, or the wrong kinds of data. A good guide is that the data you collect should be closely linked to your objectives. If you have run a careers lesson where you have aimed to improve young people's skills and confidence in applying for work, then you should think about how you can measure skills and confidence. You should also take care to think about whether your measures are exactly the right ones, so a good example of this is measuring a person's 'confidence' before and after a careers session might not always be a good measure on its own, as individuals can sometimes be quite confident about topics that they know relatively little about, and the process of learning more about them can result in a reduction of confidence – but we would argue this is not necessarily a bad thing if it means they access the support they need. It is also useful to keep a critical perspective on whether the measures you use are explainable solely by the services you have provided or if there are alternative explanations. A classic example of this is that measuring the effectiveness of careers provision through employment figures is not always a good indicator, as employment levels are impacted heavily by factors outside of the control of career services or individuals, most notably the state of the economy.

A key means through which you can strengthen the quality of the data you collect and the interpretations you make of it is to collect a range of different forms of data from different sources. Comparing different data sets helps you to check your understandings and assumptions and prevents you from coming to incorrect conclusions. This is sometimes called data 'triangulation'. Examples include when you are designing a survey, you might collect numeric data (quantitative) and data in the form of written feedback (qualitative), and here the written comments can offer additional insights or context to help you interpret the numeric data. You might also collect data from different sources; for instance, when delivering a careers education programme, you might collect data from the students in a school class or year group and also the teachers, which might give you different perspectives on how and what students have learnt or how their behaviour has changed after a careers intervention. You might collect data not just on your own graduates' employment figures each year but also on general graduate employment figures and on local employment figures to check what wider contextual influences might be impacting your client outcomes.

💡 Resources

The Better Evaluation website offers some insights into different evaluation approaches and methods at www.betterevaluation.org. Pawson and Tilley's book *Realistic Evaluation* offers a comprehensive overview of conducting realist evaluations, which is a popular form of theory-led evaluation.

Pete Robertson's chapter 'Evidence-Based Practice for Career Development' explores the importance of evidence in delivering effective career services and identifies some of the challenges and opportunities for collecting and making sense of this evidence.

In a nutshell

In this chapter, we have looked at how career services are led and managed and considered the way in which you can participate in that, both as an ordinary team member and as a leader or manager. It has covered:

- how services respond to and evolve with their context and the various drivers that they face;

- how services can be effectively led and managed;

- how you can engage with leadership and management and potentially move into a leadership and management position; and

- how you can monitor and evaluate your service, including how you can gather and make effective use of data.

Chapter 12
Reflecting and
moving forwards

Introduction

The aim of this book was to introduce the knowledge, information and skills that you need to be a career development professional. We suspect that most people will have been engaging with this book alongside a course, but there are undoubtedly a few people who have tackled it solo.

However you have engaged with the book, we hope that it has met your needs, answered your questions, made you think and in a few places surprised you. The field of career development is too big for one book to have given you everything that you need for a lifetime of practice, but hopefully it has served as a stepping stone towards becoming a career development expert.

In this final chapter we will try to draw together the strands and encourage you to think about what you have learned and how you can take this learning into a lifetime of practice.

What have we learned?

The book has introduced you to the concepts of 'career' and 'career development work' and encouraged you to think about the skills that you need to first study as a career development professional and, second, to practice. We have also introduced you to the fact that career development is a profession and encouraged you to think about what the concept of professionalism really means.

Career development work helps people to reflect on their own capabilities and think about how they are going to use these capabilities to navigate the worlds of learning and work, as well as the wider context within which they pursue their own lives. In most countries career development services are funded by the government to meet a range of policy aims and so the way that the government organises the career development system can make a big difference to your work.

Our practice as career development professionals is underpinned by an extensive body of career theory which seeks to understand how careers work and the best ways of helping people with their career development. We argued that all career theory is interested in the relationship between the individual and the wider context and that theories typically focus more on either the self, the environment or the nature of the relationship between the two.

Reflection

To consolidate what you have learnt so far, consider the following questions.

- Why do careers matter so much? Why is it worth putting this concept at the centre of your professional life? (Consider the content of Chapter 1)
- What study skills have you learnt while becoming a careers professional? How will these skills continue to be useful in your professional life? (Chapter 2)
- What does being a career development *professional* mean to you? What responsibilities does it give you? (Chapter 3)
- What are the key issues and trends that you are noticing in your context? How are these shaping the lives of your students or clients? (Chapter 4)
- How is the career development system within which you are working organised? How does this shape your work in both good and bad ways? (Chapter 5)
- What career theories speak to you? How will you use them in practice? (Chapter 6)
- How do you approach one-to-one work? What models and approaches guide your interviews? (Chapter 7)
- What is your approach to career learning? How do you translate this into impactful work with groups? (Chapter 8)
- What information sources and resources do you use? How can you be sure that you keep up to date? (Chapter 9)
- How do you work with the systems in your organisation and beyond? What partnerships are key to your work? (Chapter 10)
- How do you feel about taking on leadership and management roles? What do you think are key leadership qualities in others? (Chapter 11)
- How are you going to ensure that you continue to develop as a professional and move your own career forwards? (Chapter 12)

The work of career development professionals can take a variety of forms. Traditionally, the dominant approach has been a variety of one-to-one approaches which draw on counselling and coaching. But the modern careers professional also has to be able to work with groups and play a role in the creation of career learning opportunities and the teaching of careers education. They also need to be able to work with labour market information and other resources to support the career learning of their clients and to work with systems and partners to enhance the opportunities available.

Finally, we asked you to think about how career services operate and how they are best led and managed. While some of this is asking you to think forward in your career and consider whether you want to become a leader or manager, we would also argue that everyone should think about how the organisations that they work for operate and be willing to take up both formal and informal leadership roles.

Continuous development

As the last section shows, you have already learnt a huge amount about being a career development professional. Hopefully, by now you have had the opportunity to start to put this into practice, but don't worry if you haven't had the opportunity to use all your learning yet. During your career, you are likely to move through a variety of different roles which will each require you to use different skills. Because of this, it is important to keep up to date and be prepared to refresh your knowledge when necessary and learn new things. After all, the field of career development itself continues to evolve, and new theories are developed and researched, and new practices evaluated.

We have already looked at continuing professional development (CPD) in Chapter 3 and offered a range of different ways in which you can access this. The most important thing is to recognise that CPD is a key professional responsibility and that it involves a lot more than just attending the occasional course. As you move through your career, you have an ethical responsibility to continue to update your knowledge, pay attention to changes in the worlds of education and work, ensure that you are up to date with developments in theory and practice and, perhaps most importantly of all, reflect on and strengthen your own professional practice by understanding and (where necessary) addressing your strengths and weaknesses.

Becoming a professional is a commitment to lifelong learning and development. In Chapter 3, we discussed a range of ways that you could fulfil this commitment through reading books, articles and online resources, shadowing and visits, accessing and providing mentoring, observation, attending conferences and events, participating in courses and training programmes (including further qualifications) and participating in communities of practice and professional associations. As you become more experienced, you might also want to get involved in various forms of professional representation (e.g. joining the committee of your professional body), the mentoring and training of career development students and professionals, research and leadership. There is a lot of learning in these forms of advanced professional practice, and it will also give you the opportunity to contribute to the profession and the development of younger career development professionals.

💡 Resources

We mentioned it in Chapter 3, but we would strongly recommend you get hold of Neary and Johnson's book, *CPD for the Career Development Professional* to help to guide you in the next stages of your development as a career development professional.

Managing your career

Just as the builder often lives in the most tumbledown of houses, career development professionals can sometimes be guilty of neglecting their own careers as they work diligently to develop the careers of others. We would argue that you should view your own career as evidence of the message that you preach. This means spending time thinking about how your career is developing and what you can do to develop it further in the future. We can self-exemplify the possibilities that skilful career management opens. After all, who wants to seek careers advice from someone who is miserable in their own work and life.

The imperative to develop your own career should not be confused with pressure to climb the 'career ladder' and increase your status and wealth. Effective careering is about finding the right balance of life and work, at the right time for you, while also allowing you to find meaning and make a contribution. Sometimes this will be about reducing your paid work, sometimes about committing to the professional practice that you have trained to do and only sometimes will it be about changing jobs or seeking promotions. The important thing is to be purposeful in your actions and to have self-compassion and the awareness that none of us can achieve everything all at the same time.

CASE STUDY

Shona has now been working as a career development professional in a community centre for almost a decade. Although it was something that she drifted into, rather than a lifelong ambition, she has loved it and feels passionate about it. But after a decade, she is feeling in need of some new challenges. She still loves helping her clients with their careers but is occasionally feeling that she has 'seen it all before' and that she isn't being stretched.

She starts to look for jobs and finds that there are actually quite a lot of roles that call for her skills and which relate to careers, progression, employability and a host of other terms that she is familiar with. She eventually decides to apply for a role as 'Careers and Progression Lead' at the local university's medical school. The role appeals to her because it will involve working with a very different set of clients, with very different career aspirations from those that she is used to in the community centre. She is also excited by the role because they are looking for someone who can set up a new service from scratch and think about how it connects to the wider teaching and learning that is going on in the medical school. The opportunity to think more strategically and set things up the way she believes they should work is very appealing.

She applies for the job, attends an interview where she speaks passionately about the power of career development, displays a lot of research on medical careers and gets the job. It seems that a new chapter is about to begin in her career journey.

We thought that it would be useful to include a few thoughts about how careers in careers can develop so that once you get comfortable in your new role, you can begin the process of deliberating about where you might go next. We have presented these as a series of 'career shifts' that you might make, with some of the shifts being bigger or more radical than others.

- **Career shift #1. Keep on keeping on!** You've trained for a long while to become a careers professional. If you are enjoying it, helping people and paying the bills, then there is no need to change. Just keep learning and working to change lives and develop careers. There will likely be new ways of reaching and helping people to try, evaluation and feedback to take into account and responses to changing contexts needed (see Chapter 11).

- **Career shift #2. Changing sector.** In Chapters 3 and 5, we introduced you to the wide range of different roles associated with the career development profession. Many of these are strongly linked to different sectors, so careers work can look and feel quite different in a school, a university or in the adult sector. If you get to the point where you have had enough of doing the job in your current context, it can be reinvigorating to move into a new context and explore both what is transferable and what new ideas and ways of working you need to learn.

- **Career shift #3. Moving on up.** In Chapter 11, we looked at leadership and management in the careers sector. If you found this interesting, one option for your career development is to seek these kinds of leadership roles. Such a move is likely to place you further away from practice but will give you the potential to make an impact through the people and activities that you manage. It is also important to recognise that leadership roles do not always involve direct line management. For example, you may become the coordinator of a local network of practice, where you do not line manage anyone but have the opportunity to influence the development of practice in your area.

- **Career shift #4. Going independent.** Most careers professionals will start their careers working in an organisation such as a school, university or public employment service. But, as we discussed in Chapter 10, working within organisations comes with its own opportunities and challenges, and so at some point, you might decide that you want to step outside of the structure of an organisation and go independent. There are lots of ways to organise careers work outside of an organisation, and for many people, making a living is likely to mean doing a mix of these activities. These may include setting up a private practice in which individuals pay you for career development services, selling your services to organisations such as schools or employers, getting involved in research, development, writing and other activities, and many more types of work. Going independent can be financially challenging (at least at first), but it can also be hugely rewarding.

- **Career shift #5. Research and development.** The career development field is underpinned by a huge amount of research and development. This includes everything from the kinds of scientific research that go on in universities to the development of resources, handouts, websites and books (like this one). There are relatively few formal pathways into this kind of work (although taking a doctorate may be helpful for the more scientific end of the spectrum). So, ask people who are involved in this kind of work to give you help, advice and ways in. The Careers Writers Association and scholarly bodies like the National Institute for Career Education and Counselling (NICEC) might be good first stops.

- **Career shift #6. Education and training.** In Chapters 2 and 3, we talked about the training of careers professionals. Someone has to organise and deliver this training, and this offers another possible career pathway that you might like to consider. People involved in the education and training of careers professionals can be located in universities, vocational colleges or in other kinds of learning organisations.

- **Career shift #7. Entrepreneurialism and social entrepreneurialism.** There are always lots of good ideas around the careers field. Maybe you have developed a new kind of career assessment or a serious game that will engage young people in their career development. Maybe you have identified a group that is poorly served by existing services or a new way of delivering services. In such cases, there can be opportunities to be entrepreneurial and set up something new. This could involve doing things like finding funding, building a new organisation or delivery mechanism, or in convincing a lot of other people to get involved in your idea.

- **Career shift #8. Policy and representation.** We have talked a lot about the intersection between career development work and politics and public policies. We have also said that the profession itself is important and something that you need to actively advocate for. Maybe your next career move might be to get involved in some of these issues by working for the government, a trade union, a professional association or some other body that campaigns for people to have access to decent work, good careers and professional career development support.

- **Career shift #9. Do something else.** Of course, you do not have to spend the rest of your life involved with anything to do with careers. Career development work gives you lots of transferable skills which you could apply to many related 'people focused' areas such as human resource management, teaching, counselling or youth work. Alternatively, there are always opportunities to change sectors and role or to retrain. There are undoubtedly ex-careers advisers out there working as everything from accountants to stand-up comedians to zookeepers. One of your jobs as a careers professional is to stimulate the career imagination of others, so you should be willing to let yours fly free. Finally, it is worth remembering that work is only a part of life and your next role might be caring for a loved one or retiring to enjoy the sunshine (or to energetically engage in a pletoria of voluntary work).

The nine career shifts outlined above are just ideas. You don't necessarily have to pick one; they can be combined or undertaken in sequence. The point is to note that while you have trained as a career development professional, this is just the start of a new phase in your career and that you have many choices ahead.

💡 Resources

Depending on which country you are in, the best websites for finding new opportunities are likely to vary. It is important to figure these out and keep an eye on your own labour market (see Chapters 4 and 9).

If you are in the UK, you may be particularly interested in Careers in Careers (https://jobs.thecdi.net/), Jobs.ac.uk (https://www.jobs.ac.uk/), the IEP Jobs Board (https://jobs.myiep.uk/), Guardian Jobs (https://jobs.theguardian.com/) and TES jobs (https://www.tes.com/jobs). But remember, these are just some good starting places, and it is important to do your research to find out where jobs are advertised.

You may also be interested in finding out about the Career Writers Association (https://careerswriters.com/) and NICEC (https://www.nicec.org/) to explore some different kinds of careers in careers.

With great power comes great responsibility

Through your training in career development, reading this book, and your ongoing CPD, you are becoming a fully fledged careers professional. This hopefully gives you a huge range of advantages that you can be proud of. You know how to undertake a range of careers work, you understand the theory that underpins this work and the context in which it is delivered. Hopefully, this should open a wide range of new jobs and possibilities for finding meaning in your work and developing your own career. Sadly, careers work is unlikely to be your pathway to the top 1% of earners (we perhaps should have mentioned this before), but it can offer you decent work, a high level of employability and perhaps most importantly, something worthwhile to do with your life and career.

This kind of deep understanding of the operation of a career is a kind of superpower. You will start to notice that career infuses everything and recognise when friends, neighbours and colleagues are making bad career choices or neglecting their career development. But you need to remember that with this great power comes great responsibility. To finish this book, we want to encourage you to reflect on some of these responsibilities carefully.

The responsibilities of a career development professional

- **Look after yourself.** Careers work can be exhausting. There are always lots more people to help than you have the capacity to help. Make sure you pay attention to your own energy levels and set good professional boundaries for yourself. If you find yourself researching LMI for a student at midnight, think carefully about whether your approach to work and/or your workload is sustainable. Similarly, if you find that every party you go to turns into a series of career counselling sessions, then try setting some clearer professional boundaries and enjoying yourself a bit more!

- **Behave ethically.** We discussed professional ethics in Chapter 3. These are at the core of your practice, and it goes without saying that you should always have them at the front of your mind. Behaving ethically is a responsibility to yourself, to your client and also to the whole profession. Cutting an ethical corner can sometimes feel like the right thing to do for you or a client, but if it brings the whole field into disrepute, then it is very much the wrong thing to do.

- **Be collegiate.** As a professional, you are signing up for a community of practice. This is a huge resource for you, which you should make the most of. Whenever you are stuck, reach out to other professionals, and you will be amazed at the help, support and resources that come your way. But this is all based on the principle of reciprocity. Others will help you, so you should help others. This is not a question of quid pro quo between individuals, but rather a sense that all career development professionals are in this together. A profession is a cooperative structure rather than a competitive one, in which we all gain if the profession is more effective and perceived more positively. At different points in your career, you are likely to take and give different amounts from the profession, but the whole thing only works if we are all prepared to do both.

- **Speak out for the profession.** Sadly, the careers profession is often the target of (we think typically unwarranted) criticism. Whether it is a pop star or a footballer complaining that they were told they would never make it, a politician trying to cut funding for career services or just your uncle giving his always-ready opinions after a few drinks too many, there are plenty of people who want to bash career development professionals. This means that we all have a responsibility to speak positively about the profession in public and to defend it against attacks where they are made. While there may be little point in arguing with your relatives, it is important to state clearly that this is an important profession which you are proud to be part of. When the attacks are in the public domain, think about writing a letter to the newspaper that is carrying the attacks or engaging with critics on social media (be careful with this one). The point is that this is our profession, and if we don't speak up for it, we can't expect others to.

- **Pay attention to the big picture.** Finally, it is important to pay attention to the worlds of politics and the economy and to think about how to respond to them. A new government may decide to cut or reform career services. It is important to find out what they are proposing and decide where you stand on this. Talking to your trade union or professional body is likely to be very helpful in this regard. Sometimes, the challenges won't be so direct; perhaps school funding is being cut or the employment system is being overhauled. Where some new shift in policy or the economy is going to have a major negative impact on the profession or your clients, you should be interested and you should take some action. Whether that is signing a petition, writing to your political representatives, going on a demonstration or voting in an election is up to you to determine, but it is important to remember that a profession is only as powerful as its members, and this power can only be exercised if people ensure that they are informed and willing to take action.

To finish, we want to welcome you into (what we think is) the greatest profession in the world. You are going to have an enormous amount of fun and do a huge amount of good as a career development professional. Our careers are our pathways through life, learning and work, but as we have learnt, these pathways often have many twists and turns and require us to navigate many obstacles. This is why people need help and why the role of a career development professional is so important. We wish you luck as you move into practice and look forwards to seeing the way in which you put all your learning into action and begin the process of moving the profession onwards and upwards.

In a nutshell

This concluding chapter has encouraged you to think about what you have learnt and the values that you should take forwards as you move into practice. It has argued that

- the structure of the book provides an ideal way for you to think about what you have learnt and to reflect on how you are going to take this learning forwards into practice;

- being a professional means that learning does not end with your initial training and that it is vital to commit to an ongoing process of continuing professional development;;

- becoming a careers professional is a step on your own career journey and that you should continue to think about where your career will lead you next; and

- with great power, comes great responsibility. Being a careers professional brings with it a range of important professional responsibilities that should guide you as you move forwards in your career.

Notes

Chapter 1

1. McCash, P., Hooley, T., & Robertson, P. (2021). Introduction: Rethinking career development. In P. Robertson, T. Hooley, & P. McCash (Eds.), *The Oxford Handbook of career development* (pp. 1–19). Oxford University Press.

Chapter 2

1. For more on this model, see Brookfield, S. D. (2017). *Becoming a critically reflective teacher.* John Wiley & Sons.

Chapter 3

1. Hooley, T., Johnson, C., & Neary, S. (2016). *Professionalism in Careers.* Careers England. https://repository.derby.ac.uk/item/92q50/professionalism-in-careers
2. Neary, S., Marriott, J., & Hooley, T. (2014). *Understanding a 'Career in Careers': Learning from an Analysis of Current Job and Person Specifications.* iCeGS, University of Derby. https://repository.derby.ac.uk/item/937vv/understanding-a-career-in-careers-learning-from-an-analysis-of-current-job-and-person-specifications

Chapter 4

1. Elias, P., Dickerson, A., & Bachelor, N. (2023). *A Skills Classification for the UK: Plans for development and maintenance.* Department for Education. https://www.gov.uk/government/publications/a-skills-classification-for-the-uk

Chapter 5

1. See, for example, Organisation for Economic Co-operation and Development (OECD). (2004). *Career Guidance and Public Policy: Bridging the Gap.* OECD. https://www.oecd.org/education/innovation-education/34050171.pdf

Chapter 6

1. Einstein, E. (1933). *On the Method of Theoretical Physics.* The Herbert Spencer Lecture, Oxford, June 10.
2. Law, B. (2006). *Which Way Is Forward? Fewer Lists, More Stories.* https://www.hihohiho.com/underpinning/cafbiog.pdf
3. Savickas, M. L. (2012). Life Design: A Paradigm for Career Intervention in the 21st Century. *Journal of Counseling & Development, 90*(1), 13–19. https://doi.org/10.1111/j.1556-6676.2012.00002.x
4. See for example Sultana, R. G. (2014). Rousseau's Chains: Striving for Greater Social Justice through Emancipatory Career Guidance. *Journal of the National Institute for Career Education and Counselling, 33*, 15–23. https://doi.org/10.20856/jnicec.3303
5. Flouri, E., & Buchanan, A. (2002). The Role of Work-Related Skills and Career Role Models in Adolescent Career Maturity. *The Career Development Quarterly, 51*(1), 36–43. https://doi.org/10.1002/j.2161-0045.2002.tb00590.x

6. Sultana, R. G. (2022). Four 'Dirty Words' in Career Guidance: From Common Sense to Good Sense. *International Journal for Educational and Vocational Guidance, 24,* 1–19.

Chapter 8

1. This reflection is informed by the concept of 'pedagogic stance', which we take from D'Errico and colleagues' article 'Pedagogical Stance'.
2. This is a qualification taken by young people in England and Wales around the age of 16. The full specification can be accessed at https://assets.publishing.service.gov.uk/media/5a7bfd7640f0b63f7572aa8b/GCSE_English_language.pdf
3. See Gatsby's website at https://www.goodcareerguidance.org.uk/
4. See further details on Advance HE's website at https://www.advance-he.ac.uk/knowledge-hub/framework-embedding-employability-higher-education-0

Chapter 9

1. The Careers & Enterprise Company (2016). *Moments of choice.* The Careers & Enterprise Company.

Chapter 10

1. Some important historical definitions of guidance which sought to expand the range of activities available to career professionals are found in the work of the Standing Conference of Associations for Guidance in Educational Settings (SCAGES) and the Unit for the Development of Adult Continuing Education.

Chapter 11

1. See Pawson and Tilley's *Realistic evaluation.*

References

In this section we provide a complete list of references that we have used in the book. This list should provide you with a good starting point for accessing the wider literature on career development.

Abele, A. E., & Spurk, D. (2009). How do objective and subjective career success interrelate over time?. *Journal of Occupational and Organizational Psychology, 82*(4), 803–824. https://doi.org/10.1348/096317909X470924

Advance HE. (n.d.). *Framework for embedding employability in higher education*. https://www.advance-he.ac.uk/knowledge-hub/framework-embedding-employability-higher-education-0

Alexander, R. (2023). Why LMI? Questioning the role of labour market information in career guidance. *Journal of the National Institute for Career Education and Counselling, 50*(1), 5–15. https://doi.org/10.20856/jnicec.5002

Alexander, R., McCabe, G., & De Backer, M. (2019). *Careers and labour market information: An international review of the evidence*. Education Development Trust.

Ali Abadi, H., Coetzer, A., Roxas, H. B., & Pishdar, M. (2023). Informal learning and career identity formation: The mediating role of work engagement. *Personnel Review, 52*(1), 363–381. https://doi.org/10.1108/PR-02-2021-0121

Ali, L., & Graham, B. (1996). *The counselling approach to career guidance*. Routledge

Allingham, M. (2002). *Choice theory: A very short introduction*. Oxford University Press.

Andrews, D., & Hooley, T. (2022). *The careers leaders' handbook* (2nd ed.). Trotman.

Arthur, N., Neault, R., & McMahon, M. (2019). *Career theories and models at work: Ideas for practice*. CERIC.

Atkinson, S. P. (2022). *Writing good learning outcomes and objectives: Short guide to creating well-structured intended learning outcomes that ensure effective course designs*. Sijen.

Atwell, G. (2024). AI and career counseling, advice, information and guidance and Generative AI. *AI Pioneers*. https://aipioneers.org/ai-and-career-counseling-advice-and-guidance/

Bakke, I. B., & Hooley, T. (2023). Neither online, nor face-to-face, but integrated career guidance: Introducing new ways of engaging undergraduate students in career learning and reflective careering. In M. Buford, M. Sharp, & M. Stebleton (Eds.), *Mapping the future of undergraduate career education* (pp. 138–154). Routledge.

Bandura, A. (1977). Self-efficacy: Towards a unifying theory of behavioral change. *Psychological Review, 84*(2), 191–215. https://psycnet.apa.org/doi/10.1037/0033-295X.84.2.191

Barnes, A., Bassot, B., & Chant, A. (2010). *An introduction to career learning and development 11-19*. Routledge.

Bassot, B. (2020). *The reflective journal*. Bloomsbury Academic.

Bassot, B. (2021). Client-centred career development practice: A critical review. In P. J. Robertson, T. Hooley, & P. McCash (Eds.), *The Oxford handbook of career development* (pp. 325–336). Oxford University Press.

Bassot, B. (2023). *The reflective practice guide: An interdisciplinary approach to critical reflection* (2nd ed.). Routledge.

Bassot, B., Barnes, A., & Chant, A. (2013). *A practical guide to career learning and development: Innovation in careers education 11-19*. Routledge.

Bates, B. (2023). *Learning theories simplified: … and how to apply them to teaching*. Sage.

Bernadette van Rijn, M., Yang, H., & Sanders, K. (2013). Understanding employees' informal workplace learning: The joint influence of career motivation and self-construal. *Career Development International, 18*(6), 610–628. https://doi.org/10.1108/CDI-12-2012-0124

Bernard, A. (2021). *The ladder: Supporting students towards successful futures and confident career choices.* Independent Thinking Press.

Bimrose, J. (2016). Constructivism in online career counselling. In M. McMahon (Ed.), *Career counselling* (pp. 210–221). Routledge.

Bimrose, J. (2021). Labour market information for career development practice: Pivotal or peripheral? In P. J. Robertson, T. Hooley, & P. McCash (Eds.), *The Oxford handbook of career development* (pp. 283–296). Oxford University Press.

Bimrose, J., & Barnes, S. A. (2007). Styles of career decision-making. *Australian Journal of Career Development, 16*(2), 20–28. https://doi.org/10.1177/10384162070160020

Blackwell, S. (1999). *Think: A compelling introduction to philosophy.* Oxford University Press.

Blustein, D. (2006). *The psychology of working: A new perspective for career development, counseling, and public policy.* Routledge.

Bourdieu, P. (2018). The forms of capital. In M. Granovetter & R. Swedberd (Eds.), *The sociology of economic life* (pp. 78–92). Routledge.

Bourdieu, P., & Passeron, J. C. (1990). *Reproduction in education, society and culture.* Sage.

Briggs Myers, I. (1998). *Introduction to type: A guide to understanding your results on the MBTI instrument* (6th ed.). CPP. Inc.

Bright, J. (2023). *Modern management and leadership: People, places and organisations.* University of Buckingham Press.

Brookfield, S. D. (2017). *Becoming a critically reflective teacher.* John Wiley & Sons.

Brown, S., & Lent, R. W. (2021). *Career development and counseling.* John Wiley and Sons.

Butler, C. (2002). *Postmodernism: A very short introduction.* Oxford University Press.

Clarke, M. (2015). Dual careers: The new norm for Gen Y professionals?. *Career Development International, 20*(6), 562–582. https://doi.org/10.1108/CDI-10-2014-0143

Cobb, F. (2019). 'There's no going back': The transformation of HE careers services using big data. *Journal of the National Institute for Career Education and Counselling, 42*(1), 18–25. https://doi.org/10.20856/jnicec.4204

Colley, H. (2011). 'Ethics work' in career guidance: navigating ethical principles and ethical pressures in an under-resourced service. *Journal of the National Institute for Career Education and Counselling, 26*, 15–21. https://doi.org/10.20856/jnicec.2604

Collins, A. (2012). The systems approach to career. *Journal of the National Institute for Career Education and Counselling, 28*, 3–9. https://doi.org/10.20856/jnicec.2802

Collins, J., & Barnes, A. (2017). *Careers in the curriculum. What works?* The Careers & Enterprise Company. https://www.careersandenterprise.co.uk/media/oq0bqhmp/careers_in_the_curriculum_report_what_works.pdf

Cottrell, S. (2019). *The study skills handbook.* Bloomsbury Academic.

Covey, S. (2020). *The 7 habits of highly effective people.* Simon & Schuster.

Cramp, P. (2011). *Labour markets: The economics of work and leisure.* Anforme Ltd.

Crisp, R. (2010). A person-centred perspective to counselling in educational and vocational agencies. *Journal of Psychologists and Counsellors in Schools, 20*(1), 22–30. https://doi.org/10.1375/ajgc.20.1.22

Daubney, K. (2021). *Careers education to demystify employability: A guide for professionals in schools and colleges.* Open University Press.

Dawson, C. (2019). *Introduction to research methods: A practical guide for anyone undertaking a research project.* Robinson.

Deniers, C. (2019). Experiences of receiving career coaching via Skype: An interpretative phenomenological analysis. *International Journal of Evidence Based Coaching and Mentoring, 17*(1), 72–81. https://doi.org/10.24384/r4j8-hm94

D'Errico, F., Leone, G., & Poggi, I. (2012). *Pedagogical stance: The teacher's position and its social signals.* 2012 International Conference on Privacy, Security, Risk and Trust and

2012 International Conference on Social Computing, 926–931. https://doi.org/10 .1109/SocialCom-PASSAT.2012.121

De Phillips, F. A., Berliner, W. M., & Cribbin, J. J. (1960). *Management of training programs.* Richard D. Irwin.

De Vos, A., & Soens, N. (2008). Protean attitude and career success: The mediating role of self-management. *Journal of Vocational Behavior, 73*(3), 449–456. https://doi.org/10 .1016/j.jvb.2008.08.007

Dirksen, J. (2015). *Design for how people learn* (Voices that matter). New Riders.

Dunn, K. (2023). *Working online in the counselling professions.* British Association for Counselling and Psychotherapy.

Eby, L. T., Butts, M., & Lockwood, A. (2003). Predictors of success in the era of the boundaryless career. *Journal of Organizational Behavior, 24*(6), 689–708. https://doi.org /10.1002/job.214

Einstein, E. (1933, June 10). *On the method of theoretical physics.* The Herbert Spencer Lecture, delivered at Oxford.

Elias, P., Dickerson, A., & Bachelor, N. (2023). *A skills classification for the UK: Plans for development and maintenance.* Department for Education. https://assets.publishing .service.gov.uk/media/652fdb9d92895c0010dcb9a5/A_skills_classification_for_the _UK.pdf

Fallows, S., & Steven, C. (2016). *Integrating key skills in higher education: Employability, transferable skills and learning for life.* Routledge.

Flouri, E., & Buchanan, A. (2002). The role of work-related skills and career role models in adolescent career maturity. *The Career Development Quarterly, 51*(1), 36–43. https://doi .org/10.1002/j.2161-0045.2002.tb00590.x

Friedman, S., & Laurison, D. (2020). *The class ceiling: Why it pays to be privileged.* Policy Press.

Frigerio, G., Mendez, R., & McCash, P. (2012). *Re-designing work-related learning: A management studies placement module.* Career Studies Unit. https://warwick.ac.uk/study/ cll/about/cllteam/gfrigerio/wrl_final.pdf

Garavan, T., Hogan, C., & Cahir-O'Donnell, A. (2020). *Learning and development in organisations: Strategy, evidence and practice.* Oak Tree Press.

Gatsby Charitable Foundation. (2014). *Good career guidance.* Gatsby Charitable Foundation. https://www.gatsby.org.uk/uploads/education/reports/pdf/gatsby-sir-john-holman -good-career-guidance-2014.pdf

Gibbs, G. (1988). *Learning by doing: A guide to teaching and learning methods.* Oxford: Further Education Unit, Oxford Polytechnic. https://stephenp.net/wp-content/uploads/2015 /12/learning-by-doing-graham-gibbs.pdf

Ginzberg, E., Ginsburg, S. W., Axelrad, S., & Herma, J. L. (1951). *Occupational choice: An approach to a general theory.* Columbia University Press.

Goddard, T. (2021). *Online career learning: integrating ICT for service transformation.* PhD thesis, University of Warwick. https://wrap.warwick.ac.uk/156331/

Gottfredson, L. S. (2005). Using Gottfredson's theory of circumscription and compromise in career guidance and counseling. In S. D. Brown & R. W. Lent (Eds.), *Career development and counseling: Putting theory and research to work* (pp. 71–100). John Wiley and Sons.

Gough, J., & Neary, S. (2020). The career development profession: Professionalisation, professionalism, and professional identity. In P. Robertson, T. Hooley, & P. McCash (Eds.), *Oxford handbook of career development* (pp. 556–568). Oxford University Press.

Gravells, A. (2010). *Delivering employability skills in the lifelong learning sector.* Learning Matters.

Grey, M. (2023). How to cope with the complexity of careers service leadership. *WonkHE.* https://wonkhe.com/blogs/how-to-cope-with-the-complexity-of-careers-service -leadership/

Gribbon, J. (2005). *Deep simplicity: Bringing order to chaos and complexity*. Random House.

Griffin, C. (1985). *Typical girls?: Young women from school to the full-time job market*. Law Book Company of Australasia.

Hansen, E. (2006). *Career guidance: A resource handbook for low-and middle-income countries*. ILO.

Hartung, P. J. (2015). The career construction interview. In M. McMahon & M. Watson (Eds.), *Career assessment*. SensePublishers. https://doi.org/10.1007/978-94-6300-034-5_13

Harvard Business Review. (2014). *Managing up*. Harvard Business Review Press.

Henrich, J. (2020). *The WEIRDest people in the world: How the West became psychologically peculiar and particularly prosperous*. Farrar, Straus and Giroux.

Hersey, P., & Blanchard, K. H. (1977). *Management of organizational behaviour: Utilizing human resources*. Prentice Hall.

Hill, L. A. (2003). *Becoming a manager: How new managers master the challenges of leadership*. Harvard Business Review Press.

Hodkinson and Sparkes, A. C. (1997). Careership: A sociological theory of career decision making. *British Journal of Sociology of Education, 18*(1), 29–44. https://doi.org/10.1080/0142569970180102

Holland, J. L. (1997). *Making vocational choices: A theory of vocational personalities and work environments*. Psychological Assessment Resources.

Hooley, T. (2022). Building a radical career imaginary: Using Laclau and Mouffe and Hardt and Negri to reflexively re-read Ali and Graham's counselling approach to career guidance. *British Journal of Guidance and Counselling, 50*(4), 660–675. https://doi.org/10.1080/03069885.2022.2058697

Hooley, T. (2023). Impartiality: A critical review. *Journal of the National Institute for Career Education and Counselling, 50*, 41–53. https://doi.org/10.20856/jnicec.5005

Hooley, T., & Godden, L. (2022). Theorising career guidance policymaking: Watching the sausage get made. *British Journal of Guidance & Counselling, 50*(1), 141–156. https://doi.org/10.1080/03069885.2021.1948503

Hooley, T., Johnson, C., & Neary, S. (2016). *Professionalism in careers*. Careers England. https://repository.derby.ac.uk/item/92q50/professionalism-in-careers

Hooley, T., & Staunton, T. (2020). The role of digital technology in career development. In P. Robertson, T. Hooley, & P. McCash (Eds.), *The Oxford handbook of career development* (pp. 297–311). Oxford University Press. https://doi.org/10.1093/oxfordhb/9780190069704.013.22

Hooley, T., Sultana, R. G., & Thomsen, R. (2018a). *Career guidance for social justice: Contesting neoliberalism*. Routledge.

Hooley, T., Sultana, R. G., & Thomsen, R. (2018b). The neoliberal challenge to career guidance: Mobilising research, policy and practice around social justice. In T. Hooley, R. Sultana, & R. Thomsen (Eds.), *Career guidance for social justice: Contesting neoliberalism* (pp. 1–28). Routledge.

Hooley, T., Sultana, R. G., & Thomsen, R. (2019). *Career guidance for emancipation: Reclaiming justice for the multitude*. Routledge.

Hooley, T., Sultana, R. G., & Thomsen, R. (2021). Five signposts to a socially just approach to career guidance. *Journal of the National Institute of Career Education and Counselling, 47*, 59–66. https://doi.org/10.20856/jnicec.4709

Hooley, T., Watts, A. G., Sultana, R. G., & Neary, S. (2013). The 'Blueprint' framework for career management skills: A critical exploration. *British Journal of Guidance & Counselling, 41*(2), 117–131. https://doi.org/10.1080/03069885.2012.713908

Hughes, D. (2017). Careers work in England's schools: Politics, practices and prospects. *British Journal of Guidance & Counselling, 45*(4), 427–440. https://doi.org/10.1080/03069885.2017.1346234

Inkson, K. (2004). Images of career: Nine key metaphors. *Journal of Vocational Behavior*, *65*(1), 96–111. https://doi.org/10.1016/S0001-8791(03)00053-8

Inkson, K., Dries, N., & Arnold, J. (2014). *Understanding careers*. Sage.

Johnson, M., & Majewska, D. (2022). *Formal, non-formal, and informal learning: What are they, and how can we research them?* Cambridge University Press & Assessment. https://www.cambridgeassessment.org.uk/Images/665425-formal-non-formal-and-informal-learning-what-are-they-and-how-can-we-research-them-.pdf

Jones, G., & Stokes, A. (2009). *Online counselling: A handbook for practitioners*. Palgrave Macmillan.

Kahneman, D. (2012). *Thinking fast and slow*. Penguin.

Kellerman, B. (2008). *Followership: How followers are creating change and changing leaders*. Harvard Business Review Press.

Kelly, A. (2021). *Dynamic management and leadership in education: High reliability techniques for schools and universities*. Routledge.

Kidd, J. M. (2002). The career counselling interview. In A. G. Watts, B. Law, J. Killeen, J. M. Kidd, & R. Hawthorn (Eds.), *Rethinking careers education and guidance* (pp. 127–141). Routledge.

Killeen, J. (1996). The social context of guidance. In A. G. Watts, B. Law, J. Killeen, J. M. Kidd, & R. Hawthorn (Eds.), *Rethinking careers education and guidance: Theory, policy and practice* (pp. 10–22). Routledge.

King, S. P., & Mason, B. A. (2020). Myers-briggs type indicator. In B. J. Carducci, C. S. Nave, J. S. Mio, & R. E. Riggio (Eds.), *The Wiley encyclopedia of personality and individual differences*. https://doi.org/10.1002/9781119547167.ch123

Kolb, D. A. (1984). *Experiential learning: Experience as the source of learning and development*. Prentice-Hall.

Košťálová, H., Cudlínová, M., Blake, H., Clark, L., Dimsits, M., Kavková, E., Graungaard, E., Moore, N., Sigaard H., J., Neary, S., Nemcova, L., Nogueira Perez, M., A., Fernandez Rey, E., & Ceinos Sanz, C. (2021). *A practitioner's guide to uncharted waters of career counselling, a critical reflection perspective*. EKS. https://repository.derby.ac.uk/item/936q1/a-practitioner-s-guide-to-uncharted-waters-of-career-counselling-a-critical-reflection-perspective

Krumboltz, J. D., & Levin, A. S. (2010). *Luck is no accident: Making the most of happenstance in your life and career*. Impact Publishers.

Krumboltz, J. D., Mitchell, A. M., & Jones, G. B. (1976). A social learning theory of career selection. *The Counseling Psychologist*, *6*(1), 71–81. https://doi.org/10.1177/001100007600600117

Law, B. (1981). Community interaction: A 'mid-range' focus for theories of career development in young adults. *British Journal of Guidance and Counselling*, *9*(2), 142–158. https://doi.org/10.1080/03069888108258210

Law, B. (1996). A career learning theory. In A. G. Watts, B. Law, J. Killeen, J. M. Kidd, & R. Hawthorn (Eds.), *Rethinking careers education and guidance: Theory, policy and practice* (pp. 37–53). Routledge.

Law, B. (2006). *Which way is forward? Fewer lists, more stories*. https://www.hihohiho.com/underpinning/cafbiog.pdf

Lewin, K., Lippitt, R., & White, R. K. (1939). Patterns of aggressive behavior in experimentally created 'social climates'. *The Journal of Social Psychology*, *10*(2), 269–299. https://doi.org/10.1080/00224545.1939.9713366

Mallows, R., & Walker, J. (2021). CDI guidance on the benefits and delivery of supervision in the career development sector. https://www.thecdi.net/resources/cdi-resources/supervision

McCarthy, J., & Borbély-Pecze, T. B. (2021). Career guidance living on the edge of public policy. In P. Robertson, T. Hooley, & P. McCash (Eds.), *The Oxford handbook of career development* (pp. 95–112). Oxford University Press.

McCash, P., Hooley, T., & Robertson, P. (2021). Introduction: Rethinking career development. In P. Robertson, T. Hooley, & P. McCash (Eds.), *The Oxford handbook of career development* (pp. 1–19). Oxford University Press.

McMahon, M. (2016). *Career counselling: Constructivist approaches*. Routledge.

McIlveen, P., Perera, H. N., Brown, J., Healy, M., & Hammer, S. (2021). Career assessment. In P. J. Robertson, T. Hooley, & P. McCash (Eds.), *The Oxford handbook of career development* (pp. 313–324). Oxford University Press.

Meldrum, S. (2021). Group career coaching – A critical pedagogical approach. *The Journal for Specialists in Group Work, 46*(2), 214–225. https://doi.org/10.1080/01933922.2021.1929619

Minchin, K. (2019). *Always time for coffee: A down-to-earth guide for frontline managers, team leaders and supervisors*. Kate Minchin.

Mishra, P., & McDonald, K. (2017). Career resilience: An integrated review of the empirical literature. *Human Resource Development Review, 16*(3), 207–234. https://doi.org/10.1177/1534484317719622

Mitchell, K. E., Al Levin, S., & Krumboltz, J. D. (1999). Planned happenstance: Constructing unexpected career opportunities. *Journal of Counseling & Development, 77*(2), 115–124. https://doi.org/10.1002/j.1556-6676.1999.tb02431.x

Moore, A. (2012). *Teaching and learning: Pedagogy, curriculum and culture*. Routledge.

Neary, S., & Johnson, C. (2016). *CPD for the career development professional: A handbook for enhancing practice*. Trotman.

Neary, S., Marriott, J., & Hooley, T. (2014). *Understanding a 'career in careers': Learning from an analysis of current job and person specifications*. iCeGS, University of Derby. https://repository.derby.ac.uk/item/937vv/understanding-a-career-in-careers-learning-from-an-analysis-of-current-job-and-person-specifications

Neelen, M., & Kirschner, P. A. (2020). *Evidence-informed learning design: Creating training to improve performance*. Kogan Page.

Nettle, D. (2009). *Personality: What makes you the way you are*. Oxford University Press.

Offer, M. (2001). The discourse of the labour market. In B. Gothard, P. Mignot, M. Offer, & M. Ruff (Eds.), *Careers guidance in context* (pp. 76–92). Sage.

Old Treasury Building. (n.d.). *On the street: The newsboy*. https://www.oldtreasurybuilding.org.au/lost-jobs/on-the-street/the-newsboy/

Organisation for Economic Co-operation and Development (OECD). (2004). *Career guidance and public policy: Bridging the gap*. OECD. https://www.oecd.org/education/innovation-education/34050171.pdf

Parsons, F. (1909). *Choosing a vocation*. Houghton Mifflin Company. https://archive.org/details/choosingavocati00parsgoog

Patton, W., & McMahon, M. (2015). The systems theory framework of career development: 20 years of contribution to theory and practice. *Australian Journal of Career Development, 24*(3), 141–147. https://doi.org/10.1177/1038416215579944

Patton, W., & McMahon, M. (2021). *Career development and systems theory*. Brill.

Pawson, R., & Tilley, N. (1997). *Realistic evaluation*. Sage Publications.

Peck, D. (2004). *Careers services: History, policy and practice in the United Kingdom*. Routledge.

Percy, C., & Dodd, V. (2021). The economic outcomes of career development programmes. In P. J. Robertson, T. Hooley, & P. McCash (Eds.), *The Oxford handbook of career development* (pp. 35–48). Oxford University Press.

Percy, C., & Hooley, T. (2023). Lessons for career guidance from return-on-investment analyses in complex education-related fields. *British Journal of Guidance & Counselling*. https://doi.org/10.1080/03069885.2023.2186372

Pryor, R. G., & Bright, J. E. (2005). *Luck readiness index manual*. Congruence/Bright and Associates.

Pryor, R. G., & Bright, J. E. (2011). *The chaos theory of careers: A new perspective on working in the twenty-first century*. Routledge.

Pryor, R. G., & Bright, J. E. (2014). The chaos theory of careers (CTC): Ten years on and only just begun. *Australian Journal of Career Development*, *23*(1), 4–12. https://doi.org/10.1177/1038416213518506

Pope, M. (2000). A brief history of career counseling in the United States. *The Career Development Quarterly*, *48*(3), 194–211. https://doi.org/10.1002/j.2161-0045.2000.tb00286.x

Pyle, K. R., & Hayden, S. C. W. (2015). *Group career counseling: Practices and principles.* NCDA.

Redekopp, D. E. (2017). Irrational career decision-making: Connecting behavioural economics and career development. *British Journal of Guidance & Counselling*, *45*(4), 441–450. https://doi.org/10.1080/03069885.2016.1264569

Reese, R., & Egan, G. (2021). *The skilled helper. A client centred approach.* Cengage Learning EMEA.

Richardson, M. S. (2012). Counseling for work and relationship. *The Counseling Psychologist*, *40*(2), 190–242. https://doi.org/10.1177/0011000011406452

Roberts, K. (2009). Opportunity structures then and now. *Journal of Education and Work*, *22*(5), 355–368. https://doi.org/10.1080/13639080903453987

Robertson, P. J. (2021a). Evidence-based practice. In P. J. Robertson, T. Hooley, & P. McCash (Eds.), *The Oxford handbook of career development* (pp. 353–370). Oxford University Press.

Robertson, P. J. (2021b). The aims of career development policy. In P. J. Robertson, T. Hooley, & P. McCash (Eds.), *The Oxford handbook of career development* (pp. 113–128). Oxford University Press.

Rogers, C. (2021a). *Client centred therapy.* Robinson Publishing.

Rogers, C. (2021b). *On becoming a person.* Robinson Publishing.

Rosenfield, M. (2013). *Telephone counselling: A handbook for practitioners.* Palgrave Macmillan.

Rossier, J., Cardoso, P. M., & Duarte, M. E. (2021). The narrative turn in career development theories: An integrative perspective. In P. J. Robertson, T. Hooley, & P. McCash (Eds.), *The Oxford handbook of career development* (pp. 162–180). Oxford University Press.

Rowland, B. (2023). *Understanding apprenticeships: A student's guide.* Trotman.

Savickas, M. L. (1997). Career adaptability: An integrative construct for life-span, life-space theory. *Career Development Quarterly*, *45*, 247–259. https://doi.org/10.1002/j.2161-0045.1997.tb00469.x

Savickas, M. L. (2012). Life design: A paradigm for career intervention in the 21st century. *Journal of Counseling & Development*, *90*(1), 13–19. https://doi.org/10.1111/j.1556-6676.2012.00002.x

Savickas, M. L. (2013). Career construction theory and practice. In S. D. Brown & R. W. Lent (Eds.), *Career development and counseling: Putting theory and research to work* (2nd ed., pp. 144–186). John Wiley & Sons.

Savickas, M. L., Nota, L., Rossier, J., Dauwalder, J. P., Duarte, M. E., Guichard, J., ... Van Vianen, A. E. (2009). Life designing: A paradigm for career construction in the 21st century. *Journal of Vocational Behavior*, *75*(3), 239–250. https://doi.org/10.1016/j.jvb.2009.04.004

Schiersmann, C., Einarsdottir, S., Katsarov, J., Lerkkanen, J., Mulvey, R., Pukelis, K., & Weber, P. (2016). *European competence standards for the academic training of career practitioners: NICE handbook volume 2.* Verlag Barbara Budrich.

Schiersmann, C., Ertelt, B. J., Katsarov, J., Mulvey, R., Reid, H., & Weber, P. (2022). *NICE handbook for the academic training of career guidance and counselling professionals.* Heidelberg University.

Sharples, M. (2019). *Practical pedagogy: 40 new ways to teach and learn.* Routledge.

Smith, I. (2014). *Assessment and learning pocketbook.* Teachers' Pocketbooks.

Standing Conference of Associations for Guidance in Educational Settings (SCAGES). (1993). Statement of principles and definitions. In C. Ball (Ed.), *Guidance matters: Developing a national strategy for guidance in learning and work* (24–30). RSA.

Staunton, T., & Rogosic, K. (2021). Labour market information and social justice: A critical examination. *International Journal for Educational and Vocational Guidance*, *21*(3), 697–715. https://doi.org/10.1007/s10775-021-09466-3

Stewart, M. (Ed.). (2023). *A history of the careers services in the UK from 1999*. NICEC.

Sultana, R. G. (2012). Learning career management skills in Europe: A critical review. *Journal of Education and Work*, *25*(2), 225–248. https://doi.org/10.1080/13639080.2010.547846

Sultana, R. G. (2014). Rousseau's chains: Striving for greater social justice through emancipatory career guidance. *Journal of the National Institute for Career Education and Counselling*, *33*, 15–23. https://doi.org/10.20856/jnicec.3303

Sultana, R. G. (2022). Four 'dirty words' in career guidance: From common sense to good sense. *International Journal for Educational and Vocational Guidance*, *24*(1), 1–19. https://doi.org/10.1007/s10775-022-09550-

Super, D. E. (1980). A life-span, life-space approach to career development. *Journal of Vocational Behavior*, *16*(3), 282–298. https://doi.org/10.1016/0001-8791(80)90056-1

Swanson, J. L., & Schneider, M. (2021). The theory of work adjustment. In S. Brown & R. W. Lent (Eds.), *Career development and counseling* (pp. 33–38). John Wiley and Sons.

Thaler, R. H., & Sunstein, C. R. (2022). *Nudge: Improving decisions about health, wealth and happiness*. Penguin.

The Careers & Enterprise Company. (2016). *Moments of choice*. The Careers & Enterprise Company.

Thomsen, R. (2012). *Career guidance in communities*. Aarhus University Press.

Thomsen, R. (2017). *Career guidance in communities: A model for reflexive practice*. iCeGS, University of Derby. https://repository.derby.ac.uk/item/94vq0/career-guidance-in-communities-a-model-for-reflexive-practice

Thomsen, R., Hooley, T., & Mariager-Anderson, K. (2022). Critical perspectives on agency and social justice in transitions and career development. *British Journal of Guidance & Counselling*, *50*(4), 481–490. https://doi.org/10.1080/03069885.2022.2106551

Thomson, B. (2020). *How to coach: First steps and beyond* (2nd ed.). Sage Publications.

Thornton, S., & Gliga, T. (2020). *Understanding developmental psychology*. Red Globe Press.

Tobin, L. (2023). *A guide to uni life*. Trotman.

Unit for the Development of Adult Continuing Education. (1986/2003). *The challenge of change: Developing educational guidance for adults*. Republished as an occasional paper from the National Association for Educational Guidance for Adults.

Van Vianen, A. E. (2018). Person–environment fit: A review of its basic tenets. *Annual Review of Organizational Psychology and Organizational Behavior*, *5*, 75–101.

Vela, K. N., Pedersen, R. M., & Baucum, M. N. (2020). Improving perceptions of STEM careers through informal learning environments. *Journal of Research in Innovative Teaching & Learning*, *13*(1), 103–113. https://doi.org/10.1108/JRIT-12-2019-0078

Watts, A. G. (1999). *Reshaping career development for the 21st century*. Centre for Guidance Studies. University of Derby. https://www.derby.ac.uk/media/derbyacuk/assets/departments/icegs/documents/1999a-watts-reshaping-career-development.pdf

Watts, A. G. (2014). Cross-national reviews of career guidance systems: Overview and reflections. *Journal of the National Institute for Career Education and Counselling*, *32*(1), 4–14. https://doi.org/10.20856/jnicec.3202

Watts, A. G. (2016/1996). Socio-political ideologies in guidance. In T. Hooley & L. Barham (Eds.), *Career development policy and practice: The Tony Watts reader* (pp. 171–185). Highflyers.

Watts, A. G., & Sultana, R. G. (2004). Career guidance policies in 37 countries: Contrasts and common themes. *International Journal for Educational and Vocational Guidance, 4*, 105–122. https://doi.org/10.1007/s10775-005-1025-y

Whiston, S. C. (2021). Career counselling effectiveness and contributing factors. In P. Robertson, T. Hooley, & P. McCash (Eds.), *The Oxford handbook of career development* (pp. 337–352). Oxford University Press.

Whiston, S. C., & Rahardja, D. (2005). Qualitative career assessment: An overview and analysis. *Journal of Career Assessment, 13*(4), 371–380. https://doi.org/10.1177/1069072705277910

Whiston, S. C., Rossier, J., & Barón, P. M. H. (2016). The working alliance in career counseling: A systematic overview. *Journal of Career Assessment, 24*(4), 591–604. https://doi.org/10.1177/1069072715615849

Whitmore, J., & Gaskell, T. (2024). *Coaching for performance* (6th ed.). Nicholas Brealey Publishing.

Williams, K., Woolliams, M., & Spiro, J. (2020) *Reflective writing – Pocket study skills* (2nd ed.). Bloomsbury Publishing.

Willis, P. (1977). *Learning to labour: How working class kids get working class jobs.* Saxon House.

Wilton, N. (2022). *An introduction to human resource management.* Sage.

Yates, J. (2017). A meta-theoretical framework for career practitioners. *The Indian Journal of Career and Livelihood Planning, 5*(1), 15–25.

Yates, J. (2018). *The career coaching toolkit.* Routledge.

Yates, J. (2022). *The career coaching handbook* (2nd ed.). Routledge.

Young, R. A., & Friesen, J. D. (1992). The intentions of parents in influencing the career development of their children. *The Career Development Quarterly, 40*(3), 198–206. https://doi.org/10.1002/j.2161-0045.1992.tb00326.x

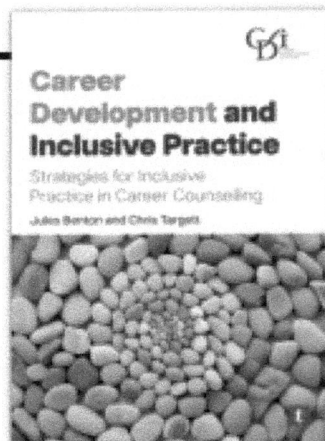